BATFISH

BATFISH

The Champion "Submarine-Killer" Submarine of World War II

Hughston E. Lowder with Jack Scott

PRENTICE-HALL, INC., Englewood Cliffs, New Jersey

BATFISH: *The Champion "Submarine-Killer"*
Submarine of World War II
by Hughston E. Lowder with Jack Scott
Copyright © 1980 by Hughston E. Lowder and Jack Scott
Address inquiries to Prentice-Hall, Inc.,
Englewood Cliffs, N. J. 07632
Printed in the United States of America
Prentice-Hall International, Inc., London
Prentice-Hall of Australia, Pty. Ltd., Sydney
Prentice-Hall of Canada, Ltd., Toronto
Prentice-Hall of India Private Ltd., New Delhi
Prentice-Hall of Japan, Inc., Tokyo
Prentice-Hall of Southeast Asia Pte. Ltd., Singapore
Whitehall Books Limited, Wellington, New Zealand
10 9 8 7 6 5 4 3 2 1

Library of Congress Cataloging in Publication Data

Lowder, Hughston E, date
Batfish, the champion "submarine-killer" submarine of
World War II.

Includes index.
1. Batfish (Submarine)   2.   World War, 1939–1949—
Personal narratives, American.   3.   Lowder, Hughston E.,
date   4.   World War, 1939–1945—Naval operations—
Submarine.   5.   World War, 1939–1945—Pacific Ocean.
6.   United States.   Navy–Biography.   7.   Seamen–United
States–Biography.   I.   Scott, Jack, date   joint author.
II.   Title.
D783.5.B37L68   940.54'51   80-12155
ISBN 0-13-066563-0

ACKNOWLEDGMENTS

A number of people cooperated unselfishly with the writing of this book. Grateful acknowledgment of their efforts is herewith extended with the deepest appreciation.

June S. Lowder understood the problem and suggested a way to solve it.

Rear Admiral John K. Fyfe (USN ret.) read all drafts, made invaluable suggestions and corrections, and loaned most of the photographs that appear in this book.

Former Lieutenant Commander Wayne R. Merrill and Rear Admiral Walter L. Small (USN ret.), also clarified events abbreviated within their original war patrol reports, adding strength and depth to the story.

Captain Robert G. Black (USN ret.), Captain James M. Hingson (USN ret.), and Captain Peter G. Molteni (USN ret.) shared their thirty-five-year-old recollections in detail, as did Admiral Lewis S. Parks (USN ret.), who clearly reconstructed the episode in which he participated.

The war patrol reports were furnished by Karen A. Pritchard, Curator of the Pacific Submarine Museum at Pearl Harbor, Hawaii, and Dr. Dean C. Allard, head of the Operative Archives Branch of the U.S. Naval Historical Museum in Washington, D.C.

The personality sketches of Merrill, Fyfe, and Small from "The Lucky Bag," the Naval Academy Yearbook, were provided by Richard M. Barone, Reference Librarian of the Nimitz Library and are reprinted through the courtesy of the United States Naval Academy.

Yasuyoshi Komizo, Attaché of the Embassy of Japan, Washington, D.C., translated the Japanese submarine records into English.

Portions of the Epilogue are reprinted with permission of Major Books, from the book *I-Boat Captain* by Zenji Orita with Joseph D. Harrington, © 1976 by Joseph D. Harrington.

Batfish's "Eighth Patrol" was based largely upon files loaned by Admiral John E. Kirkpatrick (USN ret.), then elucidated through correspondence and conversation with some of its principals: W. E. Battenfield, Dr. Glen Berkenbile, Harold Hooper, Admiral Kirkpatrick, Ken Meyer, Jr., and Captain Karl R. Wheland (USN ret.).

Grateful acknowledgment is also given to the *Daily Oklahoman, Muskogee Phoenix and Times Democrat, Oklahoma City Times, Southwest Times*

Record, Tulsa Tribune, and *Tulsa World* for permission to reprint excerpts from articles about *Batfish* during her period of acquisition by Muskogee.

The use of all photographs is gratefully and individually acknowledged.

The perceptive observations of Captain Edward L. Beach (USN ret.) persisted through several rough drafts and into the final revision. His enabling interest in *Batfish* could not possibly be more warmly appreciated. Clay Blair, Jr., was also kind enough to read an earlier draft of *Batfish*, make helpful comment, and encourage its resolution.

Betsy Geishen not only typed thousands of pages throughout the evolving drafts, but helped to shape the thoughts upon them with a sure and graceful hand.

Others who assisted in important ways are: Ken Barnes, George J. Bergling, Edwin C. Buxbaum, John Corun, Pat Corun, Florence Williams Dowling, James R. Foard, Bill and Patty Hoke, Paul Hotvedt, Earl E. Ihle, Jr., Ruth Jamison, Chris Kozak, Sharon Lynn, Jim Maslousky, Diane MacDonald, John Miles, Dick Parr, Mrs. Vivian Pierson, Albert C. Stein, Wallace Waynick, Christy Wolfe—and M.R.T. Their thoughtfulness was indispensable.

Baltimore, Maryland

CONTENTS

ACKNOWLEDGMENTS ☆ v

PROLOGUE ☆ 1

7 December 1941 ☆ 8

SHAKEDOWN ☆ 17

PASSAGE TO PEARL ☆ 27

FIRST WAR COMMAND, FIRST WAR PATROL:
    11 December 1943 ☆ 41

SECOND WAR PATROL: 12 February 1944 ☆ 78

TRANSITION ☆ 89

SECOND WAR COMMAND, THIRD WAR PATROL:
    26 May 1944 ☆ 93

FOURTH WAR PATROL: 24 July 1944 ☆ 119

FIFTH WAR PATROL: 8 October 1944 ☆ 137

SIXTH WAR PATROL: 9 January 1945 ☆ 155

THIRD WAR COMMAND, SEVENTH WAR PATROL:
    12 April 1945 ☆ 181

EPILOGUE ☆ 199

THE "EIGHTH PATROL" ☆ 208

APPENDIX: Roster of U.S.S. *Batfish* ☆ 227

INDEX ☆ 229

PROLOGUE

Arriving in Muskogee, Oklahoma, on a Sunday afternoon, I drove out to the foot of the Arkansas River Bridge. And there, equally sought and unexpected, was U.S.S. *Batfish* (SS 310)—history's foremost submarine-killer submarine.

Few Americans would expect to find a United States fleet submarine over a thousand miles from the nearest sea. Yet folks around Muskogee have become accustomed to this former underseas raider resting docilely in the little park just off the Muskogee-Tulsa Turnpike. After twenty-six years of service to her country, *Batfish* was struck from the naval register on 1 November 1969 and donated the next year to the state of Oklahoma as a perpetual memorial to the veterans of our armed forces. She finally arrived at the Port of Muskogee on 7 May 1972, and a year later was eased into her permanent berth in an artificial lagoon overlooking the "navigable" McClellan-Kerr Waterway. Nearly restored to her original condition, *Batfish*—albeit immobile and unarmed—now looks much as she did poised on the Portsmouth ways in 1943.

Boarding this incongruous exhibit from the stern, I walked forward along the black, slatted deck. Thirty-five years before, I would have merely flung myself at the old torpedo room hatch and dropped to the deck below in a matter of seconds. This time, however, I descended with a firm grip on both handrails of the new stairway cut for the visiting tourists.

As I stood in the forward torpedo room, the shafts of late afternoon sunshine slanting down the stairway diffused an eerie half-light within *Batfish.* I found a place to sit out of the way of sightseers, and tried to align this presence with the memories it suddenly provoked.

Gone were the bunks that used to line the bulkheads from deck to overhead. The racks for spare torpedoes were empty. The red lights from the overhead glinted back from the six shiny brass torpedo tubes sporting miniature Japanese flags—representing the men-of-war and merchantmen sunk by torpedoes fired from these tubes. This sleek killer, once loaded with deadly ton-and-a-half torpedoes—cocked, everready to be fired at any enemy target worth the torpedoes' cost of $10,000 each—was now crowded with camera-toting tourists and wide-eyed youngsters who wondered unaffectedly at such a large, expensive *toy.* She did not seem to touch any of them as she touched me. Her spirit had receded within her steel and brass, like water into sand upon a high, dry beach. But I could sense the spirit within her, within my memory.

In that teeming Sunday midst spoke a voice, heard by me alone. It was Captain Jake: "Gentlemen, we've just sunk a 3,500-ton Japanese training ship, and we can expect to catch hell. Take her down. Rig for depth charge and rig for silent running."

We had just fired three torpedoes at the ship, hitting it with one, sinking it almost immediately before the second or third could hit. Our captain's voice described her crewmen as he saw them through the periscope, desperately looking for a place to hide from death and, finding none, jumping into the burning sea. All hands put their practice to the test and passed with honors, as *Batfish* went deep. We eluded the subsequent depth charging and, obviously, we survived.

My fingers played their long-lost roles, and my eyes scanned the lights flickering upon dead instruments. On the way aft, moving as in a dream, I looked up and panicked. At 450 feet, under the Makassar Strait, a deadly Q-ship had located us precisely; an exploding depth charge had blown out the torpedo loading hatch gasket. The sea was pouring in. Somehow I found the presence of mind to reach for a block and tackle. Not in its locker! The torpedo gang already had it and, nearly drowning in the waterfall, were dogging the hatch down tighter, tighter until the ocean merely trickled in. Here I was—half a lifetime later—drenched with real sweat.

Stepping through the hatchway, I entered the forward battery. In the officers' galley I saw Nat Kelly fixing a salad, humming a tune to himself. On down the passageway I glanced into the wardroom upon Lieutenants Walker, Longfellow, McCann, and From, solemnly intent on their game of pinochle; the executive officer, Lieutenant Commander Hingson, studiously kibitzing. On the other side of the passageway I stared at the single short bunk in the captain's quarters. Somehow I'd remembered him as being taller.

On past the chief petty officers' quarters and Yeoman Schlief's office, I stepped through the hatchway into *Batfish*'s control room, home of the gyro compass, depth gauges, diving planes, and rudder controls. This was where an intricacy of levers and valves controlled the flooding and unflooding of her ballast tanks, and guided her on and under the sea. Chief Bohreer was peering over the backs of two sailors, intent upon the diving angle gauges glowing in front of them. Below, through an open hatch, the pump room was dark, vacant, and humming.

More memories and faces converged on dim red lights. The metallic click of a depth charge's detonator, an instant before the explosion, was larger than the silence. Eighteen-year-old sailors silently mouthed, "Though I walk through the valley of the shadow of death, I will fear no evil . . ." then danced like puppets beneath some drunken unseen hand. Cork insulation flying, valves springing a leak in a steady stream, deck plates rippling, instrument glass and light bulbs shattering . . . waiting, praying, and sweating, as *Batfish* groaned, moved on, and lived.

Then, the Klaxon: *ah-ooga, ah-ooga, ah-ooga.* A voice bellowed from the conning tower: "Battle surface! Take her up! Man the deck gun!" Nervously I obeyed, climbing the ladder into the conning tower. There, with his hat on backward and crouched as near the deck as possible, Captain Fyfe was glued to the eyepiece of the periscope he hugged, waiting for *Batfish* to pop up to the surface so we could scramble to the bridge. Three other busy men were crowded expectantly in the small compartment. On the ladder, the quartermaster had his hand on the hatch dogs, ready to open the instant it was clear of the surface. The memory was so clear it made my nerves tingle.

"Fantastic ship."

A change of focus. "Yes," I replied to the elderly woman standing below me in the control room, "she's a great boat." But I wasn't ready to come back. The connections were too precious. Something of *Batfish* and something of myself were in tune, too tantalizing to analyze, too potent to avoid.

Retreating into my daydream, intact, I backed down the ladder and headed aft, as if there were something I had to find before returning to the present. Tourists and guides flowed invisibly around me.

I walked back through the crew's sleeping quarters, absently peering into the head and shower room on the way past. Now that I wasn't waiting my turn, there wasn't any line. In the forward engine room, on either side of the passageway, lay the two big diesels for surface running. Chief Cox and Pete Morreale were tinkering with a gauge on the bulkhead above one of them.

The smell of diesel oil biting my nostrils, I passed on through the hatchway into the after engine room, between two more diesels, and

3

through another hatchway into the maneuvering room. In muffled tones, Leasure was explaining something to Evinger about the switchboard. Joe Tuma had his face buried in an electrician's manual.

Lest my eavesdropping disturb them, I stepped softly past, through the hatchway and into the after torpedo room. Chief Rogers was pointing out the little Japanese flags painted on each of the four gleaming torpedo tubes, just like those in the forward torpedo room. The brass and steel reflected more memories, more remembered faces. Odd, I thought, they look so young. The shiny brass emergency flare gun jutted out from the port bulkhead behind the ladder. In the light from the bare overhead bulb, I saw a face reflected in it, and realized this graying stranger was the one I wanted most to see. Among the phantoms walking with me in my mind, one of them was me.

With gooseflesh standing out all over my body, I hurried back to the control room and the one place I had overlooked—the radio shack. Its door was closed, blocked by tourists conversing with a guide. I squeezed along the wall to the door and opened it slowly, my back to the crowd. Someone was sitting at my seat, vague in the dim light, his back to me, my headphones on his head, pecking steadily at the typewriter with two fingers that must surely be mine. I was afraid to look. Approaching his side, I leaned cautiously to peer at his hidden face. I could almost hear the message he transcribed coming in, leaking past the earphones. As I bent, the typing and the message stopped. Looking slowly upward, our senior radioman, Chief Farnsworth, smiled in recognition and disappeared.

With this flood tide of memories rising higher, I climbed the stairway in the after torpedo room to go topside. Walking forward past the after battery hatch once more, I climbed up on the cigarette deck and then on up to the lookout station. My back pressing against the cool steel of the periscope shears, I looked down upon the now darkening bridge. Again I could see the officers playing pinochle in the forward battery wardroom; the practiced shuffle, the deal, the play.

In the lulls between torpedo and depth charge, there were always two card games going on board—one a gentlemen's pastime, sportingly played; the other pursued with a kind of bloodlust. The game and rules were the same for officers and crew alike. But the play in the forward battery wardroom and the play in the after battery crew's quarters were worlds apart.

In the after battery, the ice-cream machine would be shining in

4

the glow of light coming out of the galley. Against the after bulkhead the boat's Victrola was playing "Don't Fence Me In." My old radio buddy Stan Javorski was having a cup of steaming hot coffee from the urn beside the galley partition. Wearing cowboy boots and completely oblivious to those around him, Dave Dennis was picking out a tune on his trusty Gibson. At the back table, Cartmill, Duefrene, and Glace were hot at a game of cutthroat pinochle. "You reneged, you dirty bastard!" "The hell I did!" "The hell you didn't! You trumped my king of spades two hands ago." "Bullshit! I played a ten of spades." "You lyin' sonofabitch." "Who you calling a liar!" To hear them, a stranger would disbelieve these three such mortal enemies could habitually refrain from killing one another.

The cutthroat game in the after battery crew's quarters was the war I knew: an acting-out of readiness. The boredom and the cards, obscenity and roughness, all discarded in a flash when the Klaxon snatched us to our valves and knobs and switches. Then, performance without question. A hand for every valve, a one-to-one accommodation to metal parts when there could be no pause, no reflection, no delay. Then *Batfish* was something greater than all its parts—a one, a unity.

Batfish was her captain, whoever he might be: timid or daring, butcher or fatted calf, and his officers who steered and aimed and drove her. She was her crewmen, mechanics married one to one with the machine, commanded by her captain and her needs. We were as one as many ones can ever be. We helped win a war none of us could bear to lose. Regardless how we each got there, we submitted, which was our only choice, did our jobs, obeyed our captain, served our machine. And by that submission we survived. Surviving, we felt lucky; winning, we felt proud, but our only glory was to live on.

We won the war; it is for others to say how close we may have come to not winning it. I grew up during this period, in a submarine. How odd! And the man now looks back to see what the hell really happened to the boy he had been.

⌐ I had long wanted to understand those historic days aboard *Batfish,* to comprehend an experience that introduced me to death a thousand times before I came of age. But the Silent Service remained silent even long after the war. By the time enough of the truth was known to be told, very few remained interested enough to listen, including those of us who were there, too young and inexperienced, too *specific* to see beyond the jobs our hands were doing. As suddenly as it came, the war was behind us, fading inexorably into the past; our myths and images of it had been cast and were reluctant to change. Most of us had been willing simply to let it go.

Generally, history books continue to attribute our eventual victory to an air war supported by battleships and cruisers, generally minimizing the cumulative submarine attrition that did so much to humble the Japanese. With a few exceptions, most submarine novels and movies are cast in an aura of perpetual glory with impossible heroes dispensing death and justice in the most improbable ways.

There were indeed real heroes: Slade Cutter of *Seahorse*, Dick O'Kane of *Tang*, Sam Dealey of *Harder*, Reuben Whitaker of *Flasher*, Dusty Dornin of *Trigger*, Mush Morton of *Wahoo*, to name just a few— and obviously, great crews to back them up.

The submarine *Batfish*, her skippers, and her crew were typical, not great. In service for less than two years during World War II, *Batfish* and those who manned her earned a Presidential Unit citation, nine battle stars, sank fourteen enemy ships, damaged two others, and rescued three Army bomber pilots from the East China Sea. Still, in a large war, in a large ocean, that was not uncommon.

In seven war patrols, *Batfish*, her three captains, and her officers and enlisted crewmen did most things common to submarines in that war under the Pacific—and one thing that had never been done before, or since. In February 1945 only four Japanese submarines remained in Philippine waters. Operating in the Luzon Strait on her sixth war patrol, *Batfish* encountered three of them and, in as many days, sank them. As a "submarine-killer submarine," *Batfish* became unique.

The accomplishment went generally unheralded. *Time* and *Life* had prepared fitting articles that were at first preempted for reasons of security, but *Batfish*'s story was finally upstaged by larger events. Deprived of her moment in the sun, she served modestly in the postwar Navy. Then in 1973 she made the world press in a controversy that threatened to destroy her. At the hands of Oklahoma submarine veterans, she had been transported to Muskogee, where spring floods and politicians almost did to her what the Japanese had never managed to accomplish.

Born 16 January 1925 in Alcolu, South Carolina, I dutifully attended elementary school in Oswego. After two years of high school in neighboring Sumter, with the lazy flies buzzing just enough to keep us barely awake, I found that the maps in the hot classroom remained flat on worn pages. But the maps in the newspapers were becoming exciting. Even though I hadn't reached my seventeenth birthday, as one of ten children in a farm family on the hungry heels of the Great Depression, I had little difficulty persuading my mother to sign the papers for me to join the Navy in late November 1941. On 1 December I received train tickets and Navy travel orders directing me to proceed on 6 December to Raleigh, North Carolina, for swearing-in proceedings on 8 December. En route, history happened.

7 December 1941

Early on this clear, quiet Hawaiian morning, the United States warships seemed to slumber at anchor by their docks. There had been increased patrols in the Pacific waters surrounding Hawaii like a vast moat, but—despite the scare talk of some unheeded few—there had been no actual event to provoke alarm. Should diplomats fail to negotiate a continuing peace with Japan, the American fleet and Army units were supposedly on the alert.

Since the turn of the century, overpopulous Japan had turned her gnawing need for space and materials into Russia, then China, in an attempt to reverse her increasingly unfavorable balance of trade. Of the many opposing factions contesting for control of her government and her destiny, General Eiki (Hideki) Tojo and his party took over and immediately planned aggressive expansion.

When Japan had begun encroaching upon French Indochina, the United States countered by stopping the export of scrap iron, steel, and other basic war materials to all but England and our closest allies. Hoping to regain materials blocked by this partial embargo, Japan moved major military forces into southern Indochina in July 1941. President Roosevelt quickly froze all Japanese assets in the United States, snapping trade between the two countries; then on 17 August, warned the Japanese that we would take "any and all steps" to protect "the safety and security of the United States."

American military leaders believed that sooner or later the United States would be drawn into the raging Atlantic-European war. If we entered the war against Germany and Italy, it followed that we would automatically be at war with Japan, due to her Tripartite Alliance of 27 September 1940. But most Americans considered it absurd that a tiny group of islands across the Pacific Ocean could ever be a threat to anyone but their even less civilized neighbors. The consensus of American opinion regarded the Japanese Pacific threat as a grandiose bluff.

On 14 November a Japanese submarine fleet departed the Yokosuka Naval Base for Pearl Harbor. Nine days later, a major Japanese task force consisting of two battleships, six aircraft carriers, with supporting surface and submarine forces, left its Kurile Islands base for the same destination. As they approached their rendezvous on 5 December, the code message "Climb Mount Nitaka" was received, and under concealing weather they proceeded to a point two hundred miles north of Oahu, Hawaii.

At 6 A.M. on 7 December a Japanese midget submarine crept into the harbor to reconnoiter the massed presence of our Pacific fleet. The midget was detected, but the report was regarded more as a curiosity than an alarm. Likewise, an Army radar station gave notice of two reconnaissance planes, but a subordinate with more pressing matters disregarded the message.

Japanese reconnaissance confirmed that most of our naval eggs were indeed in one basket. Eighty-six surface vessels and four submarines were crowded in the harbor, afloat or in some stage of repair in dry dock or at their piers. It was jokingly rumored that Roosevelt had ordered the fleet in to appease Honolulu shopkeepers; they lost money when the fleet was out at sea.

One hundred eighty-nine Japanese torpedo planes, horizontal and dive bombers were launched from their carriers. At 7:50 A.M., upon sighting the north point of Oahu, they split up into three groups to attack Pearl Harbor from the north, south, and east.

Five minutes later, the methodical devastation began. Bombers swept in low through the mountain passes and struck unalerted aircraft on the ground at Hickam, Wheeler, and Bellows fields. Most Army and Navy planes were destroyed within the first few minutes. Rushing to their remaining planes, pilots were incinerated in the multiple explosions of accurately placed Japanese bombs. A following wave of fighter planes, finding little in the air to fight, refocused on strafing runs on barracks and hangars.

The torpedo planes and other bombers concentrated on the sleeping fleet. The seven giants moored in Battleship Row were first-priority targets. All ships that could respond mustered gun crews, but for many, it was too late—it happened that quickly.

Mortally wounded by torpedoes, *Oklahoma* capsized. *Nevada* was struck, but managed to get under way and was trying to head for sea when five more bombs hit her. Her skipper ran her aground to keep her from blocking the channel. Hard hit in the first minutes of the attack, *California* caught a fifteen-inch armor-piercing shell converted into a bomb and began to sink. Afire and out of control, *West Virginia* listed sharply, wedging *Tennessee* against the pier where she in turn was hit. Wood-covered for target practice, ancient *Utah* was mistaken for an aircraft carrier, bombed, and capsized. Destroyers *Downes* and *Cassin*

9

in dry dock along with *Pennsylvania* were incinerated by a bombing; *Pennsylvania* fared somewhat better. A Japanese bomb penetrated *Arizona*'s forward magazine and exploded the battleship's ammunition, ripping apart her steel body. Over 1,000 men died instantly.

Heavy black smoke and fire surged skyward, intermittently concealing the Japanese attackers as they zoomed over and around for another attack. An airborne torpedo badly damaged the cruiser *Helena* as she lay alongside Ten-Ten Dock. Nearby, the shock of explosions capsized the unhit minelayer *Oglala*. Like *Nevada*, repair ship *Vestal* was beached in sinking condition. The *Curtiss*, a seaplane tender, was severely hit.

Onto the water flowed gasoline and diesel fuel from broken, burning ships. Men jumped, could not hold their breaths long enough to clear the blazing scum, and drowned or gulped a final breath of fire. Survivors were fished from the water and dragged from wreckage, then laid out upon any flat surface that wasn't aflame.

Upon the ground and water, the stunned defenders did more shooting than aiming, so shattering was the sudden horror to professional judgment and private nerve. In the pandemonium, base communications with the outside world snapped. Nobody knew what was going on beyond sight at any given moment. Every time anything moved, someone shot at it. Only 52 of our 202 naval aircraft managed to leave the ground in our defense; many of these were destroyed by both sides in the crossfire. Carrier planes from the distant *Enterprise* caught "friendly" fire as they tried to fight or land, as did some unarmed Flying Fortresses blindly entering the ambush while running out of fuel.

To relieve the first attackers and intensify the damage, a second wave of the Japanese air strike began at 8:50 A.M. With air retaliation effectively nipped in the bud, they concentrated single-mindedly upon decimating the surface fleet. By 9:15 A.M. nineteen American warships had been hit, nine of them sunk or sinking.

Antiaircraft rallied to drive away the third and final wave of attackers. Sustaining only minor damage, these last enemy planes returned to their carrier with little opposition, and the Japanese First Air Fleet stole away as smoothly as it had come.

Honolulu newspapers circulated extras almost before the Japanese left: "War: Oahu Bombed." "Deaths over Four Hundred at Oahu." (Our own guns probably did more damage to neighboring Honolulu than to the Japanese.) "Saboteurs Land Here." But there weren't any saboteurs; it was the Japanese fleet who skillfully knocked out our Pacific surface fleet, eliminating our means to counterattack or retaliate. In less than three hours, nearly every major military installation in the Pearl Harbor complex had been reduced to scrap metal. Over 2,300 sailors and soldiers had been killed; about 1,000 more were wounded. The Japanese had lost only twenty-nine aircraft, five midget submarines, and one fleet submarine.

Although Manila immediately learned of the Pearl Harbor attack, MacArthur fared little better than Pearl's Admiral H. E. Kimmel and General W. C. Short, who had been hit with no warning whatever. Within hours, the Japanese destroyed more than half of MacArthur's planes on the ground. (And within days, Japan would begin her full-scale invasion of the Philippines. By March 1942 MacArthur was forced to retreat from Luzon to Australia. Ironically, Admiral Kimmel and General Short were forced into retirement in February, taking the rap for the event of whose foreknowledge they seemed to have been deliberately deprived.)

Simultaneous with the attacks on Pearl Harbor and Manila, the Japanese closed in on the United States Pacific outpost islands. Midway's Marines, manning inadequate defenses since the first radio alarm from Pearl, caught their first enemy fire that evening. Pinpointed by a cruiser and destroyer moving at top speed, salvos from distant Japanese warships demolished the hangar and Marine Command post. The defenders prepared themselves for overwhelming odds. But the Japanese unexpectedly ceased fire and made a high-speed withdrawal. Apparently as with Pearl, Japan did not want to occupy Midway at this time, only disarm the occupants.

The following day, Wake Island—even more vulnerable than Midway—was hit by Kwajalein-based Japanese bombers and took two days of merciless pounding before a Japanese naval task force arrived to finish the job. The 350 defenders succumbed to this irresistible force on 24 December. Also practically defenseless, Guam fell to the Japanese invaders before dawn on 10 December.

In one clean, inexpensive sweep, Admiral Isoroku Yamamoto's war plan had crippled or captured America's strategic islands and reduced our mighty fleet to a smoking shambles. But however cunning and well-executed, however overwhelming its immediate shock effect, the master plan was flawed by a curious oversight.

The Japanese attack on our surface Navy and aircraft had spared the Pearl Harbor repair facilities and fuel tank farms. Without these, surviving and forthcoming naval vessels would have had to abandon Pearl totally as a base, and retreat to mainland-based operations.

With the importance that Japan invested in her own submersibles, it seems incomprehensible that not one Japanese bomb, torpedo, or bullet was dispatched at the American submarines, tenders, or submarine facilities at Pearl. Luckily, only four submarines were docked there on 7 December; greater numbers might have drawn Japanese attention. The total destruction of *Cachalot, Dolphin, Narwhal,* and *Tautog,* and their tender, *Pelias,* would have cost only minutes but the Japanese purposely overlooked them. By precise design, they attacked only major targets.

Yet history offered Japan the obvious parallel of England—another island nation. The astounding track record of German submarines in World War I, when the U-boat blockade nearly sank England's war effort, had clearly demonstrated the submarine's fighting potential—especially against a nation surrounded by the submarines' domain.

Japan's underestimation of the United States submarine fleet was apparently based upon stale intelligence gathered when World War II first erupted in Europe. In 1939 there had been only fifty-five U.S. submarines in active commission. But when the U-boats again tightened their stranglehold upon England and proliferated throughout the entire North Atlantic, the United States—however ponderously slow to unify in advance of catastrophe—saw the sparks and felt the heat. New submarines were developed and built at an increasing rate. By 7 December 1941 most of our "obsolete" and decommissioned boats had been refitted for training and coastal defense.

The intrinsic secretiveness of the Submarine Service precluded accurate intelligence of their growing numbers and deployment. Of 111 commissioned submarines, 22 operated out of Pearl. Unlike the surface fleet, they were widely deployed throughout the Central Pacific and along the American West Coast. And until the United States could recover, replace, and increase her naval forces, these unscathed submarines and their far-flung sister boats inherited the incredible burden of a hastily improvised Pacific defense.

About three hours after the Pearl Harbor attack—with 6 million of her troops already in the field—Japan anticlimactically declared war on the United States and Great Britain. Three days later, in accordance with their Tripartite Treaty with Japan, Germany and Italy declared war on the United States. Barely prepared to meet a major enemy on a single front, we were suddenly involved in a two-ocean war on a scale the world had never witnessed (a confrontation some believed our own President had allowed in order to revitalize our economy—a vigorous, bloody solution to our national Depression). Immediately, the Navy Department issued an unprecedented, unrestricted air and submarine warfare directive against Japan.

The U. S. Navy had neither advocated nor practiced unrestricted warfare on merchant shipping before. Submariners recalled with disgust (and merchant seamen with horror) the U-boat sinkings of defenseless cargo and passenger ships which drew shocked but unavailing protests from nearly every international organization.

American peacetime personnel had been trained in the practice of a legal, traditional war, observing standards derived from honorable sea combat doctrine throughout the ages. To translate the many treaty restrictions and legal limitations each American warship Commander was issued a slender volume entitled *Instructions for the Navy of the United States Governing Maritime and Aerial Warfare.* Central to its international standards, submarines were required to place a merchant vessel's papers, crew, and passengers in a place of safety before attacking, "except in the case of persistent refusal to visit or search."

But a new code was rapidly emerging from de facto U-boat practice. The *only* advantage a submarine has over any other warship lies in its power to strike from concealment—with the element of surprise. According to those former restrictions, a submarine would be at the mercy of any armed contender the moment she rose to order "Abandon ship!" Could the United States practice traditional warfare against unrestricted enemies? With the exception of hospital vessels, all Japanese ships—armed or not, whatever their cargo or purpose—were now ships of war. For some, this transition was hopelessly abrupt. Many peacetime captains trained to regard naval regulations as gospel were slow to grasp the fact that the Japanese practiced a different religion.

If the Japanese had followed through on their attack on Pearl Harbor, they could have had it for the taking. Consequently, as Pearl Harbor frantically fortified itself for the *coup de grace* which never came, the Japanese went unpursued.

Of the four submarines at Pearl, only *Tautog,* in need of further repair but technically seaworthy, could have gone to sea on short notice. Dry-docked *Cachalot* could not be operable for weeks, and *Narwhal* was in similar straits, next in line for complete overhaul.

Dolphin, just returned from a prewar patrol off Wake Island, was in the middle of a much-needed refit. Her hull was covered with "grass"—green algae that had grown thick and long during the many submerged hours in the warm waters. Her main engines were being reringed, and most of her pistons were sitting topside or over in the Engineering and Repair Shop. Several soft patches were off, and the hull was open so that submerging even alongside the dock was impossible. Defective battery grounds, electrical faults, and inoperable water distillers also mitigated against her going anywhere until some repairs were made.

During the following days other submarines arrived: *Argonaut, Gudgeon, Plunger, Pollock, Pompano, Tambor,* and *Trout.* Shocked at the devastation, the submarine crews completed the overhaul and stocking of their boats, but their defensive presence was thought to be so critical that days passed before the first of them ventured forth.

Gudgeon and *Plunger* were the first to depart, on 11 December. Prewar training had been conservative: to conserve fuel, they had been ordered to make half-speed on the surface during the day and anchor by night. Now they'd been ordered to get results, but no one was yet experienced enough to tell them how.

For most American captains and crews, this was a timid time of trial and error. Trained for balanced fleet operations, many of these skippers were shaken with the idea of entering Japan's dangerous and unknown waters without a fleet's support. The prospects of coming back alive were felt to be rather dim.

In the early morning hours of 9 December, I arrived in Norfolk, Virginia, along with a lot of other youngsters. Being a farm boy, I had naturally chosen the Navy. Being young and in love with adventure, I volunteered to serve in submarines, although the largest vessel I'd ever seen had been a barge on the Santee River. After an abbreviated six-week boot-training course at the Norfolk Training Station, I was sent to the Submarine School at New London, Connecticut. Arriving in mid-January 1942, I commenced my practical apprenticeship into the Silent Service aboard the first of several of these strange undersea boats with which I would become intimately acquainted.

Electing torpedoes as my submarine specialty, I attended the Navy Ordnance School, also at New London. Upon completion in late April, I was assigned duty aboard the U.S. submarine *O-8.*

When the Pacific War had erupted, most of our training submarines were of the older class: the numerically designated short-range

O-boats, R-boats, and S-boats. Designed for neither global cruising nor prolonged submergence, they had proved painfully inadequate to patrol the expanses of the world's largest ocean. Stowage space and living accommodations were cramped and primitive. Since they lacked air conditioning, the heat during even brief submergence in tropic waters quickly became unendurable. Nicknamed "pigboats," after the porpoise or "sea pig," the name degenerated as the boats aged, into a less flattering comparison.

Like all submariners, their crewmen were volunteers, renowned as tough men—possibly because they had to fight like hell to come up for fresh air! But as training boats in the relatively friendly waters of the American mainland, they served their purpose adequately.*

Much larger submersibles had been built during and after World War I, but these experiments had been expensive failures. Ponderous to maneuver, dangerously detectable, their heavy surface guns sapped their undersea speed and diluted their prime function: the stealthy approach and swift delivery of a surprise attack. American submarine designers took a closer look at the highly successful German U-boat then concentrated positively on the essential priorities of maneuverability, speed, range, firepower—and habitability.

In late 1942, when the skipper learned I could type, I was sent off to Radio-Sound School at Groton, Connecticut. At that time there was an acute shortage of radio operators in the Submarine Service. So because I could already type, it became expedient for the Navy—despite my torpedo specialty training—to teach me radio. Following the three-month Radio School, I returned to duty aboard submarine O-8, where I soon qualified as a sound operator in addition to being able to stand radio watch. Within six months I had also "qualified in submarines," meaning that if I had to, I could operate any part of the submarine in the dark under simulated battle conditions.

Armed with four practice torpedoes, we plied the waters off the Connecticut coast in training exercises with students from the Submarine School. Once, just outside the bay, we saw an unseen U-boat's torpedo miss us closely and heard it explode beyond us at its end-of-run. We crash-dived and listened. Hearing nothing, seeing nothing further, we raced toward the sanctuary of our home base at New London.

---

*A number of S-boats fought in the early years of the war, conducting war patrols in the Southwest Pacific and in the waters around Dutch Harbor, Alaska.

Even if our vintage *O-8* had been armed, we would have been no match for the U-boat. Being enlisted crew, however, it was not my place to ponder these things; I was merely thankful to have eluded a death I could not specifically imagine, and did my job.

I felt very fortunate when, in the late summer of 1943, I was transferred to the U.S.S. *Batfish*—one of the modern long-range fleet submarines all named after fish—then in the final stages of her construction at the Portsmouth Naval Shipyard in New Hampshire.

While gestating on the drawing board, this new undersea raider had been named *Acoupa*. But on 24 September 1942, prior to her keel laying, she was renamed *Batfish* after a "small, pediculate fish resembling the stingray, which sits on the bottom, supported by its fins, waiting for its prey which consists of almost everything coming within its reach." Although the physical comparison was unflattering, the implication of our expected performance came through loud and clear.

Launched 5 May 1943 under the sponsorship of Mrs. Nellie W. Fortier (mother of six New Hampshire sons serving in the war), *Batfish* was far superior to any of her predecessors. Reflecting twenty years of research and development, she was also the best of the Gato/Balao class first constructed in 1941. Although improvements and refinements were made throughout the war, there were no basic changes in the most complex, compact, formidable war machine ever produced by man to kill men. Her vital statistics were:

Length: 311'6"
Beam: 27'3"
Height: 47'3½" from keel to tip of periscope shears
Mean draft: 15'3"
Displacement: 1,526 tons surfaced with full war load; 2,391 tons submerged
Range: 10,000 miles at economical surface speed; 75 days
Cost: $7 million
Description: hunter, killer submarine
Fate: unknown

SHAKEDOWN

Three and a half months had passed since *Batfish*'s christening in her Portsmouth cradle. We envied our shipmates in the Pacific who were already seeing action while we still trained endlessly. Many of us seriously worried that the war would be over before *Batfish* could get into it. The weeks passed anxiously, but not too slowly—Lieutenant Commander Wayne R. Merrill and his staff of six officers pushed and squeezed us hard to fit into our jobs.

Any submarine is basically a watertight, pressurized hull strong enough to withstand incredible amounts of water pressure, plus the added shock of depth charging or collision. The two basic classes of fleet submarines are distinguished by the thickness of their all-welded steel pressure hulls. Otherwise identical to the "thin-skinned" Gato-class submarine with 7/8"-thick hulls, the basic Balao-class *Batfish* was built within and around a full 1" steel pressure hull.

About eleven times longer than wide, this tapered steel cylinder was divided internally by cross-ship bulkheads into eight watertight compartments. Two decks ran most of its length: the lower deck housed the batteries, pumps, most of her heavy machinery, and stowage. Below this was the bilge; below that, the keel. A narrow passageway ran the length of the upper deck through seven 1½' by 4' watertight bulkhead doors, each weighing more than five hundred pounds. At the narrow ends, two torpedo rooms carried twenty-four torpedoes: ten ready in the firing tubes, ten stored forward, and four aft.

The conning tower—a ninth watertight compartment integral with the pressure hull—was situated above and parallel to the hull amidships. A cylinder about 8' in diameter and 15' long, the conn was separated from the control room below by an oval watertight hatch slightly smaller than the bulkhead doors. Above the conn, beyond a round watertight hatch, was the bridge, open to the sea and air except for a low armored railing enclosure. Connecting the bridge to the conning tower was a metal ladder, use-polished like a fireman's pole; another one running from the conn to the control room rotated 90 degrees so that one usually ascended facing aft rather than port. In an emergency, one or both hatches would be slammed shut and dogged down. If our conning tower were hit or flooded, *Batfish* could then be operated from the control room—although blindly, without benefit of periscope.

Crammed inside the pressure hull were four diesel engines and two electric motors for propulsion, electrical equipment for operating mechanisms, navigational and fire-control instruments, valves, pumps, gauges, operating levers and switches, smaller "vital organs," spare parts, and other necessary equipment. There were air compressors and high-pressure air banks for blowing tanks, firing torpedoes, and maintaining a habitable atmosphere approximately equal to air pressure at sea level. Into the precious remaining space were woven an intricate maze of air, oil, water, hydraulic, and electric lines and pipes—part nervous system, part circulation.

Like any other ship, *Batfish* had the space and facilities for her five or six tons of humanity to live, eat, and sleep. We worked long hours to learn our places within her as we neared readiness to enter the war.

On 21 August 1943 *Batfish* was officially commissioned into active military service. We stood rigidly proud in salute as the United States flag was hoisted above *Batfish*'s stern. Captain Wayne Merrill, in the presence of a small group of visitors, read us his orders.

Following the ceremony, Captain Merrill said he wanted to talk to all enlisted men, with no other officers present. Assembled on an adjacent barge, we stood at attention. Short, handsome, with very wide-set eyes and a contagious smile, Captain Merrill came aboard and said, "Boys, relax." We had all been so busy readying *Batfish* for commissioning we'd had little time or energy to pay attention to personalities; Captain Merrill had always been all business.

"We'll be going out soon, and this is the first chance I've really had to talk to you man-to-man. As your skipper, I have certain interpretations about Naval Regulations that I want to get across. I'm going to tell you what my policies are.

"Let's say, first of all, if the Navy says the speed limit is sixty, I'm inclined to give you sixty-five—but that's it." He looked around. "Navy regs forbid gambling aboard ship. But this is the Submarine Service, not the battleship Navy. You can gamble all you want, but these are my rules: Every game will be cash-on-the-mahogany. If I ever hear of anyone going in debt or putting out an IOU, he'll be barred from further gambling. Now—this is for you old-timers—I don't want anybody hurt. If you get one of these young kids who doesn't know his ace from a hole in the ground, but he's willing to pay something to learn, that's fine. But I don't want you breaking him so he can't make a liberty. Either get him out of that game, or give him some free lessons.

"Now, I bought a slot machine from another boat, and it's stocked with nickels. If any of you need money, see the Chief of the Boat. There will be absolutely no interest, but you've got to pay it back. If the Chief thinks anybody's borrowing over his head, I'll decide whether he's to be cut off. When we go to sea, the slot machine gets sold to the next boat. I want my nickels back then; the rest of it is your slush fund." Then his voice became stern. "There will be no drinking aboard this boat. In port *or* at sea," he emphasized. "You can get as wild-ass drunk as you want ashore—in fact, I expect you to relax off-duty. You'll need to, and I'll back you up. But come across that brow with any booze, and you'll leave the *Batfish* for good. Incidentally, torpedo alcohol is no longer ethyl alcohol with a bad taste that you can filter out through a loaf of bread. It's methyl alcohol. I guess you could say the Navy's gotten wise. Please take my word that it will kill you. Any problems ashore getting the booze you need, come to me and I'll try to see you get it.

"Family emergencies, personal crises—anything that interferes with you getting back from leave on time, I'll do what I can to help you straighten it out. That goes for emergency leave, too."

We'd heard that Merrill had been out on seven war patrols; scuttlebutt had it that all of the submarines he had served aboard had been sunk shortly after he had been detached from them. Nine days after he left his last sub, *Grampus,* in Australia, she was sunk by a Japanese destroyer.

"We're all here for different reasons to do one job," he continued, his tone quietly serious. "We're going to kill Japs. Congressional Medals of Honor are most always awarded posthumously. Well, I don't want one on those terms. I've served under some heroic skippers, and I've survived all of them. It's logical for us to do the maximum damage to the enemy consistent with bringing you guys back alive and returning the government's investment in this submarine intact. That's what I'm getting paid for. Understood?"

Shakedown training began the next day—the rigorous "final exam" of captain, boat, and crew. A good shaking-down under simulated war conditions works the kinks and bugs out of the boat and her machinery and drills the awkwardness out of the men who move her. We remained in port only when we had to provision ship, take on fuel, or perform some minor repair or adjustment not readily made at sea. Every day, Sundays included, *Batfish* headed for deep water off the New England coast. At first, we went through the basic ABCs of sailing and diving our submarine.

On the surface, *Batfish* was driven by four Fairbanks Morse diesel engines generating 6,400 horsepower and a maximum surface speed of about twenty-one knots. Before submerging, she had to stop all engines, because the instant the main air induction valves and conning tower hatch were secured for submergence, air in *Batfish* became precious. In two separate compartments, a pair of huge, powerful batteries weighing more than 52 tons would propel *Batfish* submerged on electric motors for about twenty-four hours or one hundred miles at her most economical speed, far less at her maximum speed of nine knots.

On the surface, *Batfish* could drive herself directly with one, two, or three of her diesels while recharging her batteries with at least one. It usually took four to six hours' surface running for the diesels to recharge the batteries fully, and this should be done—conditions permitting—at least every twenty-four hours. To conserve the batteries, we would have to patrol on the surface whenever possible—for safety's sake, usually at night or under cover of fog or bad weather.

Batfish also had a second hull nearly surrounding the pressure hull like a bun upside down around a hotdog. Only the inner pressurized hull offered watertight integrity for crew and all equipment that could not be subjected to water or water pressure during submergence. Although the outer hull also contained many compartments including main water ballast tanks, variable ballast tanks, and fuel tanks for the approximately 140,000 gallons of diesel oil we would need for a full war patrol, it was not as sturdy as the pressure hull, nor did it need to be—for since it always had equal pressure inside and out, it would not crush with increased depth.

These two hulls were topped by a light steel superstructure that streamlined the submarine for maximum speed and smooth steering through the water, furnished support for the outside weather deck and heavy guns, and provided storage space for hawsers, life rafts, portable guns, ammunition, and other gear carried outside the hulls.

Having all that equipment cleverly jammed inside the pressure hull and tacked to its outside and between the hulls, a submarine would seem heavy enough to sink straight to the bottom. But float she did.

When filled with air, large buoyancy tanks supplied the flotation necessary to stay on the surface. They had holes in the bottom and air valves known as "vents" on the top which, when opened, allowed the air to escape. Seawater enters through the flooding ports, the tanks lose buoyancy, and the submarine submerges.

Controlling our rate of ascent and descent (as well as pitch and depth stability) was a series of trim and "variable ballast" tanks along the hull. We learned the two kinds of dives: normal and crash. On a normal dive there was no hurry. The approximately 225 individual manipulations necessary to rig *Batfish* for diving could be checked and double-checked, and we'd take her down gradually at comfortable angle. A crash dive was an emergency maneuver to save our neck. When an airplane screams down out of the clouds, the idea is to get under as soon as possible, any way you can, later adjusting trim and buoyancy before you plunge too deep.

In an emergency, *Batfish* could plummet to 400 or 500 feet and stay there for about a day and a night. Her normal test-dive depth was 400 feet—a depth usually exceeded by fleet-type submarines under enemy attack. While submerged, neutral buoyancy—that state in which the sub weighs exactly the same as the amount of water she displaces— is desirable, but difficult to maintain. As a craft sinks deeper and the pressure on her hull increases, the steel shell compresses, decreasing her already negative buoyancy. Unchecked, she would sink faster, deeper, until the point of no return where the pressure hull collapses. Although the maximum recorded depth survived by a fleet sub is still classified material, it was believed that this would happen to *Batfish* at approximately 850 feet.

Sinking can be stopped by blowing the water out of the ballast tanks with compressed air, by mechanically pumping the water out of the internal trim tanks, or by manipulating the bow and stern planes while under power.

Over and over we dived, trimmed the boat to level neutral buoyancy, then surfaced and repeated it again and again. A tough grind became tougher as the tempo of operations picked up to include high-speed maneuvers and quick dives—as when the diving alarm was sounded with no warning. And all this while we were testing our guns, torpedo tubes, and all other equipment. *Batfish* was equipped with a sensitive array of surveillance devices—radio, radar, sonar, and sound listening gear. Below periscope and radar depth, sound and sonar become a submerged submarine's only connection with its surroundings. Training with friendly ships and planes, our sound operators learned to detect and follow an unseen ship by the noise of her screws while she was still over the horizon beyond visual or radar range, and to distinguish from sound alone whether she was a merchantman or a destroyer.

Unlike this passive listening, the sonar mechanism generates an audible *ping* that spreads out underwater in all directions. When the ping hits something, the direction from which its echo returns will indicate its bearing. The time interval from ping to echo return, converted into yards by mechanical computer upon the video scope, indicates its range as well. But sonar was a two-edged sword; it could give an enemy surface vessel the means to locate *us* through his sound reception. Sound—just plain listening—was the tactic we employed generally and most productively aboard *Batfish*.

Near the bottom in shallow water, we practiced "silent running," necessary to evade tormenting destroyers. Noises transmitted through a ship's hull—machinery, hammering, an air-conditioner, a pump, even a dropped wrench—can be heard distinctly by a listening enemy under the right conditions.

We had no idea of what *Batfish* would sound like to enemy eavesdroppers, but we got a chance to find out on 18 September, after we had moved down the coast to Newport, Rhode Island, for more sophisticated training. One morning Captain Merrill took *Batfish* out to rendezvous with a launch specially equipped by the acoustics people to capture *Batfish*'s "sound signature"—a graphic measurement of the noise levels of specific equipment so we would know what to quiet down or cut off for silent running. Seventy-five feet off our starboard beam, the launch lowered an underwater microphone over its side.

With *Batfish* at anchor in shallow water, Merrill would communicate over a telephone cable strung between the boats. At his order, we came ahead slowly to settle *Batfish* down on the muddy bottom, where we would operate or cut off specific equipment on command from our listening captain. "Rig out the bow planes . . . Start up the trim pump." Again and again we responded. "Turn off air conditioning . . ." Then there was a long silence as we anticipated his next order.

"Who's taking a leak?" blared out over the ship's speakers. "I distinctly heard a man walk across the engine room deck plates into the maneuvering room, open the head door, and start peeing against that stainless-steel toilet bowl. And he's still peeing!" A mad rush for the head ensued, and we caught the culprit. Well, now we knew how sensitive an enemy's listening gear could be.

Thereafter, we drilled at creeping away *very* quietly, our screws barely turning over, while friendly destroyers dropped hypothetical depth charges at us. We spoke in whispers. We ran submerged at flank speed, making erratic maneuvers to be used only *in extremis,* when depth charges would drown out the attacker's sonar. We simulated all sorts of casualties, pretending that important machinery had been smashed in the attack and that we were limping home.

As the days passed our confidence in ourselves and each other increased, as we changed from an amorphous body of strangers into an integrated battle team. Each of us realized that his destiny and his submarine's destiny were one and the same: if his boat dies, the odds are three to one he dies with her. So he does his job to the very best of his ability, and constantly checks that everyone around him is working with the same understanding. Submariners have a saying that "there is room for everything aboard a submarine—except a mistake."

Finally, we took on a full load of practice torpedoes from the Torpedo Station on a little island in Newport Bay and proceeded on concentrated exercises with willing escorts who let us fire at them, while doing everything they could to make us miss.

During one of these practice runs, we had been directed to fire at a barge from the deepest spot in Newport Bay—about fifteen fathoms. Upon firing, when we surged forward and up a mud slope in order to observe the torpedo's run, our props sheared an underwater cable, cutting off all electrical power to the Torpedo Station. Until the cable could be spliced back together, they had to run emergency generators on the island, and *Batfish* went to the Newport Marine Railway for replacement of her slightly bent propeller. Since we were soon to be going out on war patrol, the increased vibrations would be a liability.

Our torpedoes were straight-running missiles that had to be perfectly aimed to hit. Our TDC (torpedo data computer) automatically registered our own course and speed; we had to feed it all the other information it would need, as accurately as possible: the target's estimated speed, range, course, true and relative bearings, and any inference we could make about its zigzag pattern—all variable within an instant. With this data the TDC could calculate the ideal course and speed range a torpedo would have to travel to hit the target—under ideal conditions. With no correction possible once it was fired, the torpedo would either hit or miss, according to the skill invested in the moment of firing.

We carried the standard Mark XIV torpedoes which could be set at either of two speeds: high power, capable of forty-six knots for a 4,500-yard range; and low power, at thirty-one knots for a maximum accuracy of 9,000 yards. The depth at which they should run could be pre-set to accommodate the state of the sea and the draft of the target. But the torpedo didn't continue straight out in the direction of the tube from which it was launched, once clear of it—like a shell from a gun barrel—unless you set it to do just that. Based upon its final computation at the moment of firing, the TDC could automatically set the torpedo to deviate from "muzzle" direction to head for any gyro compass point. Since the torpedo's gyro generated its own "magnetic field," independent of the earth's polarity, an accurate track should follow in a steady sea—as long as the gyro spun.

The Mark XIV, driven by a steam turbine that burned compressed air and alcohol, left a telltale wake of air bubbles that often warned its target of its approach in time to avoid. If an enemy ship zigged upon sighting the torpedo he might not only save himself, but gain as well a pretty good idea of where it came from. We had to aim well, however quickly, for hit or miss, we would have to dodge the inevitable retaliation once the enemy was alerted to our presence. Few good targets could be expected to be unescorted. But if we hit our primary target, there would be one less adversary to deal with in the aftermath.

During our war games, we fired one exercise torpedo at a destroyer in a perfect setup. Two minutes after, sound reported high-speed propellers coming our way fast—and increasing at an alarming rate. *Batfish* bottomed in the mud, and we listened as our errant missile buzzed back and forth, sounding, as one man said, as if "it was looking for its mother." Dud though it was, we could have been out of commission for weeks if this circular running torpedo had hit us. Although it couldn't puncture our pressure hull, it could knock off a periscope, dent our superstructure out of shape, or puncture a ballast or oil tank. Three thousand pounds hitting *anything* at forty-six knots is a significant collision. So when the spent torpedo had replaced its water-filled warhead with air and floated to the top, off it went to the torpedo shop for an autopsy. One of our third-class torpedomen had failed to hook up the air lead that gave the gyro its initial spin to activate it, so it had disoriented causing the torpedo to circle aimlessly. As a result, the torpedoman was busted back to seaman and had to leave the boat.

As we awaited orders to depart for the war, a team of visiting officers and scientists from the experimental mine depot at Dahlgreen, Virginia, asked us to lay out a minefield for them. These contact, tilt, and magnetic mines had not been tested outside the laboratory. To circumvent peril, their contact and magnetic features had been deactivated; we were to test only their tilt effectiveness. The ingenious detonator involved a copper ball in a copper cup. When the ball rolled far enough up the cup's side, it detonated the charge, theoretically sinking whatever had tilted the mine.

On the morning of the exercise, Captain Merrill invited the mine's inventor to join us. He declined, but insisted we would be in no danger. He'd be on the escort vessel—the minesweeper that would have to clear the area after it was all over. "I just need objective data," he said.

"Subjective won't do?" Merrill asked.

"Don't worry about it."

By 6 A.M. we were loaded with mines, three to each torpedo tube, and on our way. At the signal from the minesweeper, we began firing mines at timed intervals while proceeding at a steady three knots, submerged. Unitized into packages, each mine had its own anchor that would release a timed interval after firing; then the mine would float upward on a tether. We fired a bow cluster, which would theoretically ascend after we passed over them. Then so many seconds later we jettisoned a stern cluster, then another bow shot. By adjusting the time of release to our course and speed, we could theoretically pattern a perfect minefield—except for one thing. A pretty rough sea was running that day in the shallow water of Long Island Sound, and the wave action and currents were setting them off as soon as they were activated. Nearly every load of mines from the bow exploded almost as we passed over them.

Our practice firing term finally completed, we were fitted in Newport with twenty-four "live" torpedoes. The detonator was kept a few inches away from the hammer that would strike and eventually fire it. Even if the detonator accidentally fired in this position, it would not explode the warhead.

On top of the Mark XIV torpedo's warhead, in a dished-out compartment, was a small propellerlike water vane that revolved when the torpedo drove itself through water. This vane's shaft was a threaded rod connected to the detonator; as it turned, it screwed the detonator into line with the firing device, completing the alignment after the "fish" had traveled a safe distance from Mama—usually 350 yards.

On 26 September, we put in at New London. We now had to pass the rigid operational readiness inspection and prove to Commander Submarines Atlantic that we had learned our lessons and were ready to go to war. ComSubLant's seasoned staff of devil's advocates gave our boat a strenuous trial, running her through every maneuver a submarine could be expected to perform. They invented unexpected damage to the diesels, torpedoes, and casualties to other major equipment. They flipped critical switches at the wrong time, secretly opened valves that should be closed, closed valves that should be open, and tried in every wily, sneaky way they knew to snarl our operations.

But Merrill had done his job well. On 9 October 1943 *Batfish* passed her exams. Back we went to New London for minor repairs and to take on fuel, provisions, and a full load of live ammunition. On 14 October we were pronounced ready for battle.

PASSAGE TO PEARL

WAYNE RUCKER MERRILL—"W.R." "Merrill" "Wayne"—
Philosopher de luxe, with a lot of airy views, and a lot more sound
ones that made up for them. So was Wayne, ever a born snake
and ever in search of whatever life had in store.

Academics—poof! Grease—two poofs! Good times—well, not
so many poofs! But the Academy was a place he never quite lost
sight of, because he knew it wasn't such a bad place after all. It
made one turn in at ten, it made chow much too regular, and it
was, oh, *so* confining. Being a good place for a long bull session,
its good points outweighed its evil ones—for Wayne. And so he
got by—which was all Uncle Sam asked.

You never really knew this Missourian until you talked with
him seriously alone. Then you soon discovered that a happy-go-
lucky soul isn't so happy-go-lucky as you think, but instead a
concoction of some very stable, sound sense. Wayne didn't
believe in letting life bore him, but neither did he look at it nor
live it, at all one-sidedly. You could tell he was from Missouri
as soon as he told you, so you were never long in finding out.

He hated greasiness and loved the femmes. He liked to do
things but balked at the marching. A "Black N" man with a
"gold N" complex—and a fellow you'd like to know—because
he'd like to know you. (Anyway, he rated his 3.4 in Bull.)

U.S. Naval Academy *Lucky Bag*
Class of 1934

A pea-soup heavy fog had rolled in over New London. Our orders for
departure for Pearl Harbor had come through with the assumption that
we'd leave at dawn, but we were now free to depart at will. Still feeling
good after saying good-bye to most of New London, it was decided to get
under way as soon as everyone was aboard.

With a sky dark as midnight in a well, Captain Merrill ordered
Batfish to cast off from the pier and get under way. We churned down-
stream through the channel and navigated blind to within a mile of the
trestle and the highway bridge that would both have to be raised for us.
Through the thick gray mist, the lookouts could hardly see each other, let
alone the bridges. The exec said he could navigate no further under these
circumstances and requested permission to go below, leaving the
problem with the captain. Permission was granted.

Captain Merrill and most of his officers were from Missouri, which engendered automatic conviviality. Another Missourian was to have been our exec upon commissioning, but he was delayed and hastily replaced. Despite the best of naval tradition, academy ties, and officers' code, the captain and the exec were not the best of friends from the very beginning. The exec had urged waiting for dawn to cast off, and this difference of opinion strained a merely civil relationship even more.

Merrill maneuvered *Batfish* to the edge of the channel, where we anchored for the rest of the night. With first light, the fog began to lift and soon we were under way once more without incident.

Connecticut landmarks passed slowly from sight. It was impossible not to wonder when we would ever see these familiar shores again. But like hangovers, these moods pass. By dusk we were off Montauk Point, our bow pointed due south, and we now sailed briskly at flank speed on all four diesels. The heavy mood of parting changed into a sort of thrill anticipating what now at last lay ahead of us.

We had a grand passenger aboard—a scientist from the Woods Hole Oceanographic Institute. Small, wiry, and bald as a knob, Dean Bumpus looked every bit the professor, yet he always had a merry glint in his eye and a quick sense of humor. Until we reached Panama, his job was to calibrate and monitor our newly installed bathythermograph, which recorded outside water temperature at any given depth to locate sonar-deflective thermal layers. Although these layers' existence was widely recognized, the body of accumulated scientific data about them was skimpy and uncoordinated.

In water of uniform temperature, density, and salinity, sound travels at a constant speed in a straight line. Usually the ocean's temperature decreases steadily with depth—which will cause a sound wave projected just under the surface to curve downward until it either dissipates at great depth or bounces off the bottom. But for a number of reasons, the ocean is seldom homogeneous: great currents of varying temperature, speed, and contour travel great distances in seasonally varying paths and convergences, carrying icy polar water into the tropics, conveying immense streams of tropic water into the far reaches of the north and south. The resulting so-called thermal layers can "trap" sound, or deflect a sonar probe much the same as a mirror reflects light. Thermal inversions—where the temperature increases with depth—can channel sound waves for phenomenally long distances. Then the sonar ping curves upward and, hugging the underside of the surface, goes far out.

A surface vessel, with its sonar and "ears" at a fixed depth, has to do the best it can with the water conditions it finds. But by learning to use the bathythermograph, *Batfish* could now sample the water from the surface all the way down to three or four hundred feet and cruise at the depth where we found the best listening conditions—or the best sound-deflective shield.

En route south, under Bumpus' enthusiastic tutelage, *Batfish* had been allowed extra transit time to probe the warm, mighty Gulf Stream. We skirted it from either side and plumbed it shallowly while contending with its current. Then our scientist said he'd like to see if we could "get to the bottom of this"—literally; he and Captain Merrill developed a bet for a round of drinks in Panama and *Batfish* dove deep while Bumpus monitored the graph. Deeper and deeper we went—then below test depth. Merrill was expectantly waiting for the scientist to say, "That's deep enough" when suddenly we bumped on something as resilient as a soft mud bottom.

"All motors stop," the captain called. "Rig for silent running."

Merrill and Bumpus grinned at each other as *Batfish* was carried along silently by the bottom of the great Gulf current, supported by nothing more than the mattress-firm surface of a twenty-degree thermal variant! It was an eerie feeling. Where would we end up, we wondered, if we went along for the entire ride? Bumpus lost his bet, but he seemed happy enough at the prospect of paying off.

Except for daily trim dives and drills, our passage southward was otherwise a high-speed surface run to keep the modified schedule ComSubLant had set for us. We maintained a zigzag course, having been warned of increased U-boat activity on the well-worn "groove" along which Panama-bound submarines were generally routed. The entire Atlantic coast and Caribbean were favorite prowling grounds for these deadly poachers, which took a frightening toll on our shipping, often within sight of shore. But another major headache was the "friendly" American aircraft heavily patrolling the areas we had to pass through. In friendly waters, standard practice prohibits aircraft from bombing submarines within established safety zones.

Just two days before our departure from New London, however, a United States bomber operating out of our base at Guantánamo had received "faulty instructions" concerning our sister fleet submarine *Dorado*—or misidentified her. Like *Batfish*, she was a new ship on her maiden voyage to the Pacific via Panama. The plane sank her in these waters with all hands aboard, and the axiom "A submarine is every-one's enemy" had been tragically proven once again. Consequently, *Batfish* became the first new boat to take a slightly varied (hopefully safer) route through the Mona Passage between the Dominican Republic and Puerto Rico, instead of via the customary Windward Passage between Cuba and Haiti.

Regardless how *Dorado* met her end, we remained healthily spooky, and our lookouts earned their keep. Past Jamaica, for a day and a half *Batfish* sliced the flat, blue waters of the Caribbean like a shark's fin. Weather was increasingly cloudy. We had to approach well east of the Canal Zone, since a large Allied convoy was now proceeding northwest out of the Canal, and we knew that every "friendly" would be especially protective until this convoy had cleared the area. We maintained maximum lookout and radar surveillance, and the sound operator's earphones never left his ears.

Slightly ahead of schedule on 31 October, we slowed our progress to fifteen knots and were zigzagging more radically when our OOD sighted a periscope sticking six feet out of the water, about three hundred yards off our port bow.

"Left full rudder! All ahead flank! Make ready two stern tubes," he shouted. "Captain to the bridge!"

Operating the fathometer in the control room, Captain Merrill heard the commotion and clambered to the bridge, immediately sounding the general alarm. "Rudder amidships and steady," the OOD ordered. The scope had slithered out of sight.

Two minutes later, we spotted the periscope being run up about 650 yards starboard off our stern. "Left full rudder!" Merrill shouted. *Batfish* heeled violently left as the scope, now exposed four feet, moved toward us through the water at about five knots. Merrill tried to fix the aft target bearing transmitter on the U-boat, but the searchlight and 20-mm gun obstructed his view. "Meet and steady her," he called to the helmsman, attempting to get a zero stern angle on the German submarine.

Below, we responded as if there were a torpedo speeding toward us. Banging heads and skinning knuckles, we moved as if the closing yards were inches—and hoped it was a drill.

"Torpedo tubes nine and ten ready, Captain," reported up from the conn. As our stern churned past the enemy periscope and our swing was almost stopped, the scope was hauled down.

"Fire nine!" Merrill called into the bridge speaker. With no confirmed reference for firing, we estimated a five-degree lead angle. As our stern steadied on the last sighting of the U-boat's periscope, we

30

"shot from the hip" a single torpedo. It sped away, its wake invisible through our engine exhaust smoke.

"Can't track it, Captain," the sound operator called. "We're making too much speed to hear it over our engines."

Right after firing, our lookout reported observing a large bubble—similar to an impulse bubble made by a just-fired torpedo—about a hundred feet to the left of our wake and about two thousand yards distant. We began making short, quick zigs at flank speed away from the scene.

Four minutes after firing, we heard a distant rumble as our torpedo exploded at its end-of-run—indicating it had run straight, hot, and normal. With so little to go on, there had been no point in firing any others. The enemy sub had had the drop on us: no doubt she'd been looking us over quite a while before we spotted her. Despite the sighted impulse bubble, there was no firm evidence that she had fired back at us. Why she didn't shoot—if indeed she didn't—we could only guess.

When we got about eight thousand yards out from our firing point, we came back to base course and slowed to standard speed to reload our empty torpedo tube. All voices were silent, all ears attuned to our sonar and sound. But the U-boat had disappeared.

Night quickly came on with a clearing sky. The silvery patch of the moon silhouetted *Batfish* on the surface. Up on the bridge, the lookouts suspected that every Caribbean whitecap was concealing a periscope. Here was war at last. We suddenly became very serious, because this boat was our home now; there was no nest to run to. Instead of returning to their bunks, those men not on watch began filing into the after battery mess. They sat silently over coffee, alone, or in groups softly talking. We knew our boat's steel hull, so thick and strong in Portsmouth cradle, could not withstand the direct impact of the smallest enemy shell, let alone a speeding 3,000-pound torpedo. No matter how well a new ship does at drills, those are make-believe affairs. Now it was firmly fixed in everyone's mind that we were no longer safe from the distant ravages of war but were, in fact, in mortal danger every minute. There is no classroom for that lesson.

After the attack, Dean Bumpus was discovered under the captain's mattress, but we couldn't decide whether he had been panicking or just pulling our leg. He now strolled into the mess, looked us over inscrutably, then drew a mug of coffee and joined us. "That fathometer brings those U-boats up every time," he said, not entirely as a joke—the fathometer was a detectable form of sonar. "I can climb under a mattress when it gets rough. The difference is you fellows can't."

Everyone who met his glance smiled reluctantly, as if it hurt. Homesickness could be read on each green face.

"Hell, I'm a damned civilian!" he burst out.

A wave of laughter went around. "Hey," someone offered, "you guys remember old what's-his-face, the quartermaster from the sub school? The one who just got out of the sack to go on watch, and asked how the weather was topside? And the Chief tells him 'It's wet topside.' So the old guy dresses full out in foul weather gear and red goggles and marches through the control room, up through the conn .·. . then up the ladder to the bridge to stand watch . . . and drives his skull down to his collar buttons trying to go through the closed hatch! We was at two hundred feet!"

We'd heard it before, but we *liked* hearing it again.

"Hey, you remember when the captain asked the cook what he was making? And Nat, he says, straight face and all, 'About a hundred and fifty dollars a month, sir!' "

On it went into the night. One by one we turned in for some shut-eye, feeling we'd earned it, and there was some hope we'd do all right.

Above, it was the kind of tropical night people write songs about. But it was too bright, too peaceful; we were too conspicuous. Our batteries were charged, and we had enough fresh air. We submerged. Come morning we would rendezvous with our escort, who would chaperone us safely through to Coco Solo in the Canal Zone. Here, German submarines would most likely congregate like hungry sharks at the mouth of a bountiful river; so here our defensive forces were also massed in strength.

Next reckoning at dawn. Morning and evening twilight were the times for celestial observations to verify our navigation, when both the stars and the horizon were visible. But it was then we could most easily be sighted by a periscope *we* would not likely perceive.

The navigator (always the exec) was ready with his sextant; we had had no navigational fix for two days. The clear dawn heavens informed us we were only about five miles from where we'd thought we were: thirty miles northeast of Cristobal at the mouth of the Canal. We radioed our position, and were told an escort vessel would soon be out to meet us.

A Navy Patrol bomber spotted us first. Since a submarine does not challenge a friendly aircraft, we reversed the procedure and flashed the coded *answer* to his expected challenge with our deck searchlight. Thereupon, he was to challenge us properly. We would then repeat our answer, thereby exchanging recognition signals in a roundabout way.

Beginning to circle us, the bomber finally beamed his challenge—and there was an immediate problem: our recognition signals didn't mesh! His were obsolete, at least twelve hours behind ours, and apparently he wasn't going to take the time to check it out. We continued to signal the correct answer and at the same time, we ran our biggest American flag up our attack scope.

"He's opening his bomb bay doors!" screamed a lookout.

Circling at only four hundred feet, there was no way he couldn't see who we were or fail to recognize his country's flag. But still he kept coming closer.

"Send off the recognition flares," Merrill snapped. Mounted on each side of the bridge, these flares were of different vivid colors, changed daily in conformance with a strict recognition code schedule. Two men rushed to them and pulled the lanyards at their bases, ducking back as they rocketed upward to explode with a Fourth of July brilliance. The plane banked closer, flattening for a dive.

We didn't have enough water to dive from sight without bottoming. And even if we did, the "friendly" could construe it as a move suspicious enough to make him release his bombs.

"Gun crew to the conn!" Merrill ordered over the ship's speaker. If he dropped his bombs, he was close enough not to miss, but that put *us* close enough to shoot him down if he tried!

Suddenly a brilliant green flare identical to our own exploded above the southern horizon. Our escort vessel loomed into sight. Apparently in radio communication with the plane, she alerted him of our nationality and he pulled upward from us—the first sign of easing from his obvious intention. We exchanged full and proper recognition signals with the escort and swung in astern to follow her for the remaining miles to the mouth of the channel entrance.

There our escort departed, leaving us in the company of two minesweepers, one forward a few hundred yards, the other aft. We proceeded slowly into the buoyed channel. It then occurred to us that our U-boat of yesterday could very well have been a minelayer—with no torpedoes—who had laid all her mines and was on her way home. German mines were insidious magnetic-acoustal death traps. Each one clicked off a different predetermined number of times as ships passed over it before rising to destroy the *next* vessel to pass over. Our forward minesweeper was busy employing every trick to bring them up and explode them ahead of us.

At midday we brought *Batfish* up to her assigned pier at Coco Solo—and enjoyed feeling safe. Captain Merrill went immediately to headquarters and reported the identification number on that bomber, then sought out the pilot. In his friendliest possible manner, he insisted that the airman join us for our evening meal—not telling him that we had nearly been his victims that morning. Merrill's idea was to show him what a U.S. submarine looked like.

Despite our irritation at his disregard of established precaution, we gave him the full tour of our boat. After dinner, Merrill invited the flyer to the bridge. While the pilot was enjoying the view, Merrill and the OOD tripped both bridge flares. Two vivid red rockets streaked skyward with a bang, showering the bridge with sparks. The young pilot almost jumped overboard.

"Now, son," Merrill calmly said. "Those are submarine recognition flares. And I tripped these flares while you were circling me with your bomb bay doors open. You mean to tell me you didn't see them?"

"Well," the pilot stammered, "I thought they were your engine exhaust. I thought your exhaust came out the sides of your conning tower."

"Even if it did, it wouldn't be red and green." Merrill ushered him aft, showed him where our exhaust ports were, then bid him a very cordial good night.

With most of the evening still ahead for all who were off duty, we collected our bet from Dean Bumpus. He paid off royally. Not a drinker himself, he pretended drunkenness so convincingly that we had to drink hard to catch up with him. Hours later, captain and crew finally managed to stagger and crawl back to *Batfish* to sleep it off.

Early next morning, our operations officer brought the captain's orders down to the boat—an unusual deviation in procedure—and slapped Merrill on the back. "You lucky son of a bitch!" he exclaimed. "First you ran into a U-boat, then you almost got bombed. Did you know that the minesweeper coming in behind you yesterday brought up a mine? If it had been set for one click less, you'd have gotten it!"

We made ready to get under way within the hour. At the pier to see us off was Bumpus, bright and cheerful, bearing a good-bye gift: a little, dried batfish preserved and mounted on a plaque. Now where in the hell did he get that?

Our passage from Atlantic to Pacific took us most of the day. We crossed four and a half miles of canal into Limon Bay, and then on another seven miles, veering slightly westward to reach Gatun Locks. Three separate locks lifted us a total of eighty-five feet to the level of Gatun Lake. Heading south again to the mouth of Gaillard Cut, the Pedro Miguel Lock raised us another thirty feet into Miraflores Lake. Across the lake, the Miraflores Locks lowered us fifty-five feet to Pacific sea level. A final two and a half miles, and we were in Balboa on the Bay of Panama, now a unit of Commander Submarines Pacific (Com-SubPac), based at Pearl Harbor. We tied up at Balboa's naval station for minor repairs, to top off our fuel tanks (the civilian in each of us still got a kick out of getting "free gas") and replace the aft torpedo we'd fired at the U-boat.

Our run-in with the enemy had been fortunate for us in more ways than one. Most of the torpedoes we were carrying were new experimental Mark XVIII electric torpedoes, not yet considered operational. We were delivering them to Pearl, where they would be exchanged for standard Mark XIV's. Since the Mark XVIII's were not to be fired, with only two Mark XIV steam torpedoes ready in our tubes we would have been at a decided disadvantage had the U-boat chosen to duel.

Still, the official endorsement to our U-boat contact report criticized us for firing only one torpedo. On top of that, shore-based authority classified the sighting itself as "possible" in spite of positive identification by the captain, exec, OOD, and two lookouts. But we couldn't always bring in prisoners to prove these things.

Our week-long stay ashore provided welcome leg-stretching along with some refreshing elbow-bending. Many of us headed for Coconut Grove, the whorehouse district in nearby Panama City, where two dollars would get the rest of our needs taken care of.

The morning of 8 November, *Batfish* nosed into the Bay of Panama in a southerly direction. Once we'd cleared Punta Mala, we set a west-by-north course and felt safer for a while. Although a canal is a river with two mouths, the southern end of this one was keeping its teeth less tightly clenched, the U-boat menace behind it. From here, it was five thousand miles to the home waters of the Japanese Empire.

35

With only daily fire-control and emergency drills to break the featureless monotony, *Batfish* forged westward across the Pacific. All memories of land faded behind us. Here was a lot of sun and clear blue ocean, with no landmarks. Progress was measured by the clock. It would be easy to imagine *Batfish* fixed and motionless, with an infinite flow of water moving past her.

And war seemed no more real than land right now, this far out on the calm vast sea.

Perhaps for this reason, our orders to remain undetected were unwittingly disobeyed. Shortly after sunrise on 15 November, we sighted two masts of a vessel about fourteen miles distant. Through the high periscope, we made her course out to be south by southwest. Surfaced with the rising sun behind us, we approached to about eight miles, well beyond her effective gun range. It was a friendly tanker of about 12,000 tons, unescorted but armed. We didn't attempt to exchange recognition signals, as it was highly unlikely she could see us against the brilliant sun. For the same reason, we didn't submerge, just kept our distance and watched her progress.

About half an hour after first sighting, we were lifted up on a thirty-foot swell, bobbing us into sight. The tanker immediately swung hard right and fired her stern gun at us. A damned good lookout with an itchy trigger finger! Well, we couldn't blame him, and dove. Thirty-five feet under, we faintly heard the single shell explode at least a mile short. At one hundred feet, we changed course and skulked away. Hell, we'd only wanted to look at something solid! When we surfaced an hour later, there was nothing in sight on the blue Pacific.

Four days later, we arrived at our rendezvous point off Oahu. As strains of Hawaiian music from our Victrola came over our PA system, we approached volcanic Diamond Head, magnificent in the early morning sunlight; those of us below pictured the spectacle in our minds. The spell was shattered by a PBY noisily closing in to see if we were on schedule; he exchanged recognition signals crisply, without threat, and gave us aerial escort. Soon *YMS 286* sped out to meet us, exchanged recognition, then flashed, "Follow me." We obediently swung in astern.

As we neared the unjettied channel entrance to Pearl Harbor, there was much efficient activity, surface and aloft, and no sign whatever of devastation. We moved through the sheltered channel, smooth and unruffled. Following our escort's example, *Batfish* throttled down to half speed, now proceeding past Hospital Point. Rounding a long bend to the left, then another to the right, suddenly we were *in* Pearl Harbor.

Indelibly familiar landmarks loomed before us, meshing into our memories of blurred, twitching black-and-white newsreels and *March of Time* movies. What wreckage had been removed, the mind supplied in detail.

In the center of the harbor was Ford Island, judiciously ringed by a small percentage of our present surface fleet. Beyond Ten-Ten Dock, 1,010 feet long, were the submarine piers. Then the dry docks, and submarine diving tank tower. Most of the ships sunk by the Japanese had been removed from the harbor. *California, Nevada, Maryland,* among others, had been salvaged and now fought in the war. Only *Arizona* remained in place, a rusting tomb with many of her dead still in her. We assembled on deck and stared at the sight. We were here at last, where the war began nearly two years before.

We found our place and docked among a number of submarines berthed at adjacent piers. Above us all, like a brood hen, rose the tender *Griffin,* whose function it was to supply office space and quarters for submarine division and squadron commanders, to house relief crews, supply food, clothing, and medical goods, and complete most ship repairs.

Within minutes we'd secured our lines to the pier and a delegation led by Charles A. Lockwood, ComSubPac, came aboard to greet us. We'd heard he looked after his men, but we didn't expect he'd meet us at the dock. It was an honor.

He briefed us on a greatly improved SJ radar with a plan position indicator (PPI) scope that would enhance our night radar surface attack—something we'd practiced somewhat short of perfection. The tactic itself had been potentially more effective than the equipment we currently had to back it up: at its most dependable, our present SJ surface search and fire control radar was often inadequate. "This innovation will give you surface-search capabilities we've never had before," Admiral Lockwood concluded. "To the best of my knowledge, no one else in the Pacific has it." And immediately following his departure, a small group of technicians swarmed aboard *Batfish* to install the new radar equipment.

When *Batfish* was running on or slightly under the surface, radar was our principal means of locating still-unseen enemy targets. Developed by the British, radar works in the air much the same way sonar works in the water; it sends out a radio (rather than a sound) wave. After striking an object such as an enemy plane or ship, the radio echo returns to the sending station to reveal range and bearing.

Batfish's fixed-antenna, non-directional, SD air search radar was like a burglar alarm—it told us that somebody was coming in, but not through which window. Our new SJ's rotating antenna could operate for effective surface-search capability. With it a skilled SJ radar operator could tell much the same about the prospective target as the sound operator with his "ears." Its PPI scope was similar to the video screen of our sonar. The following day, most of the radio gang was shipped off to Ford Island to learn how to operate this wonder of modern science. We studied it eight hours a day for six days, returning to *Batfish* every afternoon for further training.

The remainder of our three weeks at Pearl was spent preparing for war patrol. The long, hard hours were grueling but exciting—we were about to enter the arena at last! Although we were still untested within enemy territory, the results of our training were conspicuously evident. Patriotic kids with little but revenge and glory on our minds were now professional warriors, keen for our first assignment—with every hope for success.

The prolonged eve of our final departure for combat wasn't all work, however. The luxurious Royal Hawaiian Hotel was leased exclusively for the onshore accommodations of off-duty submariners and aviators. Not much sleeping was actually done here because most submariners felt they would catch up on sleep back on board their boats; whereas the Royal Hawaiian provided a fine base from which to go out and find women and a place to drink when you got tired of bar hopping—although you had to bring in your own booze.

Captain Merrill was a hardworking perfectionist when it came to running *Batfish* and training her crew. Ashore, he worked just as hard and long at unwinding. A highly social man, he delighted in women, drinking, and conversation. Whenever we encountered him off duty, he never pulled rank and usually welcomed us to join him. Even those of us who managed on a little sleep marveled at how he seemed to thrive on none.

On 25 November *Batfish* entered dry dock for repair of her starboard propeller, slightly bent when she came alongside *Griffin*. Her bottom paint was also touched up, and she undocked the same day.

28, 29 November 1943

Under way conducting radar rehearsals, radar tracking, and night radar rehearsals. Received two indoctrinational depth charges.

Log of U.S.S. Batfish (Merrill)

During this practice depth charging, our new radar antenna failed the acid test. We were supposed to hold a course parallel to our friendly destroyer escort (DE) "attacker." Submerged at periscope depth, with both scopes up, Captain Merrill watched through the observation scope. The destroyer escort was kept alert to our position by a red flag attached to our high attack periscope. Merrill decided to give the new hands a more realistic taste of what depth charging was really like, and suddenly closed the DE more narrowly then he'd been ordered. As a consequence, the DE dropped her "indoctrinational" charges almost on top of us, knocking out the packing of our number two periscope. Even the old hands turned a little green. But it was then we discovered that the SJ antenna had not been properly shock-mounted. Far better to have it happen here where we could get immediate repairs than in the Japanese front yard. While we were in, the Engineering and Repair Shop also repacked the leaking periscope.

30 November, 1 December 1943

Participated in convoy exercise with *Silversides* and *Tarpon*. Made two night surface attacks.

2 December 1943

Under way for radar rehearsals, radar tracking, night radar rehearsals, battle surface, firing all guns, and firing of three exercise torpedoes.

7, 8 December 1943

Conducted radar rehearsals, radar tracking, night radar rehearsals, four-inch night gun firing, and fired three exercise torpedoes. ComSubPac boarded for 8 December firing.

9, 10 December 1943

Loading and making final preparations for sea. Painted ship in accordance with latest camouflage instructions: flat black decks and dark gray overall.

11 December 1943

Readiness for sea date.

FIRST WAR COMMAND
FIRST WAR PATROL

11 December 1943

After we took on fuel from the dock, trucks brought the last of our provisions. Throughout the morning, every remaining niche in the boat was crammed with food and supplies, but we found room to take on a last-minute passenger—a priest bound for Midway.

When the brow was pulled ashore at 1 P.M., *Batfish* backed slowly from the dock and turned, with *YMS 286* as our escort through Hawaiian waters. Two years and four days after the Japanese struck here, *Batfish* was finally ready to strike back—there.

Next stop: Midway, standard operating procedure for all submarines departing Pearl for Japan. There we would top off our fuel tanks (thereby gaining about a three-thousand-mile extension in cruising range), effect last-minute repairs, and receive specific operational orders for our war patrol.

At 7:20 P.M. we released our escort. An hour later SJ radar contact with the island of Kaüai, 39,000 yards astern, blinked off the radar screen, leaving Hawaii behind but for radio contact. In bright moonlight, our first night out was uneventful. But the SJ sentinel earned our increased respect when it picked up a floating box at 1,200 yards.

Come daylight, we began a zigzag course. Within an hour, we exchanged recognition signals with a *PB-2Y* at six miles. We eyed him suspiciously as he circled once, then flew off. When we submerged for a midafternoon trim dive, the gasket on the crew's mess hatch began to leak badly. It mysteriously stopped at eighty feet, but when we surfaced half an hour later, it again began admitting water whenever a wave washed over the deck. Repair en route was possible, if difficult; but the Engineering and Repair Shop at Midway would not only take care of it but might prolong our brief stopover long enough for one more party.

12 December 1943

9 P.M. Our passenger to Midway, Lt. (jg) W. S. Brown, ChC-V(G), U.S.N.R., valiantly fought off an attack of minor nausea long enough to hold the first divine service in a U.S. submarine en route to a patrol area.

41

We were grateful for the service, but nausea always threatens to be contagious. Despite our determined efforts to mask hangovers, the long, high swells of the sea added a few off-shades to an already green crew. And during the evening, the heavy swells increased to the point where we began taking water down the conning tower hatch, finally to the extent of grounding out our Bendix log repeater.

At dawn on 15 December, after four days of our steaming northwest, two Navy planes approached to escort us into Midway. Numerous small surface craft bobbed into view as we neared the island and other aircraft darted across the sky. Three hours later, Midway rose into view through our high periscope. Low puffy clouds and an azure ocean enveloped the atoll, still fifteen miles distant.

During the first year of the war, Japan had seized or safeguarded for later claim nearly every territory to the west, north, and south of her home islands. Already firmly entrenched in Korea, Manchuria, and China, she had increased and strengthened her incursions into French Indochina. Hong Kong fell to the Japanese on Christmas Day; Singapore surrendered on 15 February with the Malay Peninsula succumbing in the aftermath. Siam was forced into an alliance treaty with Japan on 21 December; from this base Japan proceeded to occupy Burma by late May 1942. Striking Ceylon on 4 April, the Japanese threatened India and the Indian Ocean.

Driving southward, the Japanese swiftly claimed the Netherlands Indies. Advancing from their Marshall and Caroline Island bases, the invaders moved to the southeast into the Bismarck Archipelago, New Guinea, the Solomon Islands, and took the Gilberts in the central Pacific.

Every week, American newspapers revealed more enemy raids and conquests. In the Philippines, defending forces had been squeezed onto the Bataan Peninsula and the island fortress of Corregidor. With no relief arriving from the United States except for an occasional plane, submarine, or small boat, these remaining forces were completely overwhelmed by 6 May.

To the northeast, the Japanese seized and occupied the Aleutian islands of Kiska, Attu, and Agatta on 14 June. But this was the last outgoing conquest the Japanese were able to make.

With few exceptions, Japan's initial advance accorded with Admiral Yamamoto's prediction that Japan could have her way with the Pacific for a year or so until the "sleeping giant" awoke. The first significant resistance came in early May in the Solomons near Guadal-canal: the Battle of the Coral Sea. Opposing naval forces fought to a standoff with extremely heavy losses to both sides. Yet this was the first naval encounter of the war in which Japan was *forced* to turn back.

The Japanese returned to Midway in June 1942, and were decisively repelled by forewarned and heavily fortified defenses. The Battle of Midway secured the central Pacific for Allied forces. By the end of the year, we had made killing raids in the Marshalls and the Gilberts, Rabaul, Wake Island, New Guinea, and Marcus Island, and our home front received a much-needed morale boost with the news of a bombing raid on Tokyo. Johnston Island was outfitted for use as a forward air and fueling base; Efate in the New Hebrides and New Caledonia were taken over as support and supply bases.

Control of Guadalcanal was regained on 8 August 1942. A bloody six months' effort was then launched to regain the lower Solomons, and several major sea battles ensued. After several enemy reinvasion attempts, Guadalcanal was firmly secured mid-November.

Still, by the end of 1942, Allied efforts had been almost consistently defensive. The Japanese were digging in to repel counter-invasion. But Japan could keep only what she could defend and supply. And thus 1943 saw a reversal in American submarine deployment: instead of biting off more than we could chew by chasing after elusive enemy battleships, carriers, and cruisers, it began to make more sense to nibble at Japan's essential vessels of supply. An enemy regiment without bullets or food would be little use to the Japanese war effort. Our persistent lurking would force the enemy into roundabout routing, constant zigzagging, and other evasive tactics, plus the necessity of expensive surface and aerial escorts.

Because of the U-boats patrolling our own front door, we had lost more shipping during 1942 than we had launched. But though Japan had a headstart, having built ships for years in anticipation of war, her peak production was only 10 percent of American production at its height. During 1943, we began building more than we were losing; but the enemy's shipping losses began to increase while her capacity for replacement began to drop. Replacing her tanker losses became her first priority, and for a brief burst, construction nearly kept up with demand. But by the end of 1943, Japan was losing more ships than she could replace, no matter how hard her shipyards labored.

Early in 1943, we began to recover New Guinea, and the Japanese rollback slowly began. With General MacArthur commanding our land forces and ex-submariner Admiral Chester Nimitz our sea power, Allied forces began the bloody ordeal of island-hopping, driving the Japanese back or cutting them off from their supplies. But submarine skippers who had learned to fight effectively found their weapons dangerously defective. For a full two years after the Pearl Harbor attack, our torpedoes continued to run too deep, and too many would not detonate. Torpedoes set to explode on contact could be seen to hit the side of a ship and bounce out of the water without exploding—or conversely, when set with magnetic detonators, pass underneath to continue on until their fuel was expended. On 24 July 1943, Captain Dan Daspit of the *Tinosa* stopped an 18,000-ton Japanese whale factory with one good hit, and then proceeded to fire thirteen torpedoes broadside into her without getting any more explosions.

He saved his last fish for the Ordnance Department. Admiral Lockwood took the responsibility of test-firing it against an underwater cliff. It also was a dud! But our Ordnance officials continued to blame these results on faulty adjustments by the submariners, who were again sent out to risk their lives bringing back the same results. The Department of Naval Ordnance considered torpedoes too scarce and expensive to test, as if submariners (and $7-million submarines) were expendable.

Nonetheless, verified submarine kills increased 100 percent—335 ships totaling 1.5 million tons were sunk during 1943. The cost was not cheap. We had lost seven Pacific submarines during 1942 and fifteen more during 1943. One of them was *Corvina,* to which Captain Merrill had been briefly assigned just prior to commanding *Batfish*. She was sunk on her maiden voyage.

Yet hopes were high. Scandalously overdue solutions were finally being applied, and younger skippers with less inertia were being effectively employed. As 1943 wore on, the Japanese front-yard losses climbed, and our knowledge increased. Surviving submariners learned quickly; they could now teach better than they had been taught. Most of the logical prewar naval theory that was not in touch with the realities of *this* war was finally superseded, and the book was being thoroughly rewritten. Accelerated feedback from war patrol reports created a renaissance of material improvements.

By 1943's end, the Pacific war was in high gear. *Batfish*, freshly launched with a predominantly green crew, was about to enter this scene of combat. But until now, our submersibles had mainly been deployed as scouts, coastal raiders, troop transports, supply ships, advance fueling bases for long-range planes, minelayers, emergency evacuation ships, and lifeguards. Could this "token" submarine fleet, for so long defensively sniping at the enemy, now aggressively range out for the kill?

Father Brown stoically disembarked onto the dry sand of Midway, noticeably demonstrating the "sailor's roll" which we had all learned so well—the attempt to walk as if the ground were pitching and rolling like a boat deck in an unruly sea.

Repairs were made to the leaky hatch gasket and to the SJ radar motor generator. An experimental thermometer element intended to monitor our bathythermograph was removed completely because it leaked. But in the process, the lead wire to the bathythermograph was "accidentally" clipped, necessitating our staying overnight at Midway. A minor, inexpensive repair for the Navy: for us, a welcome stroke of providence. It was a mystery who snipped the wrong wire, but we got our party.

Early next day we fueled and reprovisioned to capacity, removed all unnecessary gear from *Batfish*'s superstructure and all unnecessary classified papers to our tender, U.S.S. *Bushnell,* for safekeeping. We turned in one TNT-loaded warhead—relatively difficult to explode— and replaced it with a Torpex warhead. After two shameful years of malfunctioning and dud torpedoes, that changeover was but one welcome element of reform.

After filling our freshwater tanks, we departed westward for the Japanese Empire. Our assigned patrol area: 6-A, a rectangular area extending southward from the coast of Shikoku several hundred miles, bounded on the east and west by imaginary lines south from Bungo and Kii straits. Our fears increased the closer we approached Japan— for most of us, every bit as vast an unknown as it had been for *Argonaut, Gudgeon, Plunger,* and *Dolphin* in December 1941. None of us really knew yet how the rest of us would react when battle action occurred, much less how he *himself* would react.

We proceeded directly into what the old-timers defined as a junior-grade typhoon. Its first rain squall appeared our first day out, as we tested our equipment, watertightness, repairs, and general operational soundness. Thereafter, squalls appeared with increasing frequency and duration, dotting the PPI scope at ranges of 6,000 to 7,000 yards. By dawn on 18 December, the downpour was continuous; the storm had clenched us with a determined grip. Gradually the sea's

45

color changed to darker shades of blue and onyx. Despite the undulations of its angry surface, the sea looked as hard and solid as sculpted stone.

Increasingly rough seas and wind at thirty to forty knots battered and tore at us from the south. The lookouts strained to see through binoculars that required constant drying with lens tissue after each wave. Already forty-six miles behind schedule, we were still making only standard speed, the most we could do on two engines while recharging the batteries.

During the very dark afternoon, SD radar reported a plane contact at six miles and coming in fast. At four miles, our lookouts identified a U.S. Army B-25 bomber. Ready to dive instantly, we identified ourselves by searchlight, whereupon he replied, circled once, and flew off. It was comforting to know the SD radar and lookouts were in top form, and that—oddly—exchange of recognition signals seemed to be more reliable closer to Japanese waters.

By nine o'clock we were taking in so much water through the conning tower hatch and main engine air induction line that we were forced to slow to nine knots. The humidity in the boat climbed. Beads of condensation clung to the cold metal and crept down the bulkheads to join widening puddles on the deck. The sky hung heavy above the open hatch, dark gray, splotched with low white clouds. Now standing shorter, more tolerable watches, the bridge lookouts dropped through the hatch one by one and laboriously peeled out of their wet rain gear, as four fresh men pulled themselves up the ladder. No sooner had they scrambled through the narrow opening than a mountainous wave crashed over the hatch, drenching the quartermaster standing below waiting to dog it down. He slammed it shut, cursed and turned to dry several pairs of sopping binoculars.

The bridge hatch remained shut most of the time to keep out the water. For the lookouts atop the periscope shears of a pitching, heaving, twisting submarine in the teeth of a roaring typhoon, theirs was the loneliest, most terrifying vigil imaginable. Both bridge and conning tower parties managed to find a rhythm to the storm and got reasonably adept at opening the hatch at appropriate intervals. But the typhoon had more variations than we could keep up with. Before the hatch could be closed, torrents of water made their way down, grounding out equipment and the night-lighting fixtures which had apparently not been intended to be waterproof.

Come 19 December, we were over one hundred miles behind

schedule, but slowed even more. No matter how much we wanted to reach our destination on time, there was no reason to wreck our boat or lose our lookouts doing it. Even so, they stayed lashed to their stations in the darkness that was half wind and half cold saltwater driven with great force. We radioed a weather report to Pearl in the hope it might help them in routing other boats.

The barometer continued to drop even more. Thick rain squalls spattered and jumped across the sea, and visibility closed down drastically. The ocean became literally mountainous under a wild sixty-knot wind that blew the top off every wave and churned it into stinging froth. We headed up into the sea, changing our course and slowing down to four knots. An hour later, when the wind suddenly shifted, we started working around to westward to keep the bow headed into the seas. It was impossible to average more than five or six knots against waves forty feet from trough to crest. The bridge was constantly inundated.

One fifty-five-degree roll cost us half our Victrola records and seven blueberry pies, but we suspected a little salvage on the sly, as we had "blueberry shortcake" the next meal. Our favorite surviving record, "I'm Going Back to Where I Came From," however, did not survive the attack of one hand who had warned that he would go crazy "if anybody plays that goddamned record again!" Our attempts to order the accumulated clutter and wreckage throughout *Batfish* would have to wait until the storm calmed down.

On our fifth consecutive day of bad weather, the seas were even worse. Pounding heavily at four knots, *Batfish* made only sixteen miles between dawn and noon, and with the fierce wind holding from the west-northwest, there was no respite in sight. Although our spirits held up pretty well under the continued buffeting, we knew we would be thoroughly worn out if we got no relief by the time we reached our patrol area. About two more days would be all boat and crew would be able to take without diving to routine torpedoes, water the batteries, and rest ourselves.

One ensign, suffering from a hernia, would have to be hospitalized upon our arrival in port. His fortitude in disregarding his discomfort and continuing to stand watch should have earned him some kind of medal. Only after being ordered to do so did he accept replacement—and then only for a short time to rid himself of immediate pain. No doubt the rough weather aggravated the hernia into agony, but he did not complain.

During the afternoon of 22 December, the barometer started to creep upward, and the wind gave first signs of diminishing. We took advantage of every increase of speed the sea would permit. Cleaving the still-rough seas, *Batfish* was making her best two-engine speed at last—an exhilarating gallop!

But our respite was short-lived. Less than twenty-four hours later, the weather struck again with renewed energy, forcing us to slow to a tooth-jarring, pounding, bludgeoning again—at a depressingly slow jog. The typhoon produced upon us nearly all the symptoms of an unrelenting migraine and gave our pharmacist's mate a heavy run on aspirin. At least, we had taken advantage of the slight lull to secure and resecure everything below decks, so when the storm came down on us again, we were a little less preoccupied with falling objects overhead and rolling objects underfoot. Still, one of our cooks had to field a flying coffee Silex. It burst, scalding him around the neck and arms with second-degree burns.

Scheduled to arrive in our area next morning, by midnight we still had over a thousand miles to go. If conditions didn't lighten, we'd be lucky to make it in a week. Nor could we expect much from our torpedoes, as there was no way they could run normally at less than a twenty-five-foot depth setting. It was decided that whatever the weather next morning, we would submerge to check our trim, service torpedoes and batteries, and exercise at our diving stations.

At 10 A.M., although wind and sea had subsided somewhat, we submerged. Relief was simple and surprisingly close: the harshness of the weather's effect on the sea smoothed as our depth increased. At one hundred feet, we escaped the under-turbulence of the mountainous wave action. The boat grew absurdly calm. Within *Batfish*'s steel belly, the effect was like the sudden lifting of a heavy, intangible weight.

Grateful for the relatively placid existence, we set to our chores, however exhausted. Twenty torpedoes got a thorough check, and we completed all the remaining repairs to water-damaged equipment. During the rough ride, electrolyte had spilled from the batteries. The compartment was hosed down and cleaned despite the biting chlorine odor of battery acid reacting with seawater. Should serious flooding occur in the battery compartment, chlorine gas could kill everyone on board. At long last, we had a moment to take a breather and look around us: *Batfish* was a mess, badly in need of a thorough house-cleaning. We stubbed out our cigarettes and got into the chore as if it were supposed to be fun. Anyone showing a sign of shirking the smallest detail was razzed and pushed into keeping up with the rest of us. The orgy of fanatic cleaning and scrubbing ended only when *Batfish* was spotless and sparkling once again.

Someone put a sign up in the crew's mess: "Work cuts boredom like scouring powder cuts grease." Someone else put up another sign: "What's wrong with boredom? I like grease," which began to accumulate signatures like a petition. The next sign to appear stated: "I like work." Our final act of housecleaning was to remove all signs from our submarine.

By 2 P.M. we surfaced into a calm sea with a weak and dying wind behind it. Some normalcy returned to our lives—those not on duty or standing watch turned in for some much needed rest. The weather of the past days had been a tiresome trial.

Christmas Eve found us with 820 miles to go, which we were now narrowing briskly at about fourteen knots on two engines. Captain Merrill gave us a Christmas present of enough fresh water so each man could take a very brief shower. But we had been getting the most cleanliness out of the least water down to a science. We shaved and got haircuts in shifts, sprucing up for the most unlikely Christmas most of us had ever spent. Since nature herself was smiling again and *Batfish* shipshape as she could be, Christmas Eve at the brink of war was an incongruously joyous occasion. Morale was high as it could ever be for a bunch of teenagers cruising across the Pacific in a submarine looking for someone to kill.

On Christmas Day 1943, our weatherman reported, "no snow in sight." All hands enjoyed well-prepared turkey with all the trimmings. Tokyo Rose's afternoon broadcast furnished the entertainment by saying that American submariners were forced to eat cockroaches and mice and pay $225 monthly rent to live in pigpens in Honolulu. Our cooks had their hands full serving us seconds and thirds of the delicious "cockroaches and mice." A moderate sea was now running, but with no increase in wind—a comfortably uneventful Christmas.

The next day also we were blessed with good weather, good progress, and no event or obstacle to slow us. Between watch duty, there was time for a lot of stories. The young asked the older the same questions: "What's it like? What's it really like in action?" and got the same sea stories for answers—but listened more intently.

The night turned black with an overcast sky and frequent rain squalls. Getting pretty good with our SJ radar and PPI scope, we tracked

49

one in from over ten miles away. It showed very clearly on the screen. Just before sunrise we expected to pass within sight of Sumisu Shima— a middle island in the Nanpo Shotos, the closest island chain to Japan south of Tokyo. This would mark our first contact with Japanese territory, although we would then have to proceed to our assigned patrol area, about two hundred miles beyond.

At 4:11 A.M. radar reported a contact at 18,000 yards—definitely no rain squall. The boy's excited voice filled the conn, startling overloud: our first enemy ship contact! The hollow-sounding general alarm bells rang throughout the compartments, and we slowed to one-third speed. By the time the contact was at 17,000 yards, a second pip appeared at 16,000 yards, both heading west on approximately the same course as ours. Since they were approaching Sumisu Shima at a speed much slower than our own, we put them astern by changing course to widen the range, then stopped and began tracking them carefully.

The target appeared to be a small vessel with an escort—or two patrol boats, depending on who was interpreting the PPI scope data. Since visibility was only about 2,000 yards at best, our lookouts could make no additional observation. We maneuvered to keep their range fairly steady while studying the problem of how to attack.

Theoretically, a radar surface attack would give us a decided advantage—their lookouts couldn't see us until our lookouts could see them, and we knew they were there. But just as theoretically, a high-speed end-around approach would put us in position to attempt a daylight submerged attack in the vicinity of Bayonaisse Rocks. Either way, if we missed the first chance for attack there probably wouldn't be a second. Despite our SJ's excellent performance so far and our extensive training in its tactical use, Merrill was wary of going directly for a target he couldn't actually see. And because of the time elapsed since our last fix, our own position was only approximate.

We lingered in deliberation, hoping for better data on which to base the most logical attack. Within half an hour, we had closed the enemy again to about 16,000 yards and maintained that range. On the PPI scope, its escort remained steadily about 500 yards on its starboard quarter.

Moments later, a lookout called that either target or escort was flashing a hooded searchlight. The escort then turned suddenly in our direction increasing its speed; the range closed rapidly to 14,000 yards.

50

All reports were muted to the lower ranges of audibility; no unnecessary words were spoken. We kept our "ears" on, our mouths shut, and our sound signature reduced to initials.

Merrill became convinced the escort had detected our SJ radar and was coming over to investigate. We opened the range, and at 20,000 yards, the escort turned and went back to the target's side. Merrill decided to keep the distance at 20,000 to 25,000 yards, within radar range, until daylight when he could eyeball him through the scope. A target that didn't seem to be in a hurry to get anywhere was suspect; and an escort that had detected our radar or had a comparable radar that our Intelligence hadn't yet discovered might well have the upper hand.

The morning stars proved us slightly eastward of our estimated position. SJ showed the target with the same heading—still in no particular hurry, close by Sumisu Shima and the Bayonaisse Rocks, apparently bound toward Aoga Shima. Overcast skies and poor visibility with scattered rain squalls still prevented us from sighting the target.

27 December 1943

5:02 A.M. In consideration of the appearance of the target pips on the radar screen, his apparent destination, his patrolling tactics, etc., decided that he was not worth a chase and I set course for my own area. It was a difficult decision to make, and I didn't feel particularly aggressive in letting him go, although my decision was based upon the following data:

a. Am late for my own area.
b. *Salmon* close behind me and I want to clear her area.
c. Want to avoid disclosing my presence further, if practicable.
d. Estimate target to have been either a small supply vessel running between southern islands and returning northward probably empty, under escort, or else an anti-submarine radar-equipped patrol.
e. According to my navigational position I would have to run close aboard Sumisu Shima in order to attack, with visibility very low.

We moved toward our patrol area at standard speed. The unseen target may have been larger than Merrill suspected, because radar contact with it was maintained out to a range of 27,000 yards—over fifteen miles! We lost all contact at 7:15 A.M.

Three hours later, SD made a contact moving in at seventeen miles. Low clouds prevented us from spotting the plane, but allowed him a cover from which he might suddenly drop to catch us flatfooted. Even in clear weather, theoretically, a plane can see a submarine from a greater distance than the sub's lookouts can see the plane; in peacetime maneuvers they usually do. But in wartime, when a submarine's lookouts have a much higher incentive for alertness, it often happens the other way around. If the aircraft sees the submarine first and sinks it, everyone in the plane gets a medal—and usually everyone in the submarine gets killed. When a submarine spots the aircraft first, nobody gets a medal—but then, nobody gets killed.

We made a dignified crash dive in plenty of time; by the time the plane should have been overhead, we were submerged at 120 feet.

> 9:55 A.M. In consideration of cloudiness and to avoid disclosing my presence if planes were checking up as a result of our having been detected earlier, decided to remain submerged for balance of day.

While under, we routined our torpedoes—a task that had been impossible on the surface—and kept a careful periscope watch, going deep between peeps.

We surfaced at about 5 P.M. and continued toward our area, now about eighty-two miles distant, charging our batteries on the way. We made it easily by daylight, then surface-patrolled along the Kobe-Saipan sea lanes, making high periscope sweeps at twenty-minute intervals. We saw nothing but some floating debris: teak decking, a large box, an oil drum. . . .

Shortly after midnight, 29 December, we heard a muffled explosion in the distance, but weren't even able to tell from which direction it came, much less the range. There was nothing in sight or on the radar. In half an hour we heard several more explosions, with still no clues as to what or where they were. Captain Merrill said they sounded like night battle practice for five- or six-inch guns, but they could as well be depth charges at a great distance. Over the next three hours we heard more explosions at random intervals, all at great distance; and left the area with their source still a mystery.

At 10:30 A.M. we submerged to avoid an SD contact coming in

from thirteen miles. This plane also went unsighted due to low clouds. Because of the continuing cloud cover, we again spent the day submerged, rising briefly to conduct periscope surveillance. Before surfacing that evening, we dropped to 350 feet to get a bathythermograph reading: absolutely no temperature variation between that depth and the surface. Sound reported a noticeable absence of fish or suspended matter in the water; background noises were low and none of the unexplainable sounds commonly reported were heard.

29 December 1943 _____

Not such a good spot in which to get tangled up with the ping-and-drop boys.

After an uneventful night, the morning sea became glassy for a change. There were no contacts during the day, but about 8 P.M. we picked up a radar signal on our PPI. Since interference became stronger, we suspected it was from *Salmon* or *Finback*, supposed to be crossing our area at about this time.

The Japanese were not known to have radar similar to ours. The signal emanated from an SJ like our own on very nearly the same frequency, using the characteristic PPI sweep. Now and then it trained directly on us, "listening" electronically. By using our PPI as a direction finder, we were able to track the other boat, though we couldn't get any ranges. For a while she appeared to be trying a high-speed end-around, not close enough to be detected, to reach a point ahead of us from which, presumably, to attack. Believing the unknown ship to be "friendly" (our plot of her course coincided with that assigned to *Finback*), we left it far behind, finally losing all contact at 1:30 A.M., 31 December. The interference had been continuous for almost six hours, giving us a lot of confidence in the reliability of our sensitive new "toy"—and chills at the thought that the enemy might have gotten one just like it for Christmas.

In three hours we detected another similar radar interference. Judging by its course, it could not be *Finback*. We maneuvered to avoid whatever it was, but within a hour picked up a second interference before we had lost the first.

4:45 A.M. Strongly suspected enemy radar, although all characteristics indicated our own forces. I am anxious to check this with the other submarines concerned. If it was not them, then the Japs have radar very similar to our own and apparently fully as efficient.

We realized that if these were "friendlies," they were playing the same guessing game and might shoot us. If they were enemies, they *would* shoot us. We decided to get clear of that dilemma, and dived. While moving away, Merrill made frequent periscope scans, but in our retreat we were unable to pick up anything.

Dawn approached with low black clouds and rain all around. Although visibility gradually improved throughout the day, there was absolutely nothing to see. We remained submerged.

Our New Year's Eve celebration was subdued—and sober. We all went home early, a little under the weather.

With the weather clear to partly cloudy over a moderate sea, we spent the first two days of 1944 patrolling along the Kobe-Palau and the Tokyo-Balabac Strait routes—uneventfully. Finding clear skies on 3 January, we surface-patrolled all day along the Kobe-Palau route. Shortly after sunset, the lookout reported a small dark object on the horizon. Radar picked up a pip at 5,850 yards, and soon the moonlight revealed a small sampan. It showed a white light, intermittently visible in its southerly course until it passed out of range at 7,000 yards. Wanting to avoid detection, we changed course, putting us to westward of the moon's bright path. It was doubtful that the small craft sighted us.

> 6:20 P.M. Believe sampan was an observer rather than a fisherman, as this isn't a likely fishing ground. Would like to have sunk sampan, but consider it inadvisable as I haven't revealed my presence to date. This was our first visual contact during the patrol. Something better should be turning up in his wake.

Still patrolling far out to sea along established Japanese traffic routes, we again encountered nothing during the day. As night approached, the skies clouded into complete overcast, so we submerged until dark to avoid airplanes.

At about 9:30 P.M. our lookouts sighted two lighted sampans at about five miles, which we could not pick up on radar. Apparently these wooden-hulled craft were too small or too low in the water for us to get a return from their engines.

About an hour later, a darkened enemy patrol boat was spotted in the immediate vicinity of the two sampans. It could be that those sampans were serving as "bait," the patrol boat lurking nearby to attack us if we revealed ourselves. We avoided him on the surface and worked our way around to the southward to get back on our line along the Kobe-Palau convoy route.

4 January 1944

11:04 P.M. It begins to look like something may be coming along soon on this route. I intend to stay on it until I find out.

Although the sea was picking up and the sky overcast with frequent rain squalls, we patrolled on the surface the entire day with varying visibility conditions. After nine days in our area, we longed for a contact of any kind.

5 January 1944

Have concentrated on covering likely traffic routes, but if something doesn't show up soon, I'm going to search every square mile of the area irrespective of them. It appears entirely possible that the enemy is purposely avoiding the normal routing between ports, even this far off-shore.

Next day, we encountered heavy seas, rain squalls, varying cloudiness—and nothing else. At 1:35 P.M. an SD radar contact coming in from twenty-six miles broke the monotony. Since the clouds made it impossible to see aircraft even at close range, we submerged for the rest of the day.

We were beginning to realize that in order to surface-patrol during the day, it was necessary to disregard the state of the clouds; conditions changed drastically from hour to hour. We had never before experienced such frustrating and varying visibility, not even with the notorious heavy fogs of New London. We would have to place more trust in our SD radar's capabilities to warn us from cloud-concealed planes, no matter what the potential hazard.

7 January 1944

I have a hunch something is coming through here soon. It is my intention to cover every possible part of the area until I find something. For the present, this seems to be the most likely spot.

Midday, 8 January, we sighted a faint trace of smoke on the horizon, possibly diesel engine exhaust. Through the high periscope Merrill glimpsed what appeared to be either a sampan or submarine as it rose on a wave about nine miles away. There were no masts visible. In case it was an enemy submarine, we played it safe and submerged to investigate further. Manning battle stations, we closed the target's probable track. Sighting nothing further in an hour's approach—not even more smoke—we secured from battle stations and remained under the rest of the afternoon.

If only something would happen! What we really wanted was to attack—anything, even a sampan, with our fists if necessary!

The next evening, while routinely searching the horizon before surfacing, we sighted smoke again. The sea was calm and surface visibility very good despite ever-present clouds. The target was about twelve miles away, changing his bearings to the left.

We surfaced and began to close the smoke while charging our batteries, although this restricted our speed. Battle stations were manned as we worked our way eastward to intercept the target. As the full moon rose, we momentarily lost sight of the smoke, but our lookouts soon spotted it again. At 7:14 P.M. SJ radar reported contact at 27,000 yards. A minute later, three distinct pips dotted the PPI scope at 25,000 yards, increasing to five pips as we neared. Twenty minutes later we picked up a sixth. Belowdecks, the air was electric. At last!

In full moonlight, three large AKs (cargo ships) in column with a DD (destroyer) loomed into sight from the bridge. A smaller escort ship trailed behind the column. The sixth pip could not be sighted.

We turned to keep our distance at 17,000 yards until our battery charge was complete. Visibility began to vary; the moon was intermittently obscured by low clouds piling up in the west, concealing the radically zigzagging enemy ships. The wind and sea had begun to pick up quite noticeably.

9 January 1944

8:15 P.M. It was apparent that an attack would have to be made before long, or I wouldn't be able to see.

Nearly three hours after first sighting the smoke, we secured the battery charge and speeded up to work around ahead of the convoy.

8:47 P.M. Lookout sighted patrol boat or sub-chaser on starboard bow at range of 8,200 yards. Managed to avoid, but this inter-rupted my end-around run on the convoy necessitating a longer run. Apparently he did not sight us.

While running around the patrol boat at a range of six miles, radar picked up a second patrol boat in the same vicinity that had not been sighted from the bridge. Suddenly the moon broke through the cover, and both were visible—one at 8,500 yards, the other at 9,650 yards. Merrill said they looked like sub-chasers.

Apparently the patrol boats, now between us and the convoy, were then sighted by the port flanking convoy escort. He sheared out of formation and closed them rapidly to investigate, then returned to shepherd the convoy. By ranges on our PPI, it was evident that he had sighted them at over 6,000 yards, which gave us a good indication of our own visibility. But logic also insisted that if the escort had surface-search radar, he would have detected them much sooner and at a greater range. Our SJ radar seemed to give us an enormous edge with relative impunity.

By the time we had attained a position ahead of the convoy, the visibility fluctuated unpredictably between 500 and 16,000 yards. At times we couldn't even see our own bow.

> 9:27 P.M. Several times I started in for periscope attacks, but each time it would get dark and start raining. Decided to stay ahead of the convoy until the weather makes up its mind.

Three hours passed with no improvement in visibility. After twelve anxious hours at battle stations we turned and headed toward the convoy. When we had closed to 9,000 yards, the moon suddenly pierced the clouds. Visibility instantly increased to about 16,000 yards, but the convoy itself was obscured by a local rain squall, leaving us safely undetected for the moment.

10 January 1944

> 1:28 A.M. By this time it was too rough for a night periscope attack (we were shipping water down the conning tower hatch) so I broke off the approach and opened out again to about 12,000 yards ahead of the convoy. I could see the futility of further attempts at a night attack under the existing conditions, par-ticularly since all the AKs were light and high in the water and

in that sea, a torpedo couldn't have run normally at less than a fifteen-foot depth setting. I decided, therefore, to attempt a dawn submerged attack, hoping that the sea would abate or as a last resort I could fire sound shots.

Our sound gear was operating quite satisfactorily; even in this storm, it could distinguish between the ships in the convoy efficiently at ranges up to 16,000 yards. When and if the need arose, sonar was ready to send out a single ping to confirm range and bearing. And our SJ radar had proven faultless to the point of excellence. Yet Captain Merrill tended to trust only what he could see with his own eyes.

By daybreak, although we were keeping him on the same true bearing, his speed had decreased to four and a half knots and we were 23,000 yards ahead along his base course. I wanted to look the convoy over through the periscope before diving, as by this time the seas were mountainous and I knew I wouldn't be able to see much farther after submerging.

6:30 A.M. I was able to take bearings with the periscope, but couldn't make out any more detail than I had seen during the night.

About half an hour before sunrise, we submerged on the convoy's track. It *was* rough! Even though our trim was right, it took *Batfish* over two minutes to get under sea. We ran with the convoy for about an hour until it became light enough for a clear observation.

The scope silently slid up from its well, and Merrill pressed his eyes to the lens. All fell silent in the small compartment of the conn. Without warning, a heavy sea swell heaved us upward forty feet, broaching the boat—surfaced and exposed. But even if the enemy were still there, the sky was so dim and dark he could not possibly have seen us. With twenty-seven feet of periscope out, nothing was in sight, and waves were still crashing over the lens.

"Trim her under! Get her down," Merrill called to the diving officer below. From the control room, orders were quietly passed and obeyed.

"According to the plot, Captain," the exec spoke, "target should be within eight thousand yards."

Merrill made another periscope exposure. Again we broached, this time from forty-one feet, but still nothing was in sight, not even the convoy's smoke. Still not ready to give it all up, we concentrated on a careful sound search which also gave negative results.

The weather's gloom was nothing compared to the atmosphere of disappointment that settled over *Batfish*. We'd been at station for seventeen continuous hours, tensely keyed up for battle.

> 9:05 A.M. I decided the enemy had too valuable an ally in the weather, so secured from battle stations and gave it up as a bad job. I am convinced the convoy made a change of base course at sunrise, probably a radical one and to the westward.

Our tightly charged anticipation plummeted. The letdown was so total that it was as if *Batfish* had changed crews instead of just stations. To darken our mood even more, rumors had been circulating among the crew: there had been dissention by members of the attack team, who argued that there was no reason to distrust the radar, no reason to require visual verification when it could not be made. Both sides of the hypothetical argument—submerged periscope attack versus surface radar attack—became a matter of shipboard speculation. The sullen buzz of scuttlebutt now sounded like a depressed hornets' nest. We could argue about anything among ourselves as long as it did not affect the boat. Our officers could advise the captain and even differ with him to a point, but after his orders, our procedure was automatic.

> The convoy contacted on 9 January, on which no attack was made because of developments in the weather, might have been effectively attacked had I not waited to recharge the battery. I'm now convinced that it doesn't pay to delay an instant in launching an attack once contact is made. Anything may happen to frustrate an attack if delayed to gain more advantageous conditions.

We remained submerged the remainder of the day to rest—exhaustion had magnified the worst aspects of our situation. Finally, at 5:49 P.M., we surfaced and headed back to where we had lost our convoy. The sea continued heavy throughout the night, but showed some signs of abating toward morning. With the barometer rising, all things indicated a change for the better come morning.

At dawn, we sighted a sampan at 2,500 yards and maneuvered to avoid it on the surface.

_____

> 6:05 A.M. . . . am sure we were sighted. He was a typical observer-type boat with two light radio masts, which are not common to the fishing types. Decided to clear the area as soon as possible so as to be able to continue surface patrol if planes come out. Radar was unable to pick up this sampan, except for one tiny pip at 3,800 yards, and another at 6,900 yards.

Shortly after noon, SD radar reported our third enemy plane contact. We were just twenty-eight miles from where we had sighted the sampan this morning, which probably accounted for the plane being in this vicinity. We submerged without sighting the plane and stayed down for the rest of the afternoon, servicing our torpedoes. That evening, we surfaced and began patrol toward the east.

> 5:37 P.M. Want to give the southwestern corner of the area a couple of days' rest in order to avoid arousing suspicion that might jeopardize our chances of later success.
>
> 8:20 P.M. Put two men on deck to work on four-inch gun. May need it on some of these sampans at any time.

We changed course to avoid possible contact with U.S.S. *Steelhead*, known to be in the area, and submerged to avoid contact with a plane reported by radar at twenty miles. Because of a low overcast, we remained submerged for the remainder of 12 January, then surface-patrolled all night along the Bungo Suido-Palau route.

The days passed slowly, and gradually our means of entertainment dwindled. Cards grew limp and sticky from perspiration; pinochle was played simply to fill empty hours. By now, the movies had all been memorized and our small supply of books long ago exhausted. We had no favorite Victrola records left. Captain Merrill did his best to keep us busy, training and qualifying the green men, running them through drills and operations—good for the morale of all to keep occupied. And the captain himself seemed to be holding up well under the pressure of uneventfulness. He kept his log well up to date, and spent what free time he had in the wardroom with the other officers. His otherwise dull moments were spent swapping stories and quizzing the officers on engineering problems. Having a marvelous capacity for problem-solving, Merrill would grin as the others struggled to compute an answer in their heads, and when they failed, would then pop out the correct answer.

But each of us knew that all we really needed for morale was a damned good scrap with the enemy. We had been in our assigned area almost three weeks, and not one torpedo had been fired. True enough, you couldn't sink ships that weren't there—yet here we were, at the height of the war, in the middle of the *Japanese* Pacific, not sighting any! We remained optimistically anxious for better weather, for ships—for battle.

At dawn we sighted a sampan, identical to the one we encountered yesterday. He may have seen us, too, for he showed a white light as we avoided him on the surface. We dived as soon as we had gotten a few miles clear, expecting the inevitable planes.

On coming up to periscope depth an hour later, a fast low-flying plane popped down out of the clouds less than two miles away. We pulled the plug and went to one hundred feet.

13 January 1944 _____

7:40 A.M. If this plane appeared as a result of our second encounter with the radio-equipped sampan, then he certainly didn't waste any time arriving on the scene. My decision to submerge was quite fortunate because he was flying too low for the SD to have picked him up very far away. Before I leave the area, I'm going to eliminate that sampan if I can locate him. I would have done it before, but there is always a chance he is innocent and I would merely jeopardize my other chances by giving away my location. Changed course to eastward to start patrolling center part of area on surface. Have a hunch something may be coming along soon in that sector, as it has been quiet of late.

Captain Merrill's "hunch" coincided with a message received and decoded earlier that day; according to our eavesdropping Ultra (for ultrasecret) code-breakers, the Japanese battleship *Yamato* would be passing through our area within the next few days.

The news crackled through the boat like wildfire. "Battleship coming!" "*Yamato!*" Biggest bastard they got!" Visions of fame and glory danced in our heads.

Yamato was not just *a* battleship; she was *the* largest warship ever built by any nation. Flagship of the late Admiral Yamamoto, this

59,000-ton super-battleship mounted nine eighteen-inch guns—more firepower than any ship in history—and was rumored to be shielded by torpedoproof armor plating. The Japanese believed her to be unsinkable. Her elite destroyer escorts were alleged to have the best marksmanship in the Imperial Japanese Navy.

If ever there was a target worthy of a torpedo expenditure, *Yamato* was it. To sink or even damage her would be well worth all the twenty-four *Batfish* still carried. The tension of expectancy was delicious—a recipe that stirs men's hearts and quickens their blood.

Maybe Merrill was really on to this all along. Maybe he was saving us for the big one; that's why we avoided all those sampan spotters. We're on the biggest goddamn secret mission of the war, and that old son of a gun kept it quiet all this time!

At dawn, when we'd arrived in the center of our area, we managed to avoid another observer-type sampan at about 6,000 yards. Everybody aboard had now become extremely concerned that we not be observed and blow our cover.

Under an overcast sky, we began a day-long submerged patrol without sighting anything further. After the quartermaster had obtained a good navigational fix at dusk, we settled down to our night surface search.

14 January 1944

5:46 P.M. Sky was clear, sea slightly choppy, and when the moon rose at 8:42 P.M., visibility was excellent—a perfect night for a submerged periscope attack.

Any night would be a perfect time to sink *Yamato*. She had every advantage over us except the element of surprise. We knew she was coming. If she detected us in any way, her screen of destroyers would immediately turn to attack. Her shells, each packing nearly as much explosive as a torpedo, could reach us in a fraction of the time it would take us to dive and evade. And her top speed of twenty-five knots gave her quick mobility to zigzag, retreat, or attack.

The entire issue would hinge on the single element of surprise. Our aim would have to be precise, our calculations exact, for there would be no possible chance for a second attack. If through some quirk we damaged *Yamato* at all, we would be heroes. If we pierced some secret chink in her steel hide and actually sunk her, we would be immortalized. On the other hand, if *Yamato* even grazed us with a shell, if her destroyers placed their depth charges on target, we'd become "missing, presumed lost." Heady stuff for young submariners yet to make their first kill!

Two hundred and fifty miles south of Shikoku, we zigzagged southward at flank speed to increase our search path for the homeward-bound battleship. Throughout *Batfish,* one could distinguish those mesmerized with visions of glory from those restrained by more mundane matters. A mix of elation and fear hung in the air, like static.

About 11:30 P.M. Merrill and the exec were on the bridge, silently searching the horizon with binoculars. Up the conning tower hatch came a shout: "Radar contact bearing one three oh! Range two five eight five zero! Very large pip!"

Merrill went immediately down the hatch to verify the PPI picture. After several scans of our rotating radar antenna, there was no doubt the contact was very large, and coming toward us.

Within seconds, the contact was general news. In such a close, closed community, even when word is not passed over formal circuits, other kinds of communication are passed by other kinds of electricity— at almost the same speed. There was a commotion of energetic response.

"Come right to zero three zero," Merrill ordered. "Sound battle stations." (We were already at or near our battle stations.) He returned to the bridge, training his binoculars toward the southeast. Each lookout scanned his sector of the horizon, resisting the temptation to turn and look toward the reported contact.

In the brightness of the full moon, visibility remained excellent. A slight overcast drifted high above, allowing a clear line of sight to the horizon. In the steady wind, the sea remained choppy, almost rough, but gentle compared with the beating we'd taken since Midway.

"Range two three five oh oh. Bearing steady on one three zero," drifted up the hatch. The distance was quickly closing. The radar operator continued to call the ranges at regular intervals.

Within minutes, the high upperworks and mast of a large ship appeared down on the horizon. It appeared to be a battleship. Moments later there was no doubt. It was *Yamato!* SJ reported two smaller pips at each side of the target. Soon the closer of the two destroyers slid into view.

"Well, I'll be damned," Merrill quietly exclaimed. High up on *Yamato's* foremast, a big bedspring type radar antenna slowly rotated.

Our worst suspicions congealed as fact. Here was our first actual proof that the Japanese had surface-search radar. We remembered our own radar's ability to detect floating boxes and other small objects in the water. It followed logically that whatever radar equipment *Yamato* had was the very best and latest the Japanese could produce.

As long as *Batfish* remained on the surface, our discovery was inevitable—simply a matter of time.

"Stand by to dive," Merrill called. Without taking his binoculars from *Yamato* growing larger in the moonlight, he announced, "When we close to her gun range, we'll approach submerged."

Until the captain ordered our next move, there was an opportunity to debate the attack plan. The exec took advantage of it: "Captain," he offered, "if she changes course or zigs radically, we'll never close at six knots submerged."

"If we get under before she spots us, she'll have no reason to change course. She may have spotted us already."

"There aren't any signs of that."

"Her effective eighteen-inch gun range is twenty-one thousand yards, which we're now approaching," Merrill said. "If she can fire accurately at that range, you can be sure she can see even farther."

"We're low in the water, pitching around."

"She's very high and stable." The captain paused. "How many lookouts do you think she has?"

"Probably dozens," the exec conceded. Although we were a much smaller dot on their horizon than they on ours, we knew *Yamato* wouldn't be manned with amateur lookouts. And from *Yamato*'s higher lookout stations they could see much farther than ours.

SJ sang out, "Twenty one thousand yards and closing."

"Secure the radar," Merrill ordered. Instantly the little dish atop the periscope shears stopped revolving. The enemy's radio DF (direction finding) gear could detect and locate any of our signal emissions—including radar. The captain collected one last look at *Yamato,* then lowered his binoculars until they hung on their straps. Turning to the men around him, he said, "You fellows want to get her awfully bad, don't you?"

"Captain, I'm just as scared as you are," said the exec. "But this is the biggest damned target we'll ever get this close to. And it's not close enough to attack, even with low power torpedo settings. We've got the best radar in the world, and the best we can do on another submarine is about half this range. With the sea that's running, we could halve the distance before diving. She won't shoot if she doesn't know we're here."

"What do you think our chances are?" Merrill asked.

"Of getting a shot at her? Maybe ten percent. But it's our job to take chances."

"Pete, it isn't my job to take long shots like that. With any luck at all, maybe we'll get a better chance. But more likely it'll be the whole damned Seventh Fleet and half the Air Corps that gets her. Right now, if God spoke down out of this clear sky and said you can have *Yamato* but I'm going to charge you one sub and seventy-six lives—I'll tell you, I'd probably take the deal. But I don't see even one tenth of one percent for us. It's simply ninety-nine and nine-tenths against."

"But if we submerge," the exec persisted, "we won't have any."

"A zig toward us could put her right in our lap. It's my decision to approach submerged so we won't lose even that opportunity." Merrill hit the diving alarm twice. "Clear the bridge! Dive!"

The bridge party and lookouts scurried down into the conn, as the main inductions slammed shut with a heavy wheeze. Water gurgled into the ballast tanks as air hissed and sputtered out. All diesels stopped in unison, the shift into electric drive smooth without pause. The hatch clanged shut and *Batfish* slid under the water. Her bow planes groaned as the down angle began to increase.

"Level off at eighty feet," Merrill ordered.

Even though our chances of success were the slimmest, we began our submerged approach with high hopes. At 11:42 P.M. sound picked up heavy screws at about 18,000 yards. At 16,000 yards the listening gear could distinguish the screws of the destroyer escorts.

Six minutes later, we rose to periscope depth. *Yamato* had taken a radical change of course to the right, away from us. We altered our course to close her new probable track as much as possible, using an assumed speed of eighteen knots, to try to head her off before she could complete her long circle around us. Had she spotted us or hadn't she? Her escorts made no sign of leaving her side. Possibly her zig had no significance beyond a routine pattern of evasion.

Target and company continued bearing strongly to the east, working far around us toward the north. When it appeared that we were not going to be able to close her unless she zigged back to her left, Merrill ordered all torpedoes set at low power for maximum range. We waited for the slightest increase in our very small advantage.

Sound reported loss of contact with the escorts, with no change in the heavy pounding of *Yamato*'s mammoth screws. Prompted by routine or suspicion, they were investigating farther eastward—unaware of our impotent presence. Then at 12:21 A.M. the light, high-speed screws began blending in once more with the steady throb of the target's ponderous propellers.

Nine minutes later, Sound said *Yamato* was nearly seven miles east of us, as close to the Bungo Suido as we were—as close to us as she would come if she didn't change course. She drew off northward, her silhouette retreating into a large gray blur in the periscope.

Ten minutes later, a zig back to the left swung *Yamato* back into 11,000 yards—still out of range. From that point the distance increased quickly and steadily. Too late; she was past us. Her superior speed made a surface chase impossible; at flank speed she could outdistance us by five knots. At 12:48 A.M. we lost sound contact with the target.

We surfaced a half hour later. Nothing was in sight; nothing appeared on the SJ. After trying for five minutes to spot her, we secured from battle stations and picked up our patrol to the eastward as *Yamato* continued northward, out of sight, toward home. TGB (Target got by).

15 January 1944 _____

1:25 A.M. Either we were unlucky enough to get in the middle of a long, looping zig to the eastward, or else the target picked us up by radar about the same time we did her and purposely ran out around us. The conditions were perfect to carry out the approach as planned, putting the target between us and the moon, avoiding radar detection, etc., but the breaks just weren't with us. I earnestly believe a zig to the left would have put her in a beautiful position for a successful attack.

Three and a half hours later, we sighted a lighted sampan four miles to the north and maneuvered to avoid it. At dawn, we submerged to conduct patrol because of a complete overcast. The following days were dismally uneventful; our only enemy encounters were sampans.

Batfish still carried every round for her four-inch deck gun. Occasional practice for the gun crew (using our floating trash bags for targets) had dipped into our smaller guns' ammunition supply. We were also lighter by about half of our provisions, yet we continued to eat well—fresh lettuce, eggs, and ice cream were still on the menu. But so far, every torpedo was still in residence, regularly serviced.

7:20 P.M. We have had but two contacts worthy of torpedo attack. Our first contact did not develop into an attack because of typhoon weather. Our second contact was a radar-equipped battleship which we were unable to close to firing range. In spite of it all, morale is still quite satisfactory. It's no joy to anticipate a return to base with no damage having been inflicted on the enemy. I still have hope that during our remaining five days in the area this situation will be completely altered. This type of patrol is undoubtedly the toughest you can make. We are the first boat to patrol this area for a long time, and I doubt if it will ever prove very productive. The western half of the area may have possibilities if its western boundary is extended to meet the adjacent area to the westward, but the eastern half appears to be used only on very rare occasions.

Shortly after noon, 19 January, we periscope-sighted smoke on the northern horizon and changed course to close it. In less than ten minutes, we saw two tall masts. Manning battle stations, we came about to a normal submerged approach course.

Seventeen minutes after sighting the smoke, sound could hear the target pinging. Merrill ordered the scope up. A single-float seaplane circled slightly to the right of the target. Taking another look thirty minutes later, we made out the masts of three large ships in close convoy.

Abeam of the convoy's base course, we approached as close as possible. As the distance narrowed, the three ships were identified as large freighters or passenger transports with an as-yet-undetermined number of escorts. Then another, smaller transport appeared from behind a larger. While it was still daylight, its air cover kept us from surfacing for an end-around. We secured from battle stations and trailed submerged in the hopes of an after dark high-speed surface chase. At an estimated speed of eight knots, the convoy slowly drew away from us to the north. At 4:30 P.M. we lost contact completely.

An hour later the sun finally crept below the horizon and we surfaced for the chase at standard speed while recharging our batteries. The sea was moderate, visibility fair, although the moon was not due to rise until 1 A.M. Merrill went topside to search the horizon with the OOD and lookouts. For two hours we plowed ahead, following the convoy on the base course we had determined in the afternoon. At 8:15

the exec came topside to join them. "We've regained radar contact at twenty-three thousand yards, Captain. Convoy's bearing three three seven."

Merrill nodded in satisfaction. We had picked them up exactly where predicted. Soon, radar was continuously monitoring three large pips. "Secure from the battery charge," he ordered. "All ahead full."

Two diesels sputtered to life and rumbled louder in pitch, blending with the roar of the other two. *Batfish* surged forward with more speed. A pale shimmer of phosphorescence followed our wake, widened, then dissipated.

Just as we were about to pass the convoy, our gyro compass follow-up system suddenly went out of commission. There could be no accurate torpedo attack until it was fixed. A very determined repair crew immediately went to work, and repairs were effected within about ten minutes.

In the dimly lit control room, two men stabbed in slow motion at the plotting board. A series of dots marked the steady approach drawing *Batfish* ahead of the enemy formation. The target's shorter track was penciled in beside ours; the end-around run was almost complete. Hopes were again high, but unspoken—we'd had enough frustration.

By 11:55 P.M., well ahead of the convoy, we began a radar surface approach. Although the moon was still down, there was excellent visibility from starlight. The ships were roughly in two columns: two ships and one escort in each, one escort patrolling the port bow, the other on the starboard quarter, apparently oblivious of *Batfish* stalking them only a few thousand yards to starboard. The alarm for battle stations sounded.

We began to approach the nearest ship—the second in the left-hand column. The second ship of the right-hand column had dropped back until there was only about a third of a ship's length of open water between his bow and the stern of our target ship. With only 300 yards between them, Merrill decided to fire three torpedoes from the bow tubes at the first target, then three more at the further target.

The bow fish were made ready. Acknowledgment was relayed to the conn. So as not to alert our second target with our first firings, lower tubes four, five, and six were set to go first; no splash would be observed when they left their tubes.

Merrill took over the TBT on the bridge, training its powerful binoculars on the principal target. Closing to 6,000 yards, he pressed the button mounted on its side, which automatically registered the range into the TDC. Constantly updated gyro data was fed via the TDC into the waiting torpedoes. As the radar rotated in silent surveillance, Merrill alternately tracked the primary and secondary targets, keeping a careful eye on the potentially menacing escorts. He sent down another bearing.

The range narrowed to 3,400 yards. *Batfish*'s bow pointed directly at the target to minimize our approaching silhouette. Suddenly the starboard escort turned away from his station at the convoy's quarter, heading behind the formation toward *Batfish* with a zero angle on the bow.

Uncertain as to the effectiveness of our new camouflage paint, Merrill stared briefly at the oncoming escort, then made a quick decision. "Stand by to fire!" he called into the speaker. He focused the TBT on the target once more and sent a final bearing below. Believing the escort had seen us, he yelled, "Fire four!" The firing range of 3,400 yards was greater than he had planned.

The first of six torpedoes leaped from its tube and sped toward our closest target, a 9,000-ton AK. Two more followed at eight-second intervals. A minute later, torpedoes one, two, and three were fired at the second ship, a 7,000-ton AK, at a range of 3,600 yards.

"All ahead flank! Come to zero one zero!" *Batfish* listed heavily, maneuvering to avoid the oncoming escort.

Sweat-soaked silence filled the conning tower; not a word was spoken on the bridge. Everyone waited. The assistant attack officer timing the torpedo runs, his shirt wet with sweat, glanced at the stopwatch in his hand.

A heavy muffled roar hit *Batfish* like a giant slap, jarring our teeth. A vivid blossom of fire burst into the darkness, momentarily blinding us. "Sound reports heavy explosion," the talker reported in a jittery voice.

We got our cherry!

A flash of orange flame showed at the waterline and up the stack of the first target, stopping her dead in the water. The second ship belched a tremendous cloud of black smoke and sank just beyond the first, already disappearing from the radar screen and from sight behind a heavy shroud of smoke. We braced ourselves as four distinct explosions rumbled the air. The torpedo officer believed that the number four torpedo had missed ahead, but number six probably passed astern of the first target and hit the second. Number one and number two torpedoes hit right where expected on the second ship, but the third must have passed astern.

Listing to port and settling down by the stern, the first target began to signal frantically to the escort pursuing us. He swung around to her assistance and began dropping depth charges randomly, while hugging the stricken ship. We continued to withdraw to the sound of crackling, exploding noises from the dying AK. The leading two ships of the convoy sped off to the northwest, one escort following, depth-charging at irregular intervals.

The absolute preoccupation with attack and evasion abated, and the first waves of jubilation swept over us. We had done it! Now we could join the ranks of seasoned crews, no longer bashful in their company. We had tasted our first blood this night—and found it strong drink.

With moonrise at 1:07 A.M. and plenty of light, we slowed to observe the damaged ship during our reload. Merrill decided to finish off the cripple.

The exec argued against allowing two undamaged *marus* to escape when this cripple obviously wasn't going anywhere; we could deal with her after we had cleaned the rest of the slate. "Captain, two targets are making port at best speed."

"As long as there is a chance the Japanese can repair this one to freight again, we can't claim it as a sinking," Merrill replied.

He ordered the preparation of a contact report so that a sister submarine might get a crack at the two escaping ships.

Batfish continued to withdraw southward; when we were out of visual and radar range of the cripple, we steered on an easterly course to transmit the message. At 3:50 A.M., with message off, we started back toward the target. Sound reported pinging and occasional depth charges from its vicinity. Between the scattered clouds, moonlight had increased to its brightest.

In minutes, SJ picked up the target at 24,000 yards—now a considerably smaller pip, indicating she had sunk much lower in the water. The escort appeared to be circling her at about 1,500 to 2,500 yards, but not adhering to a fixed patrol pattern. We manned battle stations and prepared to close for the kill.

At 14,000 yards we could sight the stricken ship from the bridge. Dead in the water, she had drifted about two and a half miles to the southeastward since we had hit her. She was now listing about fifteen degrees to port with water up to her main deck at the stern. With a draft of thirty feet aft and five feet forward, her bow was practically out of the water.

20 January 1944

4:49 A.M. She was lying to with the moon on her starboard beam, which forced me to approach with the moon nearly astern. There was not sufficient time before daybreak to approach from the opposite side. This fact accounts for the decision to fire low power shots at considerable range with zero gyro angle using visual bearings. This was deemed advisable because of the escort and the excellent visibility.

At 5:09 A.M. we fired one torpedo from a range of 6,000 yards. Thirty-six seconds later, while heading straight for the target at nine knots, we fired another.

A high geyser of water and white smoke was thrown up from the ship's waterline just abaft her starboard beam. The time corresponded precisely with the run for the first fish. Immediately the escort signaled the target and began to come alongside her. Her port list increased dramatically as she began to settle by the stern with increased momentum. Within a minute, water poured over her main deck and open air showed under her bow, now jutting in the air. We thought the second torpedo passed under it, unexploded.

About thirteen minutes after firing, a loud explosion was heard belowdecks. All that could be seen of the ship now was the bow and forward part of the bridge. The single pip in the radar screen separated into two smaller pips, and then soon disappeared. She was gone.

6:15 A.M. Anticipating countermeasures with sunrise, submerged to conduct patrol eight miles south of scene of attack. Nothing in sight at daylight.

Since the escort did not pursue us, perhaps she was rescuing survivors, if any. At 8 A.M. we changed course to northward to investigate the attack area. Within half an hour, we sighted a four-engine patrol bomber three miles north. Nothing else was in sight except two columns of smoke coming from the sea; the escort had departed.

We could hear a systematic search in the distance west and north of us, being conducted over a broad area. We made no attempt to count the numerous depth charges as they were not close—obviously the avengers hadn't seen us and hadn't the foggiest idea which way we went.

We continued periscope patrol to the southeast, going deep between observations to avoid planes. During the afternoon, still submerged, we periscope-sighted a fishing-type sampan four miles distant. Since there was no radio mast visible, he was probably not an observer. Come night, we patrolled to southward to get back on our convoy route of yesterday. Within minutes, our lookouts sighted a sub-chaser six miles to the north. We maneuvered to avoid him on the surface.

We made no contacts whatever the next day, but developed our first SJ radar malfunction. The repair crew managed to keep it operating, but not normally. When we submerged at dawn, we attempted repair while conducting periscope patrol. During the day and evening, we made only two visual contacts: a sampan or junk, and a bobbing white light that couldn't be identified or picked up on radar. Though eager for our next victim, we had the entire area to ourselves. Perhaps the report of our kill cleared the area of targets, but search as we might, we saw no more enemy vessels of consequence. Once more we settled down to the monotonous routine of life aboard a submarine in an empty sea.

22 January 1944

Weather has been poor for the last twenty-four hours with complete overcast and occasional rain squalls. No navigational fix since yesterday. SJ radar is still not functioning properly and cannot be trusted.

23 January 1944

Sky overcast and poor visibility. SJ radar out of commission. This last day in the area is typical of a large number of the other days in that it is completely overcast. In the entire twenty-seven days we have spent in this area we haven't had one that could be called clear. It has made it extremely hazardous to try to conduct surface patrol during daylight. Only five days were spent on the surface without being forced down by planes.

At 5:32 P.M. we surfaced and set course for Midway, departing our first war patrol area in accordance with operational order. Making three-engine speed so as to clear the adjacent submarine operating area as rapidly as possible, we transmitted our third and final serial message to ComSubPac.

At 8:44 P.M. our SJ radar was back in commission after two full days' work on it submerged.

Shortly before noon the next day, we sighted two columns of smoke over the northern horizon. Closing to investigate, Merrill could see no masts through the periscope, although the smoke was only about fourteen miles away. Twenty-three minutes later we spotted a smoke-stack, but still no other part of the ship was visible.

We went to battle stations submerged and began an approach. From 12,000 yards, although we could still see the smoke, we were diligently unable to sight the smoker. The bearings we logged were changing too rapidly for it to be very far away, but the fairly large sea swells that were making our depth control uncertain were also giving us a problem holding steady periscope surveillance.

24 January 1944

1:10 P.M. Apparently the source of the smoke was two large sampans or patrol boats without masts heading on a northerly course. As the sky was cloudy and we were still near enemy air bases, decided to remain submerged until sunset to routine torpedoes. Obviously the contact wasn't worth running down.

6:11 P.M. Surfaced and set course for Midway, three-engine speed. Wish to make as much speed as possible while the weather is favorable. We have had enough bad weather already for one patrol.

Seven uneventful days later, having passed back through some of the typhoon weather we encountered coming to our area, we moored at Midway at 9 A.M.

Midway is actually two main islands—850-acre Sand Island and 328-acre Eastern Island—rising from a largely submerged circular atoll, the eroded crater of a long-extinct volcano near the geographic center of the Pacific Ocean, 1,500 miles northwest of Pearl Harbor. Until the Navy moved in, Midway had been primarily a mating grounds for gooneybirds. Graceful in the air, these birds were ungainly and clumsy on the ground—and acted as if they owned the island. They remained so plentiful and friendly (or aloof) that it was difficult for a drunk to walk far without colliding with one.

Due to the local imbalance of nature (there were no women on Midway), the gooneybirds promised to be our basic source of amusement.

The *Batfish* branch of the Silent Service had been hoping for a last-minute rerouting to Pearl, where we could live it up at the Royal Hawaiian Hotel while *Batfish* was undergoing two weeks' refit. After *this* first war patrol, we felt we really deserved more than Midway for our well-earned Rest and Recuperation, but we kept quiet about it.

We had been at sea fifty-one days: sixteen days to our patrol area, twenty-seven days in it, and eight days returning. Almost half of these days were spent submerged. During this period, we had made twelve aircraft contacts—three friendly, six unknown, three enemy—and twenty-two ship contacts, ranging from *Yamato* to a bobbing white light. We had fired eight torpedoes, sunk two ships, and made a multitude of successful evasions. Our only real adversary had been the weather.

Remarks from U.S.S. *Batfish*, First War Patrol Report:

The anti-submarine measures observed on this patrol were more potential than actual. The area was well-patrolled by aircraft during daylight only. All convoys passing through the area during daylight can be expected to have air cover, even though over two hundred miles from land. The inevitable radio-equipped sampan was found along the path of expected convoys.

Most of the patrol boats appeared to be similar to our sub-chaser of PC classes, and I believe our submarines can outrun them on the surface. It is believed that surface escorts are light in comparison to areas nearer land and that the enemy depends a great deal on air coverage.

The closest depth charge was dropped over a mile distant while we evaded on the surface after [our] attack[s].

The SJ radar operated excellently with routine maintenance with the exception of two nights' operation. The SD radar gave good results with only routine maintenance. The minimum ranges at which low friendly planes were picked up was six miles, and a maximum of twenty-six miles. There was no indication that it was being DF-ed.

This was the first patrol for this vessel and also the first for two officers and over half the crew. The weather was unusually trying and a lack of contacts during the first three weeks in the area lent to monotony. Under these conditions the Commanding Officer has nothing but praise for the splendid performance of duty on the part of both officers and men. Morale remained high throughout, even when it looked as if we would return to base without having fired a torpedo. There was, however, a very noticeable increase in enthusiasm when we heard the explosions of our first torpedoes fired.

The dull days were shortened by continual instruction in submarines, field days, material upkeep and associated pursuits. Men fresh from submarine school found their place rapidly and are now well along in their training.

It is believed that the training periods afforded new construction submarines are of tremendous value and are adequate when coupled with a reasonable amount of caution on the part of the Commanding Officer. Once a patrol has been successfully completed by a new submarine it is felt that she has won half the battle. All hands are surer of their footing and they have ceased to be "the *Batfish* detail"—they are instead a fighting unit, "the *Batfish* crew." Admittedly this metamorphosis is largely psychological, but its importance cannot, I believe, be overestimated.

The one single factor which contributes most to morale continues to be the execution of successful attacks.

Viewing the entire patrol as conducted in retrospect, the Commanding Officer feels that he is guilty of several errors in judgment. . . . It is hoped that the experience gained on this patrol, my first in command, will aid in obtaining more impressive results in the future.

We were congratulated with endorsements on a well-conducted and successful first war patrol, and credited with sinking of one freighter and one passenger-freighter, for a total of 15,678 tons of the enemy's merchant marine.

Returning from patrol, *Batfish* was assigned to a submarine squadron commander for refit. A relief crew from the squadron took over the boat while we were bussed to the Old Pan American (or Gooneybird) Hotel to begin our two-week R & R period. Unless extensive repair work or training was required, our total period of refit and training would last about three weeks.

Although Pearl Harbor had only a beer garden, besides women, Honolulu had many bars and clubs. At Midway there was some tolerable cheap beer available, but only the officers could get whiskey. In fact, every officer was issued one bottle a week. The crew got none.

Captain Merrill followed the procedure that most submarine

skippers did. After we hit Midway, he gave all fifteen or twenty bottles of depth-charge whiskey in *Batfish*'s safe to the Chief of the Boat, and told him to take the crew up to the baseball diamond and start getting us in shape for our ship's party. No doubt motivated by more than altruistic camaraderie, he wanted no man to be tempted by "torpedo juice." Since his forthcoming whiskey ration amounted to eight bottles accumulated during our patrol, plus a bottle a week continuing through our R&R, he might have a problem drinking all that himself.

Several other crews shared the hotel with us. Since they had arrived before *Batfish*, they had nearly depleted their own skippers' largess. According to custom, all the other submariners gathered around to hear our stories, exchanging modesty and rapt attention for our booze. We told about the big one that got away, and the two that didn't—until our whiskey grew short. Then when our audience started to dwindle, we caught up on our sleep. This all took several days.

Thereafter, if we went to the baseball diamond, it was to play baseball. A physical fitness program headed by Jack Dempsey featured boxing, weight lifting, some track, and more baseball. Some men fished a little to pass the time; others swam or just lay in the sun. But you can lie in the sun only so long.

In the evenings, the USO and the Naval Special Services Unit tried to make us feel at home. Commander Eddie Peabody, the Banjo King, was stationed at Midway, and all attended his concert. There were two movie houses, one on each island. Under such circumstances, no matter how bad a movie was, no one ever saw it just once. We alternated between *Four Daughters* on Sand Island and *Mexican Spitfire's Blessed Event* on Eastern Island. But mainly we settled into sitting around and watching the gooneybirds go through their hilarious antics and mate—endlessly, it seemed.

We laughed a lot. But compared with *Batfish,* Midway had a little more room and we could take a bath when we wanted to. That was about it. It wasn't long before we began to look forward to getting back to sea. *Let's get on with it.*

It wasn't very different for most of the officers. Like crew, most of them tied on one good one and then lay back, letting time play on their thoughts until it was time to go to sea again. But after the ship's party, our captain partied with his officers. Then as they began dropping by the wayside for lack of sleep and other reasons, Merrill gravitated to civilians and his crew. Thin and well proportioned at the beginning of our first war patrol, he had grown gaunt over the past two months. But other than a few oblique references to those poor brave men of *Grampus,* he confided nothing truly personal. After their ship's parties, other captains didn't normally drink with their crews, and we grew a little edgy that our curious relationship was getting unwelcome attention.

The night before departure for our second war patrol, Merrill—with a bit too much to drink—went to the exec's room to repair the damage between them, hopefully by closing the distance with a little whiskey. The exec, who roomed with the Diving Officer, said he needed sleep. When the captain persisted, they called the torpedo and gunnery officer to their room.

"War is the most asinine thing ever invented," Merrill confided. "I'm fighting men who didn't do anything to me. God knows I never did anything to them; we're not even mad at each other. But someone in Washington and someone in Tokyo said we've got to go out there and kill each other—and only one of us is coming back."

The officers decided it had become necessary to foreshorten the evening. Two of them lifted the captain up bodily and—gently and efficiently—dropped him out the first-floor window onto the soft Midway sand a few feet below. Captain Merrill landed beside a gooney-bird nest whose occupants, after honking for a few seconds, seemed not the least inconvenienced. Merrill got up and went to his room for a very brief sleep. *Batfish* was going to sea early.

SECOND WAR PATROL

12 February 1944

Early in the morning, we took *Batfish* back from the relief crew and spent the following three days preparing for underway training, testing machinery and equipment. Following the thorough refit, our boat was in excellent condition.

From 16 to 18 February, we put *Batfish* through her paces with our Submarine Division Commander on board as training officer. We successfully completed a series of radar tracking exercises, including four day and four night radar rehearsal runs and one radar firing run at a screened target. All exercise torpedoes ran straight, hot, and normal; all hit the target! Then for two days, we loaded stores, food, fuel, and torpedoes, making final preparations for our second war patrol. Night or day, *Batfish* was ready for the Japanese—but some aboard believed that Captain Merrill was not.

We got under way at 3:58 P.M., 22 February, having aircraft escort from Midway until sunset. Again we were assigned to patrol the area off the southeast coast of Shikoku. Some of our old hands had rotated back stateside to man new boats coming off the ways, and were replaced by new men—graduates of the New London Submarine School, but otherwise new to submarine combat. En route to our patrol area, on the fourth day out, the barometer began to drop and the sea picked up accordingly, forcing us to slow somewhat to relieve the stressful pounding. Over the next three days, wind and waves increased, with visibility ranging from absolutely clear to squally.

On the clearest of these days, curious pips on SD radar appeared at about three-mile intervals between fourteen and twenty-five miles, reflecting from large, stationary objects in the sky. On observation, these strange "aircraft" proved to be the lower lobes of a large, brown, peculiarly shaped thunderhead. The lightning had a definite effect upon our radar. As we entered the rain squall, the pips gradually disappeared.

Heavy seas soon forced us down to two-thirds speed. We discovered that our freshwater hose on deck had snaked out and gotten adrift from its reel forward, but until the seas subsided, it was out of the question to put a man on deck to remedy the situation. Finally, on

1 March, two men went topside to clear it, but the seas were still too rough to reel it in. They cut the hose and heaved it overboard.

A day or so short of Sumisu Shima, we began to get SD radar contacts and dived twice within five hours to evade planes. Since neither were sighted, this might possibly have been the result of interference from defective electrical equipment on board. While submerged, we went to 410 feet to test for leaks; there were none.

The barometer was again dropping rapidly, with a full gale blowing and very heavy seas. After we nearly lost a lookout overboard, we slowed once more to two-thirds speed; anything faster pounded us extremely hard.

Several times during the day we rolled as much as forty degrees. Although *Batfish*'s hull was considerably stiffer than her predecessors', the flanged unions of the hull ventilation lines in the forward battery strained and creaked ominously with our hogging and sagging in the heavy seas. One of these unions even pulled away slightly, indicating our hull was a lot more flexible than was commonly believed. Comforting thought!

At 10:50 P.M., 3 March, we passed within twenty-eight miles of Sumisu Shima in a slightly calmer sea, now within a day of entering our patrol area. The body of one "good Jap," dressed in a Japanese Army uniform and wearing a Mae West-type life preserver, floated by close to port. The body was in such an advanced state of decomposition that we didn't attempt closer investigation. Next day, we changed course to head for the south-central part of our area where we had made contacts during the last patrol.

As the barometer crept lower, we had some recurrent problems with our TDC and SJ radar. The drastically worsening weather gave all signs of an approaching typhoon, so we altered course to miss its center. With winds of sixty to seventy knots and violent seas, our lookouts had to secure themselves to station to keep from being swept overboard. Typhoons were supposed to be infrequent in this area at this time of year—an interesting statistic in the midst of one that must have snatched quite a few rooftops from the home islands.

For a full week thereafter, the weather and the calendar hounded us, the wind howling and whining, shrieking and baying. We were going nowhere but around the clock. Visibility was often reduced to as little as a thousand yards. Compared to this, our first patrol had been child's play. When we submerged to routine torpedoes, water batteries, and make repairs, Merrill periodically attempted to conduct periscope patrol, and did so—anywhere between 25 and 150 feet. There was no respite from the storm within 200 feet of the surface. During the night of 10 March, the weather gave signs of calming, but throughout the early morning hours of 11 March, wind and seas came back at us furiously in an awesome array of force and form: rain, hail, sleet, snowstorms, and forty-foot waves, all within a four-hour period. Here and there, low clouds with frequent lightning and thunder played havoc with our SD radar. Another problem we all could have done without was the odor from the sanitary tank inboard vents; no replacement filters had been available at Midway. Perhaps this is where the phrase "Keep a stiff upper lip" comes from; it's the next best thing to holding your nose.

To worsen an already miserable situation, Midway sand had gotten into some of our equipment. While routining torpedoes, considerable work was required to remove the sharp grains from the charging and check valves, and we were having recurrent problems with both radars. Even the food was drastically inferior to the food of our first patrol. The stores we took on at Midway lacked variety; the rice and cereals had weevils; the eggs were so old we had to eat them quickly before they could hatch.

We completely crossed our area twice without making a live enemy contact of any description. A second Japanese corpse floated by about fifty feet to port, dressed in dark khaki-colored trousers and a white undershirt with no life jacket. We let him pass by as well. Both bodies had been in the water a considerable time, possibly from the ships we sank two months before. At any rate, someone had sunk a ship around here.

Undoubtedly all small craft had been kept in port because of the weather, which had also been very poor for flying. Because of this we maintained surface patrol as much as possible, except for dives to service our equipment and rest the lookouts, who were taking one hell of a beating.

11 March 1944

By now I'm convinced that this is the breeding place of all the bad weather found in the North Pacific at this time of year. Since arriving in this area, we've had one day that could be called fair. It was bad enough last time, but this time even the Japs are keeping clear of it.

On 14 March the sea was finally calm once more, under a cloudy sky. About midday, we sighted a patrol plane about eight miles away and submerged to avoid detection.

> Decided to remain submerged while closing approximate track of plane in hopes that he was searching ahead of an enemy convoy. . . . Our first plane contact in the area was made on the first day that we've had decent flying weather and appears to substantiate the contention that this area is well patrolled by aircraft as was found on our last patrol here. After eleven days in the area we still have had no surface craft contacts. It is hoped, however, that the improved weather will induce the enemy to venture out of port. In the meantime we have been making every effort to have a crew of men who are 100% "qualified in submarines." With the probable exception of two men making their first patrol, I'm sure we will attain our goal.

Two days later we had another SD contact—our fourth. Since the sky was overcast, we patrolled submerged for the balance of the day.

16 March 1944

> It appears plausible that the Japs are routing most of their shipping along the coast or southward near the islands of the Nanpo Shoto to avail themselves of land-based air coverage and the protection of defensive minefields.

Captain Merrill prepared a careful analysis of probable convoy routes that included an assumed ship's average speed, base course, and arrival and departure times from ports, with the most probable position and times of interception. In spite of the analysis, however, a lack of contacts persisted.

17 March 1944

> 8 P.M. Altered course to westward along southern area boundary. Intend to start patrolling near the intersection of the Bungo Suido-Saipan and Kobe-Palau routes. By now have completely covered the area in all directions in a general surface patrol with only two aircraft contacts and no surface vessel contacts. With only fifteen more days remaining in which to patrol, I believe it is advisable to start concentrating at most likely positions.

The next day the sea picked up again, with fifteen-to-twenty-knot winds from the southeast—not a good sign! We were forced to use SJ radar all day because of poor visibility. By 4 P.M. the barometer was down, the wind up to sixty knots. We saw numerous waterspouts in a very confused sea, as we passed through the center of a "moderate" typhoon.

18 March 1944

8 P.M. I am seriously considering sending an information dispatch to ComSubPac in the hope I may be assigned a more productive area. Have decided, however, to hold off a few more days, as an accurate DF of my position would undoubtedly result in rerouting any traffic which may be passing through the area in the near future. I am almost positive that I have not disclosed my presence to date.

The bleak and boring days passed in an unvarying ritual of one watch on, two watches off—four hours on, eight hours off, the cycle common to ships since sailing began. The "hours on" were easier to manage; doing one's job is always preferable to the monotonous vacuum of recreation. Home and Mom and the girl friend all wear thin and boring after the thousandth anecdote, like pinochle cards that lost their sparkle after having been shuffled and dealt too many times.

Halfway through this second patrol, we bludgeoned our way through typhoons that chased one another northward off the Japanese island. Any day became like any other, and we could have substituted a simpler calendar: Yesterday, Today, and Tomorrow. On this twenty-sixth day, Captain Merrill could simply have written the first half of his log backward and taken a long nap.

Not that we blamed him. He was in the same boat with us; a submarine at the mercy of the elements—destined, it seemed, to tie up at Midway exhausted and empty-handed.

Over the next day, the weather relented for brief periods—ominous, like the pause between sneezes. During these intervals we made five sampan sightings and one aircraft contact on SD radar.

These were our first ship contacts, made during the first real break in the weather so far. We concluded that either typhoons rain sampans; or these sampans could survive the recent storms at sea; or else make over two hundred miles from port within a very few hours of the storm's abating.

20 March 1944

Am remaining in this vicinity in the hope that the sampans are being used as observers, since this is not a likely fishing ground and the sampans have been distributed along a line corresponding to the Bungo Suido-Saipan route, but about fifteen to twenty miles to the northeastward. Such an offset routing would allow a sharp course change just before sunrise for southbound convoys and the same change just after sunset for northbound convoys. This observation checks with our observations during our last patrol. . . .

It was two days before we sighted even another sampan, during which time the wind and sea had moderated to very flat and calm with an overcast sky.

Beginning at 10 A.M. on 23 March, and continuing at irregular intervals for about an hour and a half, we heard a series of twenty-five depth charges. They were a long way off, probably fifteen to twenty miles, and it was impossible to tell from which direction the sounds came. This could be the depth charging of a sister sub, but it was just as likely an example of the established Japanese technique of depth-charging heavily in the path of an approaching convoy to clear submarines by intimidation if nothing else. Although a very high periscope watch was maintained, we saw nothing.

Midafternoon, we sighted a sampan about 2,000 yards dead ahead on an opposite course. We could see only one mast, aft and very low, but sound picked up his screws shortly afterward. We were forced to do some fancy maneuvering to avoid this one, as suddenly he decided to lay his fishing net across our bow in a long arc at fairly high speed. Very clever, these Japanese. The aft torpedo room got a laugh imagining *Batfish* getting hauled off to some Tokyo fish market and all of us being haggled over by geisha girls.

23 March 1944

Had a good look at him at about 500 yard range and am convinced he was an innocent, though troublesome, fisherman, without radio and unarmed. Was tempted to eliminate him, but could not feel justified in taking a chance on disclosing our presence. The net he laid was marked by eighteen bamboo poles carrying white flags which were of considerable help in avoiding it. Only nine more days in the area and still have 60,000 gallons of fuel remaining, so intend to start using some of it in wider area coverage.

Because of the U.S. submarines' increasing attrition upon their shipping, hunger was quickly becoming a major problem for the Japanese. Most of their dwindling food supplies went to the military and many Japanese civilians were literally starving. Since meat was an impossibility, this could account for greater numbers of fishermen in unlikely places.

The next four days produced one plane contact at twenty miles and three sampan sightings—the first a two-master of about thirty tons, the second unknown because he changed course away from us while we were turning, and the third another two-master about eight miles off. The sightings were apparently not reciprocal. A glassy sea with a low haze and the barometer falling, sea and wind again began to raise a storm with thirty-to-forty-knot gales.

29 March 1944 _____

> With only four days remaining in which to patrol the area and still contacting nothing but planes and sampans, am pretty well convinced that traffic is being routed closer to the islands of the Nanpo and Nansei Shotos than heretofore. Although we won't have given up hope until we're moored in our base, we are all somewhat discouraged at our lack of success. The morale problem is being solved by plenty of hard work toward qualification of new men, and in this at least we have been most successful.

The following day at about 6:30 P.M., lookout sighted two masts about 7,000 yards to the northwest. Although we couldn't pick it up on radar and it was too dark to see through the scope, both Merrill and the OOD verified the sighting. It seemed to be a submarine with her periscope and radar mast extended, but these "masts" still didn't show on radar; most perplexing. As we had nothing more to go on without approaching, Merrill ordered us to maneuver to avoid it.

By 1 April the sea was again calming with light wind and good visibility. We had made four more uneventful sampan sightings.

1 April 1944 _____

> This is our last day in the area. Have decided to delay in sending a departure message until tomorrow night when I will not be so

apt to embarrass the submarine operating eastward of me in case I am DF-ed. There's also a chance of making contact with the enemy while en route through the Nanpo Shoto. Am certainly envious of the boat which reported contacting a nineteen-ship convoy. Since we couldn't be there too, I wish I could have given her my torpedoes.

Later that morning, we received a message from ComSubPac directing us to remain an additional day on station to attempt to intercept a battleship reported by a sister sub south of us. We changed course to westward and started our search for her at three-engine speed.

8 P.M. Slowed to best two-engine speed to conserve fuel. Will be able to intercept at this speed. Routined all torpedoes in tubes and reloads during the night. Checked over entire fire-control system and overhauled one tube firing valve.

In the early morning hours, we were again enveloped in rain and clouds, high seas, and a forceful wind. With dawn, the water became highly phosphorescent and our wake shimmered and flashed for some distance behind us. By the time we were on the BB's probable track, it had stopped raining. We slowed to five knots and the exec attempted a navigational fix—impossible because of the still-dark, heavy sky.

We submerged to conduct a periscope patrol. The sky gradually cleared later during the day and the sea calmed, but despite fair visibility, no sight or sound contacts of any description were made. We surfaced at sundown.

2 April 1944 _____

6:55 P.M. We had patrolled the desired line during the day in spite of the fact that we had been unable to obtain a morning fix. Set course to eastward at two-engine speed to depart area at specified position. After today's lack of results, I'm just about convinced that our luck just isn't in this patrol.

We departed our area at dusk, 3 April. Many aboard felt that our return wasn't any too soon, either. Relations between Captain Merrill and the exec had become even more strained, and they were talking to each other only when necessary. The point now under contention was whether, in retrospect, we should have been patrolling closer to land.

Next day we sighted Sumisu Shima, thirteen miles distant. We hoped "home" would turn out to be Pearl. Not that we didn't love Midway, but no one aboard had a pinup of a gooneybird in his locker.

We touched at Midway three hours after sunrise on 11 April, following a return trip as uneventful as the patrol in general. Our patrol off Shikoku probably amounted to the most wasted fifty-one days any submarine undertook during the entire war. We longed for combat almost as much as we pined for Pearl—and this time we got the latter! After minor repairs, leaving twenty-two of our torpedoes on Midway for overhaul, we departed the very next day for the harbor of our dreams.

Looking back, we had made at least two positive accomplishments. Retaining one torpedo forward and one aft, we had successfully delivered—in the most roundabout way possible—twenty-two torpedoes to Midway to help replenish their stock. And *Batfish*'s complement now consisted of all but three "qualified" submariners.

All activity of every U.S. naval vessel must be thoroughly accounted for at every possible level—from top to bottom. In wartime this accounting is intensified. Aboard *Batfish*, each chief torpedoman, electrician, and machinist, and each major equipment operator—radar, sound, and radio—must log at regular intervals all activities of his station, even including the *lack* of activity. The quartermaster formally logged the activities of the sub as a whole, though, in the heat of battle, such accounting naturally took a back seat to more pressing matters. The quartermaster also included a summary of the logs of each chief of station. In turn, the captain based his Patrol Report upon all of these plus his own log observations. He wrote them when he could, when time was available—sometimes during the act, sometimes immediately thereafter. Sometimes he wrote it coming into port with the advantage of hindsight compensating for his waning spontaneity. Each Patrol Report then usually concluded with the commanding officer's remarks, generally summarizing the essence of the preceding patrol.

> **Remarks:** In the opinion of the Commanding Officer, the lack of success on this patrol must be attributed to the nearly complete absence of enemy traffic through the sea. At no time were there any indications of merchant shipping having passed through. . . . On four occasions attempts were made to intercept men-of-war, none of which were successful. In two instances the targets were submarines. It is believed that deviations from the supposed

tracks, or schedules, caused failure of the other two attempts on surface craft.

Anti-submarine measures were noticeably lacking and it was possible to conduct most of the patrol on the surface. It is felt that the area was thoroughly searched in as systematic a manner as was practicable. It is believed that the enemy is routing traffic both to the eastward along the islands of the Nanpo Shoto and to the westward near the coast of Kyushu.

The decision of the Commanding Officer not to ask for a more productive area was influenced by our planned fleet attack on Palau and nearby islands, which I hoped would result in combatant ships passing through the area en route to or from Japan's main islands. The decision was also based on prospects occasioned by two contact reports received earlier.

At the present time, I feel that the area can be covered sufficiently well by submarines enroute to and from other areas to justify elimination of it as an area patrolled continuously by one submarine.

Upon completion, the captain's Patrol Report was duplicated for circulation—in this case, sixty-eight copies—to nearly twenty commands and agencies, ranging from one copy each to our squadron and division commanders, all the way up to five copies to ComInCh (commander in chief).

Endorsements were then made evaluating our performance. Unless we had accomplished something spectacular—perhaps requiring the attention of even the President—those endorsements most closely affecting us were those of our division commander:

The whole patrol was a battle with the elements and it is extremely gratifying to see how well this grand submarine and crew came through a most trying experience.

In spite of disappointment after disappointment, this submarine went right ahead with instruction and training so that only three new men were unqualified on completion of the patrol. The Commanding Officer is deserving of special credit in keeping up this enthusiasm in the face of adverse circumstances of which he had no control.

It is regrettable that no damage to the enemy can be credited to the *Batfish* on this patrol, but ships can't be sunk that are not contacted. Commander Submarine Division 201 admires the sticktoitiveness and spirit displayed by the Commanding Officer, officers and men of the *Batfish* and looks forward to better hunting for them next time.

Our squadron commander:

> The absence of contacts on this patrol is a keen disappointment to all hands. The spirit and fine enthusiasm of the Captain of *Batfish* is clearly reflected throughout the ship. The Squadron Commander congratulates the Captain, officers and crew of *Batfish* for carrying on with admirable spirit despite the lack of contacts. It is confidently anticipated that the attitude displayed will pay good dividends in the near future.

And our force commander, ComSubPac:

> The Commander Submarine Force, Pacific Fleet, is pleased to note that advantage was taken of the time on patrol to conduct extensive instruction in order to qualify new men and officers. This patrol is designated as not successful for Combat Insignia Award.

TRANSITION

To summarize this officer, he is the best officer I ever had the pleasure of having under my command at sea and in combat . . .

Edward Shillingford Hutchinson,
First Commanding Officer, U.S.S. *Grampus*.
W. R. Merrill, Fitness Report excerpt.

Our Hawaiian idyl began pleasantly enough. On arrival, a relief crew from the tender *Proteus* took *Batfish* from our hands. They would see to the completion of maintenance, refit and clean her, stand all necessary watches, and then turn her back over to us as good as new.

In a sense, Pearl Harbor was to us what Midway was to gooney-birds. For fourteen days of freedom, none of us had duties at all. We could do anything we wanted to within the law—and more, if we didn't get caught.

Since room assignment was determined by officers, Captain Merrill's room was near those assigned to the crew. And as the days went by, he began spending more and more time with the latter. Captain Merrill had thinned from gaunt to emaciated, worn out from a thoroughly demoralizing war patrol. On the surface, he remained the most flamboyant person around, but from our own experience, we knew no man could live beyond his limits indefinitely.

Our unsuccessful second war patrol also became a topic of discussion in the sub base beer garden. There couldn't help but be some wounded pride when another man offered his opinion:

"Some submariners find lots of enemy ships and others don't. The reason we find them is we're out there looking; when they don't drop right into our lap, we search somewhere else. What you got to do is get so close to the beach that the Japs can't go between you and land. And then you sink them. . . . By the way, hear you guys lost another battleship."

When our two weeks of luxury came to an end, there were few regrets at the prospect of going back to sea. Compared to the Royal Hawaiian, simply a place to visit, *Batfish* was home. And aboard home, much new equipment had been installed. Twenty of us had been transferred stateside—a transfusion of experience, so to speak, to improve the bloodline of new submarines without diluting our own.

(Not only do submariners have the highest percentage of rated men in any service, but enlisted men enjoy quicker promotion than anywhere else. It was not uncommon for submariners to earn a higher rate on each war patrol.)

Having caught up with necessity, the home front was now working overtime. Fleet submarines were rolling off the ways at Portsmouth, New London, Manitowoc, Philadelphia, and Mare Island with increasing frequency, and needed to be manned with the best available combination of tested and untested men.

We also lost an officer: our exec was replaced by our former diving officer. Having been recommended by Captain Merrill for the designation "qualified to command submarines," on 28 April the exec was detached from *Batfish* and ordered to the prospective commanding officer pool on Midway to await assignment as commanding officer of his own boat.

On 10 May 1944 *Batfish* was fully stocked with torpedoes, ammunition, and provisions, but Captain Merrill seemed to be in no condition to take *Batfish* on patrol. Nonetheless, in the company of his new exec and another officer, he went to the base submarine commander and requested assignment to an area where he would find targets for his third war patrol. It was an unusual request, but Merrill was told that he could expect new operational orders at Midway on our way out.

We departed Pearl Harbor the same day, the new exec at the helm because Merrill was still in terrible condition. Four days later, when we docked at Midway to undergo minor repair, surreptitious inquiry was made into the possibility of clipping this wire or snipping that in order to stay overnight. But the exec said that wouldn't be necessary: "Something is up." We could expect an unexpected delay.

Through the grapevine, we learned that Captain Lew Parks, task group commander in charge of all submarine activities at Midway, was to conduct an official inquiry into Merrill's conduct ashore. Apparently, ComSubPac had caught wind of one too many escapades involving *Batfish*'s skipper.

Not long after tying up at the pier, our division commander came down to the dock to speak with Captain Merrill. Never a large man, Merrill's prime weight had been around 150 pounds; his present weight was 127. The Commander asked if he really felt up to going out on another war patrol—or if in his own opinion, Merrill thought he'd had enough for a while.

The captain fended the question for a while. "Well, to be honest," he began, "if you've got somebody else available, I won't resist. I'm willing to go out now, even though I don't feel quite up to it." He paused. "But I'm willing to take a break."

With a feeling of immense relief at the prospect of a rest, but disturbed with the prospect of an investigation's potential effect upon his career, Lieutenant Commander Wayne Merrill then dropped his bricks.

With fresh orders from ComSubPac, Captain John Kerr Fyfe came aboard *Batfish* to "proceed, report, and relieve" Captain Merrill. As *Batfish*'s prospective commanding officer (PCO), he immediately took command, neither giving nor receiving any explanation for the procedure.

The investigation began that evening. Captain Parks personally conducted the proceedings in his office, beginning by interrogating, one by one, each of *Batfish*'s senior officers including her ex-exec, now stationed at Midway. The investigation focused on corroborating a single event that had taken place over two months before: Merrill's being thrown out of the Gooneybird Hotel window by two of his officers, in the presence of a third. Each witness testified under oath in the absence of the others, and Captain Merrill was present during the entire testimony. At one point during the engineering officer's interrogation, the captain spoke up: "Oh, it was all done in good fun."

Despite the ex-exec's differences with Merrill, he also testified that the event in question had not been accomplished by any malice. With proof of this single event clearly established, Captain Parks summarized his conclusions:

"It is obvious to me that Captain Merrill came to his officers' room on the night in question, . . . and that his officers wanted to sleep. To solve this problem, two of them threw him out of the window. This is a terrible thing to have happen. . . . Any commanding officer who allows himself to be thrown out of any window by his subordinates has lost his usefulness to his ship. The indignity of this conduct . . . can only be interpreted as a lack of respect which will affect the entire crew and seriously undermine their morale."

In his radio dispatch to ComSubPac, Parks recommended that Merrill be relieved of command of *Batfish*, and another commanding officer be designated to succeed him.

JOHN KERR FYFE—*"Jack" "J.K." "Jake"*—Black curly hair, long dark lashes, a playful smile—that's Jack. A small-town boy with metropolitan poise, he nevertheless thinks Seneca Falls is the garden spot of New York. Jack is not one of the lads who slave for the highest grades nor has he had to even work hard to stay sat, so the end of the month never worried him. A Saturday night hop or a Sunday afternoon at Carvel is an event in his life—did we hear someone say snake! Jack doesn't specialize in athletics but he's always ready for a game of touch or a rough-house; or on a rainy afternoon, he'll supply good ideas and his share of the conversation. Jack will find and fill his niche in the Navy but we'll never forget his friendliness and pleasant nature—he's one of the boys!

Aboard *Batfish*, Captain Fyfe completed his PCO training under our division commander and was officially designated our second war commander. Shortly after Merrill's investigation had concluded, *Batfish* was again ready for sea.

SECOND WAR COMMAND THIRD WAR PATROL

26 May 1944

Under Marine Corps air coverage, *Batfish* departed Midway for a so-called Rainbow Area, spanning nearly a thousand miles of Japanese water from the mouth of Tokyo Bay off Honshu southwestward to below the tip of Kyushu, including the Kii Suido, Bungo Suido, and the coast of Shikoku. There seemed no question that we would see enough ships there to make up for the heartbreaking lack of targets in our last patrol.

Two and a half hours after departure, our air escort turned back to Midway. Knowing our destination's ominous reputation, we trained as if our lives depended on it.

Our new captain seemed efficient and competent. During our seven-day transit to Honshu, Fyfe personally and tersely assured each man that he meant for us to do what we had come to do—namely, close and kill the enemy. He indirectly paid Captain Merrill a high compliment by saying that *"Batfish* was a damned fine boat"—which, all hands knew, didn't accidentally materialize from sweat and seawater, but from rigid training and a disciplined crew. By the time we sighted that bleak stone pinnacle of Sofu Gan—Lot's Wife—on station 3 June, we were doing everything Fyfe's way. We could only wonder how a man who came aboard under these conditions could have handled the transition so graciously.

For once we were blessed with excellent weather and smooth seas, ideal for high-speed surface cruising. During our first week in the island group south of Tokyo Bay, we made only three definite ship contacts: the *Kingfish,* an American submarine; a Japanese trawler which we were thwarted from shooting by hostile aircraft; and a properly marked hospital ship—a no-no, despite our general suspicion that these vessels of mercy carried as many munitions and arms as wounded warriors and Red Cross packages. No doubt because of calmer seas, the number of sampans increased, appearing in groups of six or eight. Though their nuisance was considerable, we had no trouble remaining undetected. Aircraft sightings were also relatively heavy.

Late on the night of 9 June we surface-patrolled the island cluster just below the tip of Kyushu. The navigation lights at Toi Misaki and Hi Saki were twinkling in the dark as if there were no war. The moon was nearly full in a cloudless sky, highlighting the land clearly visible across a still-calm sea. The atmosphere in the conning tower was calm and relaxed when the radar operator's voice broke the silence.

"We have a contact, Captain. Large pip, twenty thousand yards."

Fyfe didn't hesitate. Manning battle stations, we began a fast surface radar approach on our target. It had to be large to produce such a pip at that distance. But at 12,000 yards, the target suddenly disappeared from radar and could not be sighted from the bridge. We continued down the bearing to where it should have been, but nothing was in sight. Sound and radar revealed no presence.

Two hours later, we tracked another battleship-sized pip, with the same results. An hour later, at 1:36 A.M., we tracked and closed on still another at 18,000 yards, which disappeared at 13,000 yards—as another simultaneously appeared at 19,500 yards! A very disconcerting phenomenon, especially under a full moon.

We were all scratching our heads when Fyfe came below and began riffling charts and tracking something with his finger. "I think we've solved the mystery, boys. We've got phantoms."

The radarman ventured, "There's been no problem here, Captain. Perfect performance so far on everything we've double-checked, from sampans to rocks."

Fyfe said, "If you add 100,000 yards to your pip ranges, you'll find some pretty prominent mountaintops." He tapped the chart spread in front of him. "Right here." In the unusual atmospheric conditions, our SJ had been picking up mountain peaks thirty-five to fifty-five miles away and tracking our own radar echoes bouncing back from them. Our phantom targets were these echoes, showing up as pips on the radar sweep succeeding that of the pulse that caused them. "A weather freak. These things sometimes happen." Fyfe turned to the exec. "Secure from battle stations. And pass the word down: If anybody wants to see more stars than he's ever seen, he can take a quick turn topside. It's that clear out."

We took advantage of this unexpected offer, enjoying the quiet splendor. It took a special kind of captain to admit to his crew that he had been chasing after mountains half the night and then—in the midst of war—to share the stars.

Our "starwatch" made, we patrolled northward up the Kyushu

coast against a strong current. Forced under only once by aircraft, we gained as much headway as night allowed, recharging our batteries, then took a star fix at dawn and dove to periscope depth. *Batfish* now persisted slowly toward the mouth of Bungo Suido, separating the islands of Kyushu and Shikoku.

It was almost 11 A.M. when the Officer of the Deck shouted from the conning tower, "Captain to the conn! Captain to the conn!"

Fyfe was taking a little shut-eye, having been up most of the night, but he responded quickly. Commuting from his quarters to the conning tower was only a few steps over the compartment sill into the control room and up.

"Smoke on the horizon, Captain," the OOD said, sharing the periscope with Fyfe.

Fyfe squinted, his lips beginning to form silent words.

"Bearing south," the OOD offered. "Looks like it's coming our way."

Through the periscope, Fyfe saw a tiny black spot on the blue horizon. The day was intense and brilliant, as clear as had been the night before it. Fyfe slowly walked the periscope around, observing the shoreline, inspecting sea and sky for hazard. Once again he pinpointed the target. Two masts could now be seen. "Steady as she goes. We'll let it develop."

Batfish was just holding her own against the current, making barely enough turns of her screws to keep from drifting backward. Observation was maintained as the target grew steadily larger, from a fleck on the horizon to a definite blemish roughly six miles distant.

Fyfe began another slow sweep of the horizon with the periscope. We were slightly closer to the shoreline than to the approaching target. This would be his last look through this scope; the "feather," or spray of water around the periscope shaft, was large enough to give us away. Fyfe's eyes lingered on the village of Shimoura on Shimanoura Shima on our port side. Not much moving. Some civilian foot traffic and a few carts. Deceptively peaceful: the lookout station there was in plain view. With this sight, he hurried the rotation. Nothing on the sea astern or starboard, nothing in the air, no clouds to hide an enemy flight. Horizon and sky were equally spotless but for our target, still coming closer.

"Down scope." Fyfe snapped the handles into place. The quartermaster squeezed the "pickle," and the big tube slid down into its well. "Take her down to sixty-two feet." Operating depth for the big search scope had been forty-eight feet. The attack periscope was longer and thinner. Fyfe motioned for the attack periscope to rise and met the handles with his hands as it ascended into position.

He glanced quickly to the north and saw the smoke disappear. The ship was still on course, but possibly slowing or preparing a change in course. But then she poured on the coal and the smoke resumed. A swing of the periscope to port revealed nothing to get alarmed about. Through its smaller field of vision and lower magnification, Fyfe could still see features of the sleepy village. Still no activity at the lookout post.

"Ease her up a couple of feet," he called to the diving officer below without taking his eyes from the target. As *Batfish* rose in response, he craned up on the tips of his toes and held this position for a moment to get one good peep over the fence.

"Down scope." Fyfe nodded, "She's all alone. Sound battle stations."

Musical chimes began to sound throughout the boat and all hands responded smoothly. The muted murmur of their preparation for battle filled the lower deck.

"Sound reports medium screws, Captain. Faint but increasing."

"Port fifteen degrees. Half speed," Fyfe ordered.

A moment later, "Port fifteen, sir." The orders were crisply repeated with no need for Fyfe's acknowledgment. *Batfish* surged forward, defying the strong current as her batteries put out more power. The exec stood alert for the captain's slightest gesture, having learned to lip-read over the course of recent weeks.

Minutes passed, then, "Up periscope." Squatting, Fyfe met the handles as they traveled clear of the well and snapped them out, rising with the cylinder, his eyes on the target the instant the glass eye broke water. His lips moved.

"What is it?" the exec inquired, obviously excited.

"I think we've got a sitting duck," the captain repeated aloud, motioning for the exec to join him at the scope.

Six minutes of our increased speed, plus that of the target, had drawn us together so that identification was now possible. She was an MFM (mast funnel mast) ship with a silhouette unlike anything in the Office of Naval Intelligence ship identification book. She had a high forecastle, mounting two large-caliber guns. There was a deep well forward and then a high foremast, with two yardarms just forward of the long high bridge. The aft main mast was the height of the foremast. The amidships superstructure was also high; the single funnel just barely cleared the top of her bridge. Two large guns were mounted on the high aft deck. A large number of men were topside engaged in drills; from all appearances, it was some type of training ship. Two signal searchlights were being trained on the beam with no one out there to talk to; they had to be signal drills.

Strangely, she was not zigzagging, simply steaming around, apparently headed for no particular point. If she simply drifted with the current toward us, with no radical change of course, and we held our speed and course, she would come into our shooting range within an hour.

"Down scope. Steady as she goes."

Four additional men scampered up into the conning tower to join the attack team, and the conn became a very tight little compartment. It was no bigger than your average "two-ass" kitchen, but since there were far more appliances here than a stove, sink, and refrigerator—and since all our "appliances" were major, each requiring at least one operator— our battle-ready condition required swift efficiency, however cramped. And the captain had to have room, so as a rule, a moat of relatively clear space was provided around him.

Ten minutes later, the TDC, primed with our own course and speed, whirred in readiness for further data. Fyfe ordered the periscope up once more to update the target's range and bearing. The fire-control officer at the TDC console asked in a low voice, "Target bearing?"

"Due north," said Fyfe.

"Estimated range?"

"Down to five triple oh. Target's angle on the bow is thirty starboard."

"Bearing and range noted." The TDC operator spun the dials.

"Make the forward tubes ready."

Fyfe made a quick and careful scan, then focused back on the target. She was now close enough for him to see neatly dressed sailors, some drilling in small groups upon her decks. Other figures could be seen climbing about on her masts and superstructure. Here and there a glint of metal reflected the sun.

"Seems to be a well-polished ship," Fyfe said. "Down scope. Change course to fifteen starboard." This course change would bring us parallel to both the coast and to the target's general bearing.

"Flood the forward tubes. Set depth six feet."

The talker responded in a moment. "Tubes flooded forward. Depth is set at six feet."

"The next observation will be a shooting one," Fyfe announced in the crowded compartment. "Open the outer doors forward."

There is something about certainty that disallows conjecture. Every man packed into the conning tower checked and double-checked his contribution to what was about to happen, securing its inevitability.

"Sound report."

"Sound reports one set of screws increasing. No other sound."

"Report any change."

"Yes, sir. I think they're learning how to run it. Speed varies considerably in short bursts." This matched Fyfe's observations, and he nodded.

Five more minutes passed, in which the expectancy throughout the boat became electric.

"Up scope!" Fyfe's palms were wet as the periscope handles came into them. He met them at the deck again and rode them up, his vision breaking the water with the emergent scope. Setting the cross hairs on the ship, he could see midshipmen all over the target's upper rigging. Opposite, his assistant watched the azimuth. The TDC operator was poised, waiting for data. The heavy breathing within the silent conn, from no one in particular, might well have been that of *Batfish* herself.

"Target's posing for a postcard." The ship up there was doomed, and Fyfe knew it. Etched into his memory beyond forgetting, at the level of instant recall, was that loud, bloody morning at Pearl when Fyfe had watched helplessly from *Dolphin*'s deck across the narrow harbor at Ford Island as *California,* his berth and home for two and a half years after Annapolis, began to sink. His former shipmates—classmates from the Naval Academy, personal and close friends—tried to swim the sea of blazing oil and gasoline. Hair afire, burning faces tried to gulp in lungfuls of scorched air. They were never seen again.

Then two years' service aboard *Dolphin*, spared alongside *Narwhal, Tautog,* and *Cachalot.* But his personal survival did not soften the horror and impotent rage the attack had branded into him. They made him businesslike: ship-sinking was a problem to be solved. Before Fyfe let himself see the approaching target as full of men about to die, he pictured his perished friends and countrymen, and remembered who had ravaged them. At Pearl Harbor, *Dolphin* had been unarmed. On

Midway, twenty-nine months later, John Kerr Fyfe was issued *Batfish*; she was armed!

Fyfe stole a look at the men around him. Grim-faced at their jobs, alert at the demands of their specialties, they also stole occasional looks at Fyfe.

The TDC operator tensed in anticipation, facing the firing panel, fingers poised like a pianist's above the final chord. Three red lights glowed through the windows on the slender metal keyboard.

The range narrowed to 1,900 yards. Fyfe snapped the range and bearing to the fire-control officer.

"Set!"

"Shoot!"

With his left hand, the operator snapped the switch under the first of the red lights. His right hand hit the firing key.

"Fire one!" he called into the phone. The firing key was held down for a moment, then released. The first switch was flipped upright, the second switch deftly flicked down. He pressed the second firing key. "Fire two!" The process was repeated. "Fire three!"

Batfish shuddered three times as her torpedoes leaped from their forward tubes. Fyfe hunched his shoulders, needing to look.

The torpedo tracks were clearly visible, running out on a slightly spreading pattern. The second and third looked good, Fyfe noted, but the first was going to hit. He could clearly make out the midshipmen on the target, jumping up and down, waving their arms as they sighted the torpedo tracks, acting like a stage full of electrified puppets. Familiar.

The first streak of foam led directly to a point just forward of the ship's beam. Some of the cadets were pointing at the water, others flailed their arms wildly. The target's bow began to turn slowly, lumbering, but despite her skipper's frantic efforts, she could not escape.

As torpedo #1 found its home, a geyser of water shot up from the ship's side and she blew up.

Fyfe watched as the bow section angled upward, hung there for a moment and then, with an odd grace the ungainly ship had never known in life, slid slowly backward out of sight. He saw some midshipmen thrashing briefly in the water before it closed over them.

Then came the breaking-up noises—smaller explosions piling on top of one another, diminishing sounds that meant bulkheads caving in, water rushing through gaping holes in the hull, trapping doomed men belowdecks, weighing down the shattered ship for its descent.

She sank in less than two minutes.

We dove to avoid the inevitable patrol boats and planes that the lookout station would rally. That lookout would be in for a lot of trouble for letting us poach in his front yard. Minutes after diving, as we were already descending rapidly, the explosion caught us off-guard.

Wraanngg! Momentarily deafened, we felt it with our entire bodies. Dust was raised; objects shattered and flew about. *Batfish* lurched downward in total darkness, pushed by the enormous explosion. At three hundred feet, she gradually responded to our attempts to check her dive, as the dim red emergency lighting system feebly flickered on. As we touched four hundred feet, men who had been slammed against bulkheads and shipmates could stand nearly straight again. It seemed an eternity before Fyfe's voice sounded over the intercom: "All compartments report!"

The control room hatch had slammed to when the call "Emergency!" had rung out. Now it reopened. "All compartments report no damage, sir," the Chief of the Boat called up.

"Level off at two hundred and fifty feet. Rig for depth charge and rig for silent running."

In plain sight of the Shimoura lookout, retaliation was expected. We slunk out and over the hundred-fathom curve and settled safely in the deep, setting our course to patrol Fuka Shima. For about two hours we heard distant depth charges—a bit late. Their search went on well into the night.

Our brush with death might have been an aerial bomb from an undetected escort, but Fyfe's final scan before diving seemed to preclude it. The target's exploding magazine or boiler was also an unlikely cause; she had blown up so devastatingly that by the time she slid under the waves, it was doubtful that anything major aboard her remained undetonated.

A calm postmortem produced a most awesome likelihood: our second two torpedoes had missed the target. Because of the background noise of our dying target, Sound could not hear any end-of-run explosions. One of these had apparently made a circular run and exploded directly over *Batfish*. We had almost torpedoed ourselves—a near-tragedy that a number of our submarines had experienced.

By the time we surfaced, just after sundown, we had cleaned up our shattered glass and confettied cork. Shortly after midnight, 11 June, Sound caught fast screws moving fairly close down our starboard side, sounding like a high-speed antisubmarine vessel. We then contacted a plane, then a torpedo boat, apparently searching on a westerly course. We dove.

Shortly after dawn, we surfaced for battery charging and a navigational fix and then, shortly after sunrise, dove to patrol southeast along the hundred-fathom curve off Okino Shima. Soon another A/S vessel headed directly toward the spot where we had dived, passing about 1,200 yards astern. It was rather disconcerting to be tracked so obviously, especially since we didn't know if they had us on their radar or if they were DF-ing our own, which we had been cautiously keying intermittently and at odd intervals.

Surfacing after dark, we caught another plane coming in and dove once more. Ten minutes before this contact, our APR (radar detection device) had picked up a strong signal that seemed to be sweeping back and forth across our bearing. By the time contact was made on the SD, it was strong and sharp. Apparently the Japanese had borrowed the page on radar-equipped search plane tactics from our own A/S book. Our recent plane contacts apparently were not the result of our radar being DF-ed; we were being spotted by theirs.

When we surfaced at 11:16 P.M. we caught another plane on our SD, coming in fast, so at 11:18 P.M. we sought solace in the deep.

It seemed uncanny: every time we stuck our head up before dawn, we attracted a plane. Since it was nearly daybreak, we decided to stay down, even though we were making scant progress against the two-knot current.

At noon *Batfish* got caught in a fishnet. Two miles long, it had glass floats at regular intervals and marker poles every five hundred feet, each topped with a red and white flag. We pulled the poles over and dragged the whole damned thing, floats and all. While thus encumbered, depth charging started up again like distant drums. First eleven explosions, then a half an hour later, four more.

To see what was going on, Fyfe ran up the periscope, nearly spearing a very low float-type biplane. It was a miracle he didn't see us, but he kept right on going and didn't drop anything. We must have looked like a parade, with the V of the fishnet pointing at us like an arrow. When we couldn't shake or worry it off, or even back away from entanglement, we staged a bold commando raid on it with pocket knives. Clear at last of our bunting, we disappeared from sight.

At sunset we heard ten more depth charges, but from an opposite bearing. Hoping that this barrage presaged a convoy coming through,

Fyfe alerted all detection stations and maintained an intensive periscope scrutiny.

12 June 1944

7:35 P.M. Sighted the upperworks of a ship showing a large red light and two white lights. Since it was dusk, I was unable to distinguish any particular feature except that she was large and had two stacks. She was on an easterly course, coming from the direction of Bungo Suido.

7:56 P.M. Ship is now close enough to distinguish the red light as a large, lighted red cross, reflector lights mounted on sides to show white hull and green striping burning regular running lights and in all respects looking and acting like a *bona fide* hospital ship. This is our second hospital ship in four days, and a beautiful target like that certainly makes one's trigger finger itch. I almost prayed for her to make one false move. She passed about 4,000 yards abeam heading for Ashizuri Saki on Shikoku.

The next day was utterly without event as we patrolled eastward to our new area off Shikoku. We had the ocean completely to ourselves. In her 13 June evening broadcast Tokyo Rose, who normally sympathized with "G.I. Joe," blasted all U.S. submariners, calling us the "Black Panthers of the Pacific." Quite a compliment! The Domei News Agency (the official Japanese news service) also featured an American submarine "atrocity" that evening. Normally we didn't "copy" their propaganda, but that evening, their jamming of our press frequencies was so excessive that the following news was all we could get:

"Two mornings ago about noon aye American submarine suddenly bobbed up about thousand meters to rear tiny Japanese craft *stop* Then it fired into bewildered Japanese without previous warning *stop* Submarine as it drew within two thousand meters it continued its fire *stop* Sailing ship sustained four direct hits and captain ordered all passengers overboard *stop*

"Gritting his teeth nervously captain said with ship crackling with violent flames and evacuees overboard he thought enemy ought to be satisfied with his mission *stop* But he had sadly underrated enemy intentions *stop*

"Submarine slowly drifted middle gasping survivors meanwhile crew of submarine began gather on deck submarine with machine gun rifles in hand *stop*

"As submarine weaved from one helpless group to another these masters of atrocity fired as if they were shooting clay pigeons *stop*

"Evidently submarine commander had heard faint drone war plane *(more)* Surprised crew wildly dashed for hatch and dived below like rats scurrying away from cat *stop*

"Our plane swooped low to indicate recognition relayed position survivors to headquarters then sped on toward enemy objective *stop* When they flew out of sight submarine shot up again to resume their gory target practice as if there no end to their lust for savagery *stop*

"With evident intention make their savage rite aye complete success American sailors began poking floating bodies with long poles to determine whether life remained in them or not *(more)* Captain Nishio stole glance at revolting scene while feigning death aye scene which he confessed will never erased from his mind longs he lives *stop*

"When submarine finally went on its way it was about 1700 or virtually seven hours since it began its brutal attack *stop* After enemy submarine cruised away perhaps to another campaign against unarmed vessels living victims clung to charred remains sailing ship until help arrived 1400 *stop*"

Most of us regarded this as a macabre fabrication, but some others wondered which submarine, if any, might be behind that event. A few of our submarines and skippers were bandied about by name. All of us knew the Japanese did things like that, but did we? Were we making war against ships or against men? Where is the line between fighting hard and committing atrocity?

16 June 1944

8:14 P.M. Heard the latest good war news and decided to patrol slowly across Kii Suido in hopes that some naval units would come out to try and make a dash for Saipan.

A few days before, our forces had successfully carried out a massive air strike in the Marianas Islands. Tokyo Rose hadn't mentioned this, and it was unlikely that she would. In the long, bloody battles for these strategically located islands, we couldn't help feeling that the course of our victory was picking up speed. Japanese civilians would probably be the last to know.

Early in the afternoon of 18 June, Sound picked up propeller noises from at least two ships.

"Sixty feet," Fyfe ordered in the conning tower. "Up scope." He rapidly walked the periscope through its complete arc and ordered it down. "Sound battle stations!"

As we jumped to our posts, Fyfe quickly briefed the attack team in the conn. About 12,000 yards away, a coastal freighter and a small heavily laden tanker were hugging the shore near the mouth of the Kii Suido on the Honshu side, heading in a southeasterly direction. The gray cargo ship was a large, fast MFM merchant freighter with a crow's nest on the foremast and four or five lookouts on the seaward side. The tanker resembled a slightly larger version of the United States yard oiler, painted a dirty dark red.

"Up scope!"

The quartermaster at the periscope-elevating control tensed for the order to squeeze the pickle and bring it back down. The weather had shifted to summer haze and low visibility, yet even a short exposure was risky in a calm sea only a few miles from the enemy shoreline.

"Right standard rudder," Fyfe ordered as if maneuvering through a familiar bay. *Batfish*'s bow neatly swung toward the oncoming tanker and cargo ship. "Maintain speed and course," Fyfe told the helmsman. "Range—mark!"

"Two one double oh!"

"Bearing—mark!"

"Dead ahead, Captain!"

"Set!" came the report from the TDC operator.

With a quick setup, Fyfe didn't pause. He was aiming to crack them both near their overlap with a three-fish spread. "Shoot!"

Moments later, the fire-control officer reported, "Three away."

One torpedo hit the AK and broke her in half. She sank stern first with a fifty-degree down angle in less than a minute. The oiler poured on the coal and turned toward the beach. Our other two torpedoes had passed her astern.

18 June 1944

1:31 P.M. Two end-of-run explosions at the foot of a well-terraced garden which ran right down to the water's edge. I hope we ruined their potato crop. Perhaps I was guilty of an error in judgment in only firing three torpedoes at these two targets, but at the time I didn't think so. Anyway, this attack which sunk a ship in plain sight of the city of Andakino must have had some effect on the morale of the Jap home front.

3:35 P.M. Four depth charges far away. . . .

4:56 P.M. A string of eight depth charges. I guess he thinks he's got us. All clear in the periscope.

Four days later, 22 June, we were at it again. At noon, our periscope sighted a lone, large *maru* steaming down the coast from Yokohama. When the OOD reported the sighting, Fyfe took over the periscope. The approaching 3,100 ton-AK was newly built, with two heavy cranes or derricks just forward of the bridge behind her high bow, and two masts with heavy cargo booms, one forward and one aft.

"Battle stations, torpedo!" echoed through *Batfish*'s intercom system as the general alarm was sounded. We rushed with a will to our battle station assignments. By now, Fyfe's command was little more than a formality. It was less of a strain to work hard than to sweat out indecision and avoidance. Whereas before we had stayed far out to sea and seen nothing, Fyfe patrolled close to the enemy's shore—and found ships. We were now decisively in action.

"Forward torpedo room ready . . . After torpedo room ready . . . Maneuvering room ready . . ." The stream of reports from every station in *Batfish* attested the efficient, unhurried teamwork of a battle-ready crew.

Once again the attack periscope was working continuously as Fyfe tracked and studied the approaching *maru*. In twenty minutes we were ready for the kill. "Fire four . . . Fire five . . . Fire six!"

The attack officer nearly clicked his stopwatch at the first torpedo's calculated moment of impact, but ended up shaking the watch. The unconcerned target lumbered on, as we watched the torpedo wakes pass astern of her.

We immediately came around into a new attack position, our periscope nearly slicing a sampan in half. Sweating, cussing under his breath, Fyfe coached *Batfish* back in for a fresh attack on the AK, now only half a mile from crossing into Andakino Harbor. Suddenly she zigged away and sent off two puffs of steam. For an instant, Fyfe feared the target had sighted us and was whistle-signaling for help. With a quick sweep of the periscope, he saw a heavily laden sister ship on an opposite course answer with two blasts.

Fyfe could feel the others in the conn fidgeting over our prolonged periscope exposure. He studied the problem a moment longer, muttering under his breath.

"Down scope. I guess they're just being friendly," he announced.

"We're taking on her big sister. Estimated range four thousand yards. Make ready stern tubes."

As we began our new approach, the attack team quickly changed gears to take on the second *maru*.

"Up scope." Carefully, Fyfe calculated the *maru*'s speed, keeping the periscope's cross hairs trained precisely on her foremast for final calculations. "Speed six knots," he announced. The scope was sent back down; the wheels on the TDC began to spin the solution to the firing problem.

"Come right to zero eight five," Fyfe ordered quietly. *Batfish* had worked in close to the Andakino Harbor entrance, and our only escape path lay toward the open sea behind us. If we fired our bow tubes at the AK, we would waste precious time reversing course.

Batfish swung in answer to the rudder, her stern coming to aim at a point ahead of the target, her bow set in readiness toward the sanctuary of the deep and open sea.

"Ready after torpedoes." After torpedoes are called "stingers," perhaps with the scorpion or hornet in mind. According to the book, they are usually fired to equalize expenditures from the forward tubes so you always have some fish ready in each end. But in this attack, Fyfe had good reason to prefer "stingers."

"Steady on zero eight five," the helmsman reported.

"Up scope." Fyfe focused the scope's cross hairs on the unsuspecting prey. The assistant kept his eyes fixed on the periscope's range and bearing indicators, waiting to call their readings when Fyfe gave the word.

"Range—mark!"

"One seven oh oh!"

"Bearing—mark!"

"One three five!"

Without a pause, the TDC operator snapped back, "Set!" Fyfe took an instant more for a final inspection of the *maru*, then backed away from the scope. "Fire seven! Fire eight! Fire nine! Fire ten!"

"All torpedoes away, sir."

Moments later the talker shouted, "Sound reports heavy explosion." So did our ears. Another explosion followed his words—four torpedoes, two hits. The talker had a not-too-well-concealed grin on his face.

Alone, Fyfe viewed the target through the scope. Hit forward and aft, she sank stern first with a large starboard list. He silently gestured for the scope's descent.

The talker repeated the report from the sound room: "High-speed propeller noises bearing two eight oh."

"Tell him to keep the bearing coming," Fyfe calmly directed.

There was a moment's silence. "High-speed propeller noises still bearing two eight oh and coming this way!"

"Ease her on down to two hundred eighty feet and rig for depth charge." *Batfish* began her dive for deeper water accompanied by the sound of mild explosions from the sinking *maru*. Calls from the man at the depth gauge, reading our progressive descent, filtered out from the control room into the adjacent compartments: "One ninety . . . Two hundred . . . Two hundred ten . . . Two twenty . . ." Suddenly *Batfish* shivered, groaned; an unfamiliar grating noise drowned out all familiar sounds, and everyone was flung against bulkheads.

"All stop!" called out the diving officer. But indeed, we had already stopped, brickwalled at several knots. At 240 feet *Batfish* had grounded on a volcanic peak where the charts had shown 400 feet of water. "Back one-third! Bring her up to two hundred!"

Batfish responded quickly, easing herself backward and up, away from the ocean floor.

The reports of damage were being relayed to the conn when the first depth charges came. Wham! Wham! Wham! Wham! The violent explosions reverberated through the boat's steel hull. In momentary confusion, men scrambled from the deck to their unsteady feet, and back to their equipment. These charges sounded different, heavier; perhaps the Japanese were making them bigger—or setting them deeper. Not long ago, an American congressman had thoughtlessly announced to the world press that our subs were so successful because the Japanese set their light depth charges too shallow!

For hours *Batfish* silently crept along at two hundred feet while the enemy destroyer battered at her with depth charges. She twisted and turned, but try as we might, we couldn't shake him off. It was long after sundown and more than fifty depth charges later before we got clear of him and were able to get back up to periscope depth. Knowing that a plane might be waiting to pounce on us, we checked all directions most circumspectly.

Eight hours after our attack, we finally surfaced to find *Batfish* had suffered no serious damage. The sounds and shocks of depth charging had conjured many private visions of the total destruction of *Batfish*'s hull. We did have damage from grounding, though. The starboard sound head had jammed, and the shaft was bent. We also suspected a bent propeller, because we picked up a new propeller click that became very noticeable at any speed over five knots.

For several days the Pacific above us was literally buzzing with Japanese. At one point we maneuvered to stalk a set of heavy screws that pounded directly overhead, but a combination of skillful radar-equipped search planes and pinging escorts, plus a very flat *Batfish* battery, was successful in thwarting our pursuit of this convoy. Whether we were on or under the surface, even beyond the range of visibility, they still knew our location. It seemed it was just not in the cards for us to get this one. After five days of playing underwater ballet orchestrated by the Emperor's elite, we were getting punchy enough to think that *Batfish* was going to get puckered like a prune from being underwater so long.

During the night, the fierce current had driven us twenty miles to the north. At 3:10 A.M., 25 June, we made a beautiful approach on Inamba Shima, which reestablished our position. This 246-feet-high rock gives an excellent radar pip at 22,000 yards. At first we thought we had a battleship—not improbable—but no such luck. Admiral Ozawa's fleet, retreating homeward from the Marianas, was in these waters, but still quite a way to our west.

After getting what we needed most—a good airing out and re-charging our batteries—Sound picked up a familiar tempo: irregular depth charging approaching us from beyond the horizon. Since this was far from the scene of our last crime against the Empire, all this activity seemed to be their ritual drumbeat preceding a convoy. It looked like something was coming through.

Soon, three destroyers, two of the *Asashio* class and one of the *Kamikaze* class, together with two large AKs and two or three LSTs (landing ship, tanks) appeared. The two *Asashio*'s, first sighted at 9,500 yards, were well ahead; the other *Kamikaze* destroyer was patrolling station, seaward of the convoy. The AKs were in column with the LSTs and zigzagging about a thousand yards abeam to starboard.

Since we were in front of them, we bided our time until their zig-zagging course threw them right across our bow. We opened the outer doors on our forward tubes as they came right on into a beautiful setup.

108

28 June 1944

10 A.M. Up periscope . . . Down bomb!

There was no mistaking that sound: aerial bomb! The explosion shook *Batfish* from stem to stern. It was light, but it landed so close to the periscope that the two feet or so of it inside the boat whipped around like a willow wand. Glass flew from gauges, cork exploded from the bulkheads like popcorn, light bulbs shattered. Men were flung upon decks and against bulkheads. Fans and lights went out in sudden mis-alignment. The bridge gyro repeater was smashed, and the violent bedplate shake-up set the master gyro searching wildly for true north. Suddenly we were in thick pitch-blackness.

Batfish nosed down. Somewhere below seventy-five feet the dim red emergency lights came on. "Level off at one hundred feet. All compartments report."

From the control room, the diving officer called, "We're nearing one hundred feet, Captain. Dive is under control." Moments later, the Chief of the Boat shouted up the hatch, "All compartments report no damage, Captain."

Sound bearings indicated that the AK's heavy screws had changed course to the right and speeded up. Two sets of light screws could be heard coming in on the starboard beam.

Shaking his head, the assistant attack officer said to Fyfe, "They know we're here, Captain."

Fyfe looked at him open-eyed, unable to suppress a grin. The assistant attack officer sheepishly intensified his interest in the lighted panel closest to him. When he stole a look a few moments later, all sweating faces in the conn were grinning. Fyfe turned to the quarter-master. "How did we hold our course?"

"Pretty good, Captain. We're heading on two nine five now on a steady bubble."

"Sound reports screw sound diminishing, Captain. They seem to be leaving us."

"They'll be back," Fyfe said. He winked at the red-faced assistant. "They know we're here!"

In a moment, he said, "Come to two eight five. Bring her up to sixty feet." Periscope depth! The moment of hesitation bespoke the diving officer's disbelief. Then, "Sixty feet, aye."

109

As the needle on the depth gauge slid upward, the men in *Batfish's* conning tower waited silently.

"Sixty feet."

"Up scope!" A quick sweep revealed that the convoy had zigged away and was heading to go around to the other side of Miyake Shima. One *Asashio* class destroyer was on the starboard quarter at 3,500 yards, echo-ranging. The *Kamikaze* class was dead ahead at 6,000 yards, apparently just listening. One float-type plane circled at five hundred feet, about two miles on our starboard bow.

We quickly got a setup on the *Asashio* and made ready the stern tubes. The gyro follow-up system, dizzied by our bombing, was now reoriented and proceeding to put our course circuit into the TDC. Another quick sweep of the scope now revealed two planes circling at about five hundred feet, both on the starboard beam.

As we prepared to fire the stern tubes, our gyro follow-up system suddenly went out again, and the course dial on the TDC started spinning like a top. At the same time the destroyer put on a burst of speed, closing us from about a mile. At 2,500 yards, a snap setup on such a narrow target was very remote. Fyfe decided not to fire a down-the-throat shot.

When the destroyer veered away from his feint, we quickly started an approach on the second listening destroyer, which now, for some reason, lay dead in the water ahead of us. Something on our bridge had been knocked loose; any speed over three and a half knots made us sound like a freight train. Running three knots at ninety feet, bucking a strong current, we closed the range to 4,000 yards; the target destroyer was slowly circling a heavily smoking LST, now heading at right angles to the convoy's course. Above, two scout planes and a heavy bomber were using up a lot of gas searching the water for us. If it was a decoy, the Japanese didn't give us credit for much sense if they expected us to fire torpedoes at an LST. The destroyer, on the other hand, was fair game, so we continued jockeying into position for a good shot at him.

Two of the planes spotted our periscope and dove at us. *Batfish* went deep to avoid them. We checked our descent at 110 feet and rose right back up to periscope depth.

Our target DD was still circling the blatant LST, now heading for her far side. She stopped to listen, then steamed out to investigate an area even farther away from us. The other destroyer sniffing at our trail suddenly took off on a wild-goose chase, storming off away from us. Fyfe could see only one of the planes now.

"We'll wait right here. Before long our target will start circling back our way. He should pass within a thousand yards between us and the LST."

The planes reappeared, one now circling around the LST, another looking hard for us off our port beam—a safe distance away.

Then the DD beyond the LST moved as expected—but not as close as we hoped. We swung around for a stern tube shot.

"Range . . . mark!"

The assistant read the range dial: "Three two double oh!"

The TDC operator was twisting dials, inserting the new bearing and range information.

"Make her angle on the bow thirty port. Down scope."

The TDC operator straightened and turned to Fyfe. "Distance to the track is three thousand yards, Captain."

"What's our normal approach course?" Fyfe asked.

The operator glanced back at the computer . . .

"High-speed propellers coming on fast!" the soundman's voice blared out over the intercom. "Bearing one six oh!"

"Take her deep!"

"Still bearing one six oh! Coming like hell!"

"Left full rudder!" Fyfe shouted. "Flank speed!"

"Sound reports—"

Fyfe waved for silence. Our ears received their own report loud and clear. We were quite familiar with the various sounds and sensations made by the firing and recoil of our own torpedoes. To hear someone else's coming at you is an entirely different sensation.

They came on fast—faster than we would have thought from all the times we had heard them streak away from us—at at least fifty knots, with a faster screw than any patrol boat we had ever heard. For one suspended instant, the whirr of approaching death became a shriek. A collective exhale could be heard as the two torpedoes thundered past the stern of *Batfish*, very close. Then the familiar sound of torpedoes running away from us—music to our ears. Humidity was very high in all compartments.

Some minutes later Sound reported two distant end-of-run explosions, pleasantly faint.

11:50 A.M. Whether these torpedoes were fired from the DD, the LST or were dropped by a plane (I hadn't seen the bomber for twenty minutes), I don't rightly know. From our relative positions they could have come from either. However, I was watching the destroyer and since I didn't see any launched from her, and since I hadn't seen the big plane for some time, I surmise they came from the LST. We had been running at fairly high speed, 4 to 6 knots, in order to close against the current and at this speed, the broken plating or stancheon topside is prohibitively noisy. I don't believe my periscope was sighted because of the very small amount of it exposed and because the exposures were so brief. If it was the LST, however, this is a new wrinkle to A/S warfare to the best of my knowledge. She was a large, standard design, landing craft, had one gun forward and two aft and two mounts that could have been depth charge throwers aft. Her forward deck space seemed loaded with crates, so I can definitely say she was being used as a cargo carrier. I did not see any torpedo tubes. This is a tough one to lose, and I sincerely hope someone else gets a shot into them before they reach their destination.

Fyfe kept *Batfish* at flank speed for ten minutes. Then, when we had moved about a mile and a half from the scene of the attack, he dropped her to creeping speed. As the ocean began to quiet down, the soundman strained his ears. Soon he reported, "Propeller noises, medium distance." A minute later: "Propeller noises decreasing." All hands took a deep breath.

We lost our target, but at the moment that didn't seem too bad—he had lost us, too.

At dawn the following day, *Batfish* was a little north of our encounter. With about five hours' sleep, Fyfe climbed up through the control room hatch to where the exec had charge of the conn.

"We've just got a radar contact, Captain. Two targets at about ten thousand yards. Can't periscope-sight them yet."

Fyfe ordered the scope up and searched the purple-and-red-streaked horizon, focusing on the reported bearing. Two UN-1 class destroyers suddenly emerged from the diminishing darkness.

"Change course to zero six eight. Sound the alarm. Flank speed."

Batfish broke through the calm sea surface, simultaneously switching over to all four diesels. We chased the destroyers at full speed in the hopes they would zig our way, but within an hour they disappeared completely over the now bright horizon. We patrolled submerged the rest of the day, with no further sign of them.

At 11 P.M. we picked up a contact on our SJ radar at 12,000 yards and began tracking it with an end-around approach. From the bridge, Fyfe scanned the horizon. It was a clear night with a very bright full moon.

"Think I see a ship, sir," a lookout called down to Fyfe. "Off our port quarter."

Fyfe swung his binoculars toward the sighting. A dark gray blob came into focus accompanied by a speck. From the far side of the target, just emerging from her obscuring mass, he saw a second escort ship. Soon, because of the target's low, relatively long silhouette, Fyfe labeled her as a tanker.

"Escort crossing over, sir!"

Abandoning the tanker to check the lookout's report, Fyfe saw the enemy escort's slim silhouette slide into view toward us. The tanker showed no evidence of changing course—the first move of any ship sighting a submarine. Then the enemy warship steadied down on the same heading as the others, apparently only changing station.

"Lookouts below," Fyfe ordered. The four lookouts scrambled from the periscope shears and disappeared down the hatch. Alone, Fyfe trained the TBT vane on the target, then pressed the button to send her bearing below. He hit the diving alarm and climbed through the hatch, touching the deck as the quartermaster slammed the hatch and dogged it.

"Level off at forty-three feet. Make ready bow tubes."

As *Batfish* settled down at radar depth, the PPI scope became the center of attention. With the range at 3,350 yards, Fyfe gave the orders sending three bow torpedoes speeding toward the target.

"Up periscope." Fyfe motioned for the big one which offered better night vision. The torpedoes were traveling the moon slick; there was little chance the target could see their wakes in time to avoid. But in the few seconds before the first torpedo was timed to hit, the target started signaling to her port escort with a bright red blinker. Fyfe watched our perfect setup dissolve as all three torpedoes missed.

"Down scope! Come right to two two five," Fyfe ordered, changing our course for a new attack. But the soundman reported high-speed screws rumbling vengefully in his earphones. We stopped in midstream.

"Take her deep and rig for depth charge!" At seventy feet, the first three fell.

It wasn't so bad; we had taken much worse several times recently. Loose gear was scattered about, *Batfish* pitched and rolled under the impacts, but the escort had made a significant error in depth-setting his charges. They all exploded well overhead, and they seemed lighter than usual. Maybe he didn't read American newspapers. With plenty of water under us, Fyfe took *Batfish* to 350 feet, rigged for silent running, and prepared to ride out the counterattack.

One hour, ten miles, and one depth-charging later, Fyfe brought *Batfish* to the surface for a quick survey. Damage to *Batfish*: not too serious. Damage to the enemy: zero.

At a good range, our three torpedoes had failed to score a single hit on what we originally believed to be a tanker. The TDC had generated ranges and bearings that had required no correction over a period of nearly six minutes just prior to and after firing; therefore, hindsight indicated that our torpedoes had sped under the target. Sound had tracked all three directly to, under, and beyond the shallow-drafted target to their ends-of-run. Had we fired at an LST?

As the sun rose, Fyfe took us down for a day of rest. He had considered chasing the convoy further, but by the time we could overtake them they would be in Yokohama: another bitter pill.

Next day, 1 July, we gave the area off Andakino another search, but intensive periscope and sound reconnaissance turned up nothing. We surfaced at sundown, read the stars, and started thinking about going home. About half an hour before sunup, we departed our Rainbow Area with only half a pot of gold, heading for refit at Midway—or so we thought!

At about 10:30 A.M. a lookout sighted the masts of two ships on the western horizon. Within seconds, Fyfe was on the bridge, training the TBT binoculars on the contact. A large wooden Japanese trawler and her yacht-type escort were emerging from a patch of fog over the choppy waters. At first glance the trawler seemed too small to waste torpedoes on; but if she was worth an escort, she was worth sinking. *Batfish* dove to periscope depth.

"Sound battle stations—surface! Come left to two seven oh. All ahead full."

We reversed our course and set a track that would bring us up off the trawler's starboard beam. All compartments became very busy. Our marksmen had been upstaged by torpedoes ever since our

114

commissioning, but they had missed no opportunity for practicing, during training and on patrol, at any available target: flotsam, even our own garbage sacks. All trigger fingers were especially itchy after the recent series of frustrating confinements from an enemy we couldn't shoot back at. For most of the crew this was not to be a vicarious experience, as firing torpedoes sometimes is. This was a real live show coming up; surface gun battle requires hands to be on deck, vulnerably exposed.

Doing their best to mask any signs of stage fright, the gun crews neatly focused their nervous energy on preparing for the coming attack. Ammunition supply parties were set up; ammunition was laid out in readiness. The four-inch gun crew captain, pointer, and trainer went to the conning tower for the gunnery officer's detailed instructions. The captain would command the attack from the bridge, while the exec would observe the action through the big search scope, directing the party in the conn as a backup for the captain, just in case.

It took us the better part of an hour to close for our best position, broadside as close as we dared, before streaming up on deck and getting our guns set up, loaded, trained, and firing. We would have to bring all guns to bear on the primary target before she could run or fight.

Periscope confirmed the trawler was worth sinking. She was about 500 tons with a high bow, very high foremast, bridge amidships, diesel stack, raised living quarters aft, a high mainmast—and no visible armament. Only crates and drums were stowed on deck.

Though armed with only three depth charges aft and three machine guns, the converted yacht serving as her escort was to be avoided if possible. She presented a poor return for our risk, and since she was so outgunned, in all probability she would turn tail and run the moment we broached. Preparatory bustle had subsided into alert silence. Fyfe instructed the diving officer. "When I give the word, blow her with everything we've got and surface with bow planes. We've got to pop up and get out as fast as we can." Ready, we waited at the hatches in crowded groups like paratroopers waiting for the word to jump.

Ah-ooga ah-ooga ah-ooga ah-ooga! The Klaxon blared throughout the boat. "Battle surface! Battle surface!"

At 11:25 we crash-surfaced 1,500 yards starboard of the target. "All stop!" Fyfe roared. "Crack the hatch!" Air hissed out from three hatches, bridge, aft, and forward. "Open hatches! Gun crew on deck! Open gun access trunk!"

Men scurried onto the deck fore and aft, tripping and falling on the slippery deck but missing no time getting at their stations. The instant the captain's party cleared the conn, the exec secured both conning tower hatches.

Two 40-mm guns were cast loose in seconds while other hands quickly got the .50-caliber machine guns and the 20-mm guns into their mounting sockets. The four-inch gun crew bore-sighted and loaded their gun. Then the gunnery officer signaled his readiness to the captain.

Fyfe trained the TBT on the target. We had been seen the second we burst from the concealing sea, but had given the enemy very little time to do anything about it.

"Commence firing!"

Guided by our radar ranges and the radar spotting on the splashes, the four-incher fired one overshot. Then one short, then another short but closer in. The fourth round hit so close that the spray from the splash momentarily obscured the trawler. Round five scored a bull's-eye forward, immediately setting her afire.

On her far side, her escort at first seemed homeward bound as predicted. In fact, she was edging around our bow to close us from our unengaged side. All guns were spattering away at the burning trawler, which seemed determined not to sink no matter how many times we holed her. Of eighteen rounds the four-inch fired, at least ten were *definite* hits. We could see daylight through the holes we'd put in her, but none of them seemed to connect with her fuel tanks or explosives.

She was already dead in the water when the escort, approaching us at top speed from about 2,000 yards, began firing at our starboard side. Our 20's and 50's turned and savagely strafed her. At 1,500 yards we trained our four-inch gun on her and began firing. We began to see daylight through her, too, but the escort kept bearing down on us as fast as she could run. It didn't take much imagination to realize this insignificant gnat of a boat was going to ram us if she could!

Submerged, we were the world's most lethal war machine. For this power, we had sacrificed the ability to sustain damage; one crack and our pressure hull would rupture. With half our crew strung out across the deck, we wouldn't have time to crash-dive to safety. That meant this little escort *could* sink us.

We started firing low. By the time she closed to 800 yards with her engines still at full throttle, she looked like a sieve. We tried to hit her engines, but her bow was tilted so high they must have been well below her waterline.

Light machine gun fire was popping and zinging about *Batfish*'s superstructure. It was a wonder the determined escort could see to aim from her high bow, pounding wildly up and down between the ocean swells. She did a beautiful job of keeping her bow pointed dead at us, and it took us considerable maneuvering to get decent target angles. At 500 yards two of our 20-mm gun barrels froze up. The adversary kept coming on at us. Some nerves aboard were unraveling; this was all happening too fast.

"All back," Fyfe roared, "emergency!" *Batfish* shuddered as dead water gave way to speed in reverse.

At 200 yards, full of holes as she was, we could see no men aboard her. It was as if the boat itself was attacking us. She looked to us as big as we must have at first appeared to her. We prepared for the worst as her bow approached to a scant 100 yards.

Suddenly, her engines simply stopped. The "divine wind" had claimed her in an instant. With our engines churning full speed astern, our speed increased. Even so, the silent enemy boat's momentum glided her across our bow, bumping it gently as we cleared her.

As she drifted past, now sinking rapidly, a small fire broke out aboard her, then another. Suddenly she was engulfed in flames, and hissing, quickly sank below the surface.

No sight of life, no sign of death; it was as if no one had been aboard her. One could only wonder who her brave skipper had been.

During that two-hour running gun battle, we had one casualty: the four-inch-gun loader caught a bullet in the knee. The pharmacist's mate took it out and mounted it on a plaque. The victim seemed quite happy with his wound, which netted him a couple of shots of brandy, a Purple Heart, and stateside recuperation.

En route to Midway on a sea calm as a millpond, we reported our success in the evening's Fox radio schedule. Admiral Lockwood's response was, "This was an excellent patrol, displaying good area coverage at the proper places, splendid torpedo and gun attacks, and outstanding aggression."

It was an exultant crew aboard *Batfish* that came alongside *Proteus* at Midway to refit. The gooneybirds were still there, but the island itself had undergone considerable change since we had last seen it. There were at least twice as many men on the island as before, twice as many planes, and ten times as much work being done. Instead of two submarines, there were five others at the atoll in various stages of refit between patrols.

117

Again Midway did its best for us, receiving us with a band when we tied up, dumping sacks of mail on the decks, plus ice cream and crates of fruit. What American boy doesn't just love ice cream and fruit, whether or not he gets mail? We were cloistered at the Gooneybird Hotel for two weeks of R & R.

One thing was sure—we had a fighting skipper. He might scare the living hell out of us, but he was straight with us, sank ships, and brought us back alive. And he knew all of us by our first names as well as by our jobs.

And we knew his; it was Captain *Jake.* But calling the captain by his first name was known to cause whirlpools and waterspouts. As crew, we kept it to ourselves.

FOURTH WAR PATROL

24 July 1944

It took just about two weeks to get over the strain our third war patrol had put on everyone. It would be unpatriotic to mention the strain of R & R. The singular joy of boredom is its termination. Regrettably, our stay was basically no different from our previous one, and we were glad to get back to *Batfish*, leaving "Gooneyville" to the gooneybirds and flyboys.

After two weeks away, the sight of *Batfish* after refit, immaculate and perfect once more, was a little jarring. When we left her at the pier, she'd been in the water over a year. Some 50,000 miles, over a hundred depth charges, a torpedo, Japanese bullets, shellfire, and a bomb or two had taken their toll on her appearance. She wasn't the sort of submarine you would whistle at, but if you knew her as intimately as we did, you knew she would stick by you when things got rough.

She'd had the "woiks." Repaired, refitted, and cleaned from stem to stern, she sparkled in a fresh coat of camouflage paint: dazzling dark gray superstructure with snappy black decks. At night she'd be a knockout, nearly impossible to see beyond 1,000 yards without the moon behind her. She even had a shave; after several months in the Pacific waters, submarines grow barnacle and algae beards not conducive for making more than sixteen knots. And she had her ears fixed. Midway had no spares to replace the sound head we'd damaged in bottoming, but the repair checked out just as good as new.

Loaded into *Batfish*'s after torpedo room, were the latest in torpedoes—eight electric Mark XVIIIs. Wakeless, these were the ideal weapons for daylight periscope attack. Although ten to fifteen knots slower than the twelve Mark XIV-3s and four Mark XXIIIs we carried, they were almost impossible for enemy lookouts to spot in time.

The modifications made during her sixteen-day refit by subtender *Proteus* also included more plotting equipment, more bunks, and more food stowage, all of which at first appeared highly conspicuous to us, who knew her so well. But once we were back aboard and on our way once more, she felt just like our good old boat again.

Twenty-four men were left behind to break in new submarines and to provide continuity for the rotation program. Twenty-six new hands, graduate and green, took their places. We trained vigorously for several days and fired four practice shots with our new Mark XVIIIs. Then on 1 August *Batfish* turned her bulbous prow southeast toward our fourth war patrol area—the Japanese-held Caroline Islands off Palau, nearly 3,500 miles distant.

Barely two hours out of Midway, we sighted a periscope half a mile away and evaded at flank speed. We radioed a contact report to our two just-departed Marine air escorts and cleared the area without sighting it again.

On 4 August our lookouts spotted a barnacle-encrusted floating mine which we sank with 20-caliber machine gun fire. However good our marksmanship, we welcomed all the practice we could get. Although this mine didn't explode, every one of us had his occasional personal nightmare of collision with one of these. Now there was one less to sweat about.

While submerged the next day at 3 P.M., we sighted through the high periscope another unidentified submarine running surfaced on an easterly course. We surfaced to close. Then, when the range was about 15,000 yards, we dove again to investigate unobserved. When we could not periscope-observe her at fifty feet, we planed up to twenty-five feet, only to discover that she, too, had dived. We played hide-and-seek with her for an hour and a half, then surfaced and zigzagged radically around in the vicinity at flank speed.

5 August 1944

6:30 P.M. Unable to regain contact, and since it's a big ocean out here and this is like looking for a needle in a haystack, gave up the search and continued on toward our area. A surfaced submarine, or for that matter a submerged submarine, is not very adaptable for hunting down another submarine which is submerged and which was 7½ miles away when last seen.

We spent the next five days conducting daily training dives, ship and fire-control drills as we threaded our way through the Marianas and the northern fringe islands of the Carolines. We were pretty much left alone, but after we turned right at Yap Island to approach our area on 10 August, the skies began to buzz. Our first aircraft contact tried to bomb us, but missed by a comfortable margin. Over the next two days we sighted and avoided four more planes, suspected to be "friendlies."

Late afternoon the next day we periscope-sighted another submarine about 14,000 yards on our port beam. Submerged, we tried to get in position ahead on her track, but she soon changed course and dove.

11 August 1944

4:24 P.M. This is the second time this situation has come up, and each time I've closed too much while trying to get ahead of her and on her track in order to dive, identify her undetected, and fire either torpedoes or smoke bombs. Next time we will stay out of sight and use a Ouija board.

Entering our patrol area about ten miles east of Ngaruangl Passage, we could see the Palau Islands in the far distance. When a plane came out to "greet" us, we dove and made submerged patrol for the rest of the afternoon.

Within our patrol area at dusk, 13 August, we tracked a beautiful pip at 8,400 yards. Visions of getting a ship our first day in the area faded into disappointment as the pip—and rain squall—faded into nothing.

At 10 P.M. our lookouts watched a single Liberator drop four bombs on the northern airstrip at Babelthuap, the small northernmost island of the Palau group. About an hour later a second "friendly" bomber dropped his load in the same area, but as far as our lookouts could tell, no fires broke out from either bombing. The searchlight display from the southern end of the island was very ragged, as if the operator was confused. No flak was sighted. A third Liberator dropped eight bombs on the southern airfield of the island the next day. Again no fires were observed, nor any effective countermeasures.

We patrolled the Palau-Empire and Palau-Formosa shipping routes for nine days, sighting nothing but rain squalls in the cloudy, overcast skies. Our entire area was uncommonly quiet; even in the harbors we blatantly probed: no planes, no patrols, no ships. With the tides of war now turning against the Japanese, we suspected that no ships were due in the immediate future. Perhaps they had abandoned Palau to the Liberators and the submarines.

From U.S.S. *Hardhead* we received a dispatch concerning a damaged battleship—her own TGB—but we found nothing at the reported point of attack except lots of ocean and sky, and a few boatswain birds. A second report from *Hardhead* indicated that her attacks on the BB in question might have sunk her.

121

On 20 August a bomber popped down out of the clouds on us at close range. We dove with our fingers in our ears, but went unbombed, apparently unseen. We hung around on the chance that he was scouting ahead of a ship coming our way, but no such luck.

Patrolling southwest of Peleliu, the southernmost Palau Island, during the early hours of 22 August, we got some curious SJ returns from a range of 2,500 yards. It took us two and a half hours to close our targets closely enough to identify them in the dim false dawn. Ornithologically speaking, we were observing Laysan albatrosses, of "Ancient Mariner" fame. Aloft, they were the most graceful birds above the earth. Upon it, they were ungainly gooneybirds, fresh like us from R & R on Midway. Unlike us, they'd had fun.

Other than that, we saw nothing, heard nothing, shot at nothing. This place certainly seemed to have lost its interest in the war.

That evening, radio monitored a zoomie reporting a destroyer aground on Velasco Reef, a small doughnut-shaped atoll a few miles north of the main Palau Island group. We headed north to investigate.

Rounding the reef's northern edge, we dove at dawn and proceeded down along its east coast. We finally sighted smoke at 9 A.M., but it was noon before we could make out the first ship of the Velasco Reef Task Force, a designation we coined for the occasion. Thick black smoke rose from several points across the reef from us.

Velasco was a busy place today. Not one, but two ships were aground. The nearest, beached on the northeastern side of the reef, was an MFM-type AK of about 3,000 tons. Just eastward of her, inside the ten-fathom curve, a minelayer was anchored; a small auxiliary boat was making frequent runs between them, apparently unloading stores or engaged in some sort of salvage work.

On the beach across the atoll on the westernmost edge was a *Fubuki* class destroyer, also grounded, judging from her list. We could not see water or waterlines or determine her size because of the intervening land. Two seagoing tugs, two patrol boats, and an armed sampan zealously guarded her. These tugs were making all the smoke.

A second destroyer of the *Minekaze* class was either anchored or stopped about a mile southeast of the island, directly below us; a fighter plane and a bomber were patrolling the general area. Between the *Minekaze* and the AK lay a two-engine float plane, anchored to a buoy.

Submerged, we closed the AK cautiously: the reef had already claimed two ships, and our charts of the area were sketchy at best. With coral heads, shallows, shoals, and shifting sandbars all around us, it would be fatal if we ourselves ran aground—any member of the Velasco Reef Task Force would be glad to do unto us what we now maneuvered to do unto them.

"Call the crew to battle stations, torpedo." The musical chimes of the general alarm rang forth, and *Batfish* prepared for action.

Although calm with no wind, the weather had been generally overcast and hazy. It now worsened, growing blotchy with rain squalls, intermittently concealing the stranded AK. We had encountered many of these sudden squalls during our ten days in the area. Depending on our situation, they could be merciful or treacherous. Going as swiftly as they came, they could leave us suddenly exposed.

Before we could get even an approximate shooting setup, visibility closed down to zero. Sound was little help, picking up only an uninformative bouillabaisse of noises, including the faunal emissions of the reef itself. We were liable to detect an obstacle only by hitting it. Sonar was in a similar pickle; if we sent out a ping, we could be detected if the dormant destroyer was listening in. We were confident that we'd gone unnoticed and wanted to stay that way at least until we got in the first licks.

With rain squalls surrounding us, it was a guessing game at best. Despite the best of modern science aboard, we were deaf, dumb, and blind in the midst of enemy waters, which he knew a hell of a lot better than we did. We couldn't chance groping our way blindly through this shallow obstacle course to where we thought the AK was; before too long we weren't exactly sure where *we* were. As we drifted passively, Fyfe went back for another try at the periscope. Exasperated, he called down the hatch to the diving officer in the control room. "Bring us up another three feet."

"Aye, aye, sir."

The periscope squinted higher out of the water, but it was no use. "Oh, crap, take us back down." Operating blind in the rain-swept seas, we just didn't have enough to go on. Scrambled by the reef noise and rain hitting the water's surface, Sound couldn't guess whether our presence was unknown, known, or suspected by the enemy.

Expressionless, eyes glued to the scope, Fyfe mumbled, "Get the machinist's mate to bring up some goddamned reef grease!" Not used to seeing characteristically calm Fyfe so obviously ruffled, no one snickered, but hoping to ease the tension a bit, someone relayed Fyfe's comment to the machinist's mate. However, the mate was the same who had diligently searched on a former occasion for relative bearing grease; and both he and the joke were getting a little tired. Within minutes, he dutifully produced a jar of Vaseline willingly supplied by the pharmacist's mate.

"Here's the reef grease, Skipper."

Intent again on the scope, Fyfe's lips began to mumble. Trying to pierce the rain squall by sheer willpower, he had forgotten his offhand request. He took one look at the Vaseline, then at the machinist's mate, and rubbed his burning eyes. In a single gesture, he put one hand on the machinist mate's shoulders, and firmly drew him to the periscope. "*You* look," he said. "Then would you be so kind as to tell me how and where to apply this?" This was one of the longest sentences Captain Jake had been known to make aboard *Batfish*.

Not knowing what to make of his predicament, the mate simply did as he was told and pressed his eyes against the unaccustomed eyepiece of the periscope. "I don't think you'll need it sir," he said within a moment. He slowly backed away. "I mean, there's a ship up there, sir—a big one!"

Fyfe shot to the eyepiece and grabbed the handles, nearly pitching the mate into the exec, who was crowding in to get a look. There it was: a gray silhouette looming up out of the rain squall—the *Minekaze* destroyer, and very close.

"Bearing—mark!"

The exec's voice was sharp. "One nine five."

"Range—mark!"

"Two six seven oh."

"Stand by forward."

"Set!" the TDC operator confirmed.

"Angle on the bow is now five degrees starboard. Target is a destroyer. Ready?"

The TDC operator replied, "Affirmative, set."

"We're shooting three. Anybody know anything I haven't got?" Silence. "Stand by."

"Ready one."

"Fire one!" Fyfe ordered. "Fire two! Fire three!"

The snort of high-pressure air and solid kickback heralded the departure of our first torpedo. The other two followed, their wakes trailing out into the rainswept sea. In the prolonged silence, Fyfe half-turned away from the periscope.

A flash pulled him back. An orange halo, filtered by the weather, filled the scope's eye. Through the mile of intervening rain and fog, he saw a towering sheet of flame shoot up from the target. Then with a rumble like an earthquake the destroyer rose up out of the water and blew apart with wild cracking sounds.

"Sound reports violent explosion and breaking-up noises. No report on number two and number three."

Behind the series of primary explosions came the firecrackers: pockets of ammunition, depth charges, and fuel exploding in the destroyer's hull.

"Fast screws approaching at three five oh," Sound reported.

"Take her down two feet. Maybe I can take a peek under the curtain." With two feet of the high periscope out of the water, Fyfe could not penetrate the weather. "Down another foot."

"Bearing three five oh. Closing fast, Captain."

"How big is she?"

"With all this interference, she could have four diesels or an outboard motor."

The pinging had become deafening. Whatever it was was getting close now, too close for comfort.

Still, Fyfe waited. Almost frantically, he swept with the periscope. We were blind; nothing but the heavy, impenetrable curtain of rain in all directions.

"Come on, you guys," he shouted. "Do we need a torpedo or a BB gun?"

"How about a little space between him and us?" pleaded the exec.

"Down scope," Fyfe sighed. "Take her down. Rig for silent running."

We looked up and listened. The *whiz* went right over us, *very* close. Although it was still hard to hear clearly above the reef static, Sound reported that the spitkit had slowed and was shopping around, now acting very confused. Presently some other propellers joined him, as if in conference; then they all went off in all directions.

When we came back up to periscope depth, Fyfe could finally see the target AK between squalls. The patrol boats and the sampan now formed a tight screen between her and us. Fyfe conferred with the attack team. It would be impossible to get a torpedo into the AK under these conditions. We cleared out seaward, then headed south and west around the atoll for a try at the destroyer on the far side. Behind us, we

125

could see three planes and three boats beating the water in the area we had departed. It looked like the Velasco Reef Task Force had been caught with its pants down.

The most direct route would take us through Ngaruangl Passage between Velasco and the nearby island to the south. The exec called Fyfe down to the chart table.

"Captain, this is a mineable strait. Our charts don't indicate a minefield in these waters, but, then, they indicate precious little else about the area." He came to the point. "There's at least one known minelayer out there."

A debate ensued, drawing in the other men in the control room. After five minutes and much emphatic pointing at the charts, it was decided that we'd take that chance. The enemy knew we were here and would be highly defensive against an immediate shot at the A.K. Since we could see only the tops of the ships on the reef's far side, we didn't know how maneuverable the other DD might be but definitely didn't want her to get away. The squalls seemed to have cleared, and we didn't know how much time we had before the next ones closed in. Not wanting to circumnavigate, we went through—boldly and blindly.

As we rounded the reef, heavy rain once more closed down the visibility and we got only a peep at the *Fubuki* destroyer on the beach. Wary of ending up alongside her, we decided to go out and come back later—it looked as though she would be there for a while.

At 7:14 P.M. we surfaced at sea, moving southward through the night toward Peleliu, then passing east through Yoo Passage and up on the other side of Babelthuap. No ships were traveling the normal convoy routes, but as we passed by, Peleliu caught some incoming mail from a Liberator. As before, their antiaircraft and searchlight response seemed weak and even briefer than usual. Two minutes after midnight, another plane unloaded, this time on Babelthuap.

We were just sitting down to enjoy a Hopalong Cassidy movie when our lookouts reported a PC boat at 3,500 yards. It looked like a snap. We got a quick setup and fired three stern torpedoes at her at a 1,200-yard range. Set at three feet, all three torpedoes broached and probably ran erratically. We couldn't see these electrics, but the target apparently did, for she spun on a dime and then stopped.

Now at 1,900 yards, she was echo-ranging like mad and seemed to have no idea where those torpedoes came from. With visibility unlimited, the crew could be seen topside, going cross-eyed looking for our periscope. Then she bounced a couple of pings off of our hide and started coming at us. By this time we had a fresh setup on her. We quickly fired a single torpedo, then dived deep and rigged for depth charge.

On our way down we heard three end-of-run explosions from our first attempt; and three minutes later, heard two depth charges in the near distance. The fate of our fourth fish was unknown; Sound reported too much commotion to track it.

For half an hour we held our breath as the target alternately pinged and listened aft. When she seemed far enough away to chance a look, we came back up to periscope depth, but couldn't turn either scope. At four hundred feet, the pressure had stretched their cables and caused the yokes to cock.

Half an hour later, with our periscopes back in commission, nothing was in sight. This had been in the order of a quick draw, but with fresh targets generally so scarce in the area, it was a hard one to lose. It was a double pity because we'd been led to believe the electric Mark XVIIIs were going to make life easier for us. A postmortem had us reading the fine print in the owner's manual, to wit: "Because of the slower speed of the Mark XVIII electric torpedo, the data obtained by observation and tracking of the target must be very accurate since the TDC was designed specifically for the higher speed of the Mark XIV steam torpedo. Therefore, it will be necessary for firing data to be extrapolated." Further fine print revealed nothing new either. We knew these torpedoes as well as we knew the old ones. We'd just missed!

During the night our APR operator nearly became a casualty. He heard a squadron of B-24s on their way to bomb Korror talking to each other, then passed the word to the bridge and put in a request for shore duty. Hearing them talk about what they were going to do to anything that moved, scared him half to death.

At dawn we dove and headed back across Ngaruangl Passage to check out the southwestern division of the Velasco Reef Task Force, arriving at noon. Our first periscope observation confirmed that both the beached *Fubuki* destroyer and the AK were right where we left them. A single tug was now anchored near the AK; a single PC boat patrolled seaward of the DD, with a plane circling about five hundred feet above. There seemed to be a salvage crew aboard the DD; one stack was smoking slightly as if welding operations were in progress inside her.

We waited for dusk, then closed the DD to 2,970 yards and fired a

Mark XVIII electric at a shallow three-foot setting. It partially broached three times but ran straight and exploded under the target's number two stack. Still, it wasn't quite enough to do the job, so we fired a second torpedo to run at four feet. Despite a calm sea with long ground swells, this one broached once, but also ran straight and hit near the first, breaking the DD in half. The foremast collapsed halfway up; the number two stack bent over like a limp rag, and smoke and debris flew two hundred feet into the air. The stern fell away, sinking into deeper water, but the bow stuck, impaled on the reef—looking strangely desolate all by itself. These remains seemed beyond salvage, so we decided not to waste another torpedo.

The destroyer's guardians did not harass us as we stealthily crept away, patrolling to westward. At midnight we received orders from ComSubPac to take up lifeguard station off Peleliu for the next two days. Six squadrons of Liberators were expected to hit there daylight tomorrow, 27 August.

Although none of us dared speculate too longingly on the war's end, it seemed that local real estate was changing hands before our eyes. The weak Japanese retaliation to the bombings we'd witnessed seemed a good omen. But however much we were rooting for our flyboys, we doubted the wisdom of sailing into our lifeguard area flying Old Glory and shooting flares. Six miles offshore, we decided submergence with intensive periscope watch was the better part of discretion. We dove and stayed below the rest of the day.

Shortly after dark, 27 August, we surfaced, not having seen any sign of the air strike, and patrolled to northward. We really wanted to look at the Velasco Reef Task Force, but orders were orders and we stayed on lifeguard station.

The following morning shortly before noon our planes started their bombing runs on Peleliu—a full day late. Shallowly submerged we could hear them on radio, but when we tried to announce our presence and arrange amnesty, we got no response. We sighted nine planes in formation off our stern and heard others we couldn't see. Fires erupted in the vicinity of both Peleliu airports, but very little antiaircraft fire was returned. We sighted two ships through high periscope, but since they were most likely part of our task force, we maneuvered to avoid them, all the while peeling our eyes for fallen zoomies. There were none, to the best of our knowledge.

The raid was over by noon, so we headed back up to check on our half-*Fubuki* and to see if the AK had been floated yet.

The AK was still in the same spot with a single sampan-type patrol boat alternately pinging and listening south of her. Coming in submerged at two hundred feet for a closer look at the *Fubuki*, we ran right under the patrol boat. He pinged on us several times, undoubtedly got a return echo, but took no action. Our DD remained status quo, really a beautiful mess.

At dusk we surfaced to look the AK over again. We really wanted to get a fish into her, but shortly before 9 P.M. came orders to lifeguard another air strike. We turned south to be in position for it.

Next day at 11:20 A.M. the first heavy waves of Liberators hit in the vicinity of Korror on Babelthuap. They must have hit an oil storage depot this time, for the fires were remarkable. Within six minutes the strike was over. Since none of our flyboys needed rescuing, we surface-patrolled toward the west. Shortly after 8 P.M. a thunderstorm to the south gave us a brilliant lightning display.

29 August 1944

8:10 P.M. Thought at first there was an action taking place, and headed at it doing flank speed until we realized our mistake. Felt chagrined, frustrated, and a little foolish.

Dawn found us six miles east of Velasco Reef once more. During the night we could hear planes upstairs, well overhead. We surfaced and headed south to have a good view of today's show. Visibility was remarkable, with no wind above the glassy sea.

Shortly after we heard the day's first wave hit Korror, we saw a formation of eight planes flying high above intense antiaircraft fire. On our radio we could hear the pilots talking. It seemed to be going all right. They turned west after passing the northern end of Babelthuap.

The second wave hit the same point at 11:08 A.M. Six planes were flying high, antiaircraft fire bursting after them but never quite catching up. The land behind them looked like the dumps of hell had caught fire. It was reassuring that they were on our side.

30 August 1944

8:40 P.M. Received ComSubPac serial changing our operation order, so decided to head back toward Ngaruangl Passage for a last look at our AK tomorrow before we leave, in hopes the Nips have floated her.

Itching to finish her off, we surfaced in a strange, too-calm sea. The visibility was uncanny in an almost surrealistic night atmosphere, suggestive of the calm before a storm. We set our course for the Passage for a final go at the AK.

In the clear morning daylight, and *Batfish* nearly aground, only the AK's dry husk remained. At close range, in the clear light of day, she was not what she had seemed to be under the mantle of the rain squall. We thought she had beached herself to effect repairs; instead she had been stranded by a tidal wave or its equivalent, flinging her over a forbidding sand threshold. Not only was she high and dry, but she looked rotten from the effects of rust. Her protectors had departed, leaving absolutely nothing to protect. She was not even worth a few of our four-inch rounds. We did, however, take a few photographs.

Seaward west of the reef, at a respectful distance, were the faithful minelayer and and two sampan-type patrol boats lurking around Ngaruangl Passage. There was just enough time to eyeball the *Fubuki,* so we submerged to transit the Passage.

Two-thirds through the narrow strait, an arresting sound rose the hackles on every neck. It began as the slightest of taps against our hull, progressing into a full-fledged scrape of metal on metal, chillingly audible in every compartment. One by one, we realized that *Batfish* was rubbing a mine mooring chain at six knots. The mine was above us—whether inches, yards, or feet we couldn't know. For the chain to snag on us would drag the mine down to contact.

"All stop! All stop!" The chain was past our beam. Our screws diminished, ceased. All was still except for the backward scrape along our hull—a sound like sharp chalk along the blackboard of our fate. We coasted an inch a year as the mine's chain neared our port propeller and without a snag, freed us.

This was our third transit of this strait, but our first mine. Apparently we were not yet familiar with the navigation idiosyncrasies of Ngaruangl Passage. With great relief we cleared it at a creeping speed.

The minelayer lay between us and the skewered bow of the *Fubuki,* now flooded with a heavy list. As we neared to take photographs, she blew up in our faces with an overkill explosion of a magnitude that seemed sinisterly engineered to include us. Apparently she had been heavily invested with demolition charges. The minelayer lying to our west must have pushed the button for the explosion.

We went to battle stations with blood in our eyes and approached the minelayer. For the first time, she came to life with an exasperating display of elaborate figure S's at varying speeds we didn't think her capable of. During an hour and a half of tight circles, we did everything but stand on our nose to get a shot at her. Finally she withdrew to the horizon at top speed, leaving an exasperated Fyfe and a frustrated *Batfish* with ready torpedoes in flooded tubes.

Captain Jake did a lot of pacing before he finally hit the sack.

Late 2 September, ComSubPac ordered us home. Wondering whether it would be gooneybirds or quail, we soon learned it was to be something entirely new to us—Australia. Jake Fyfe had been to Fremantle; most of us had not. There was much unsupported comparison between the relative charms of nearby Perth and faraway Pearl. (Midway wasn't mentioned.) Our next ten eventless days en route toward Fremantle made for much needed, welcome rest.

Although we continued to look for trouble, the closest we came was in trying to claim a small empty native outrigger canoe for a souvenir. As we surfaced to take it aboard, we were driven down by two twin-engine planes. When we surfaced for it a second time, our souvenir had mysteriously disappeared.

During the afternoon of 8 September, upon crossing the Equator, we were reassigned to ComSubSoWesPac.

It is a time-honored tradition that whenever a ship crosses the Equator, an appropriate celebration is held to initiate the lowly Pollywogs into the celebrated domain of *Neptunus Rex*. Despite the obstacles involved, the Shellbacks of *Batfish* tried their utmost to impress upon their less-fortunate shipmates the importance of acceptance into the Royal and Ancient Order of the Deep.

Upon our crossing the Equator, Neptunus Rex and his Royal Entourage came aboard to try before the impartial Royal Court those unworthy landlubbers who dared enter his realm and defy his authority. King Neptune's first message was read over the loudspeakers: "Now hear this, all trusty Shellbacks! Those of you who have been duly initiated into my domain at some previous time, lay forward to the wardroom with your credentials. An important meeting will be held, at which time you will be introduced to my emissary, Flangehead Ventvalve, who will acquaint you with the proper method of receiving my Royal Party. All Shellbacks, lay forward prepared to prove your status!"

At the meeting held in the wardroom, only eighteen Shellbacks produced positive proof of their loyalty. It became apparent that the few Shellbacks aboard would have to work ceaselessly if the fifty-six landlubbers were ever to arrive at the proper mental and physical attitude for the coming event.

Following the meeting, King Neptune's second message was read over the loudspeaker.

"Now hear ye! No uncouth and lice-ridden Pollywogs will be allowed in my domain. In order to prevent the spread of vermin and disease, all uninitiated will appear before the Royal Barber and his talented assistant for treatment. A barbershop will be set up in the forward torpedo room. Unspeakable Pollywogs are warned that any hesitation in compliance with these orders will be looked upon with intense disfavor, and offenders will feel the weight of my royal wrath. Signed, Rex."

As prescribed, the Royal Barber took station. Several of the other Shellbacks were in attendance to make certain that the job was impartially done. With great reluctance, the Pollywogs came forward—or were pushed. Shirkers were made to see the folly of their evasive actions, and soon a long line was formed. After a few hours, the Assistant Royal Barber took over, the Royal Barber having gotten "scissors elbow," and trimming went on with increased vigor. At nightfall, when the job was done, enough hair was collected to fill several mattresses.

Several suffered more severely than others. One was Frenchy Fontenot, who might never recover. Chief Farnsworth's sparse locks were similarly mistreated. Goldfarb's golden curls were trimmed to give a mortarboard effect, and Coleman strongly resembled a cigar store Indian with clipper tracks running vertically upward and forward from the nape of his neck. Ensign From realized that if he so much as raised an eyebrow, he would lose that, too, so he parted with his hair passively. Among those to lose just half of a beard or moustache were Robertson, whose red moustache had been so carefully trimmed, Bumpus Weis and his jet-black addition, and Schlief, once in full-bearded splendor.

After all signs of mutiny and discontent had subsided, the committee met again. Final arrangements were made, and a reception committee composed of the captain and the exec was placed in readiness.

"From: Neptunus Rex.

"To: Flangehead Ventvalve.

"All Pollywogs will stand a one-hour watch for Davy Jones and

King Neptune. The uniform will be submarine jackets and rain clothes, parkas up. Binoculars will be held to the eyes continually."

The first section of three men went on watch immediately with binoculars fashioned from two tin cans, tops and bottoms removed. The unfortunate shortage of Shellbacks prevented the enforcement of a taut watch. (Thank God the enemy didn't see us, or he would have had us then and there. It would have been mortifying to die looking like that.)

Davy Jones finally appeared, issuing a general summons to his Court; the captain then passed out subpoenas to the assembled Polly-wogs with a word of admonishment to each.

The guilty persons were brought before the captain, who assigned each a number of lashes to hold these troublemakers' spirits in check until the court could take action.

All night long the boat was patrolled by creatures in overstuffed raincoats, searching for the King. If a plan of the Mighty One could be said to go wrong, this one did, because every time a Pollywog passed a Shellback's bunk, which happened several times an hour, he called in a loud voice, "Was the King here? Have you seen him?" It was a sleepless night for the Shellbacks; not even Fyfe was spared.

Finally, the great day arrived. All Pollywogs gathered in the forward torpedo room and were given a short talk by the exec to get them in the proper frame of mind for the coming ordeal. The Royal Party was admitted; King Neptune himself appeared for the occasion dressed in a spotless gown fashioned of crushed coral, or maybe pop-corn. His right-hand man, Davy Jones, was with him. The most capti-vating member of the party was the ravishing princess, in a gown of pure gold designed to accentuate a figure such as possessed by no mortal woman. The fourth person in the party was the Royal Prose-cutor, who wore as the mark of his rank a mortarboard with tassel. The Royal Attorney for the Defense followed, adorned in cap and gown. The Royal Baby was then carried to the wardroom—and that was no small feat. There in a makeshift crib the chubby little fellow held forth, wearing only a damp diaper and bonnet.

One by one the Pollywogs were dragged aft and thrown at the feet of King Neptune. Charges against the individual were read and each accused was asked to make his plea. To these deemed unworthy of a fair trial, electrodes were fastened. The lighting motor generator supplied encouragement to plead guilty without delay. When the King saw fit, he pronounced the man guilty and forced him to entertain his charming daughter with a verse—or song and dance. Electricity was found to be a great inducement.

When this was done, the landlubbers were led to the Royal Doctor for a brisk massage of the neck and a sound hammering of the chest. Aspirins—in the form of green olives stuffed with vitamin pills—were administered to all. Next came a shot of vile, black cough medicine, occasionally applied as a liniment. One final measure handed out was a large portion of mouthwash that had to be swallowed. Quite frequently, another dose was squirted down the back of the pants before the unfortunate man was led back to the Royal Baby.

One by one the Pollywogs were blindfolded, led to the baby, and made to kiss him. The complete details of this esoteric ritual are best left unprinted, but it provided these freshwater sailors with something of a shock.

The final step in the initiation consisted of being suspended upside down in the shower and having hot and then cold water poured down one's pant legs. This was most effective when executed by the exec, who became ambidexterously adept at this procedure which he called a "thermocouple."

Minor cuts and bruises were sustained, but very few were permanently injured. At the initiation's conclusion, it was felt that all hands had a comprehensive understanding of the gravity of a trip into the southern hemisphere. Accordingly, the title of Shellback was given to all and a fine celebration came to an end.

Not even our newly bald pharmacist's mate harbored a grudge, despite his difficulty in administering iodine to the razor nicks on his head. One of his jobs, however, was giving immunization shots to everyone aboard, prerequisite to entering Australia.

As we reported to get our shots, the pharmacist's mate looked up and studied our faces, his hand gravitating between two neat rows of hypodermic needles. We asked him what was going on. Smiling, he replied, "These are sharp. And these," pointing to the second row, "have burrs on the end of them." Some Shellbacks were known to have reverted spontaneously to their Pollywog state. A submarine captain whose name shall remain undisclosed was overheard by certain submariners to have uttered several loud "Ouches" surpassing any known to have issued from his lips during the closest of enemy encounters.

On 12 September *Batfish* and her hairless crew arrived at Fremantle for refit and reassignment. The U.S.S. *Guitarro,* moored alongside in Berth Three, hooted and catcalled at our lack of locks.

Fremantle was neither an air nor an Army base; it was a submarine base. For the glorious present, we had it all to ourselves. And if ever there was a heaven on earth for submariners, it was Perth, twelve miles up the Swan River from Fremantle. Admiral Ralph W. Christie, ComSubSoWesPac, saw to that.

Perth was his headquarters and the base for his men between the war patrols; and if ever a commander graciously provided for the well-being of his men, Admiral Christie did. He worked on the theory that the way to make submariners more efficient was to give them luxurious R-&-R-ing—and he spared no pains to see that we had it. As each submarine arrived from patrol, it was assigned automobiles. The enlisted submariners had a hotel that was all theirs, the junior officers had another for themselves, and each skipper had a bungalow in a beautiful residential area known as Birdwood.

In addition to being ComSubSoWesPac, Admiral Christie was an expert crapshooter, and each evening after working hours, the admiral would invite the skippers to "a friendly little hour or so of crap shooting" at the Officers' Club. To fresh Americans, a pound note looked like a dollar bill—green with a "one" on it. Before the end of the first week of our stay in Australia, Fyfe had to take out an advance on his next pay period. The good admiral had relieved him of every cent he had. But Fyfe was in good company; *all* visiting skippers were "invited" to shoot craps with the admiral. And most, like Fyfe, ended up broke before they left Australia.

Pretty Perth girls were everywhere. Their men had gone off to the war in 1939 and hadn't been back since. Their lot was similar to ours, and we made up for lost time. Romance was everywhere. In these lovely surroundings in this brief respite from war, some of us fell in love; it seemed certain that some of us would return to marry.

After three weeks of Australian "heaven," 8 October was the day we had to leave. But we had problems with our sound gear, damaged off Andakino Harbor, then repaired at Midway. About halfway through the last patrol it had again become misaligned and, due to excessive vibration and noise, could be used only at very slow speeds. The Engineering and Repair Shop thought they had isolated the malfunction; but during our training period, a bad hydraulic leak developed in the system.

We had the classic situation in which the recurrent road problem disappears completely in the garage. Since the hydraulic cylinder had

135

been repacked several times, it was probable that the cylinder itself was cracked. Finally, repairs failing, the entire unit was replaced, courtesy of the U.S.S. *Crevalle,* donor.

The day before *Batfish* had arrived at Fremantle, *Crevalle* had accidentally planed under the waters of the Lombok Strait with her main ballast tank vents and conning tower hatch open. Suddenly flooded, she plunged like a stone at a forty-two-degree down angle—with her lookouts still on the bridge. At 150 feet and sinking swiftly toward the point of no return, someone tenaciously managed to close the upper conning tower hatch *from the outside*. Miraculously, her fatal descent stopped just short of 200 feet.

Saving his boat and most of her crew—drowning when he could have swum away—was *Crevalle*'s OOD, Howard J. Blind. His posthumous Navy Cross was given to the Australian girl he had married just before sailing. But *Crevalle* was damaged beyond local repair and was destined for complete overhaul at Mare Island.

Despite intense security, rumors of Allied reinvasion of the Philippines were rife and we wanted desperately to be on hand to support MacArthur's imminent "return." Our training period had already been prolonged by enemy submarine activity in our practice area. Solving *Batfish*'s sound gear problem added fifty-two hours to our delay.

Tied up once more to the tender *Griffin,* our submarine had been refitted, refueled, reprovisioned, and rearmed. Admiral Christie came aboard to shake hands all around, and after talking to Captain Fyfe for a while, wished us "good hunting."

FIFTH WAR PATROL

8 October 1944

We departed Fremantle under the escort of H.M.A.S. *Parker*. In company with U.S.S. *Guitarro* we trained with her all the way to Exmouth Gulf, Australia, there to top off our fuel tanks. We proceeded up and out of Exmouth Bay on 11 October, due north for Lombok Strait, just east of Java.

Within two hours, trouble struck again. Our #2 periscope jammed in the fully raised position. The auxiliaryman and two other hands worked on it without success for over eight hours, as we sped farther and farther away from our "garage." A tough decision was made to decommission the scope and force it down as far as possible so we could proceed to our station.

Using all our wits and strength until 11 A.M. the next day, we could retract only three-quarters of it, leaving the remainder sticking out above the bridge like a sore thumb. After mulling it over for six hours more, we acceded to reality and radioed for permission to proceed to Darwin—now our nearest Australian port—to effect repairs. Permission was granted.

Since it was still going to be a long war, it may sound like two or three days' delay probably wouldn't make much difference. But settled down "in the groove" on our way to station, it was hard to accept any roundabout trips or stopovers. We sensed the imminent conflict north of us, and keenly wanted to rejoin the war at its dramatic turning point. We wanted action, not riding back and forth in a damaged sub.

En route to Darwin, *Batfish* was plagued with other mechanical difficulties. Excessive sparking and overheating in two of our main motors forced us to halve our speed. Vibrations developed in all four main motors at speeds in excess of two hundred turns per minute. An attempt to reduce the clatter revealed eighty-four cracked or loose brushes.

At 6:44 P.M., 15 October, we moored at Darwin next to U.S.S. *Coucal*, whose crew and officers ably assisted us in our repairs. On pulling our scope, a half-inch steel bolt a mere inch and a half long was found wedged between the periscope and the lower bearing housing. Apparently it had been forced into the system by the greasing at Exmouth, although no one could guess where it came from. Our

137

forcible attempts to retract the periscope had badly scored the bearings and the shaft, and since replacements weren't available, we patiently filed the bulges off the bearings and ground down the periscope shaft as smoothly as we could. Although not nearly as good as new, our accomplishment sufficed.

Our motors had also undergone considerable make-do repair. Although they worsened during the patrol, they didn't fail, causing us only headaches from the excessive noise and eternal vigilance—and skinned knuckles from constant maintenance. We finally departed for our patrol area at 2:30 P.M., 17 October.

Twenty-four hours after departure, our bow plane rigging went to hell, forcing us to surface for a three-hour repair. Luckily, it grew dark, which gave us the ideal opportunity to test our camouflage for future reference. We were passed unobserved by several planes; apparently the experiment was a success. In this black night with a new moon, we had an SJ plane contact as close as 8,000 yards. Since there was no indication of plane radar on our APR, we stayed right where we were until the bow planes were fixed.

Under way once more, we passed Timor on our left at 11 P.M., heading farther north into the Banda Zee until we could turn left above the Malay Barrier.

19 October 1944

4:47 A.M. Bow plane rigging failed again. Quite a thrilling dive in the dark, but another good drill for the JOOD and the stern planesman.

We benefited from a second experiment with our camouflage while repairing the repaired bow plane.

At 9 P.M. we began tracking an SJ contact at 18,000 yards. At 12,000 yards there were three definite pips: a large target and two smaller escorts, each patrolling about 1,000 yards on each side of the target. When we picked up echo-ranging from the escorts at 10,000 yards, we went to battle stations and started in for the kill.

Sound picked up the target's fast, light screws at 5,000 yards. All three ships were now visible from the bridge. The target seemed to be a tanker, judging by her long high profile and the fact that the radar pip had been so large at the initial ranges. With Japan's oil supplies becoming increasingly precious, tankers were high-priority targets, so she seemed worth a full salvo of six torpedoes.

138

10:10 P.M. This was the most accurately solved problem I have ever seen generated by the TDC, requiring only very small corrections about every half hour.

We fired six bow torpedoes at 2,600 yards, three set for four feet and three for six feet, using a one-degree spread. *All six* ran under the target to explode at their ends-of-run!

Batfish pulled out to 10,000 yards to mull over the situation. We were sure that the enemy had seen or heard our torpedoes; right after the first should have hit, we could see her signaling to her starboard escort. Yet not one of the three ships changed course or speed. How could we reconcile the large-appearing silhouette with the light draft and the strong radar signal, the high-speed screws, and the fact that she wasn't zigzagging and took no evasive measures?

We decided to work up ahead, get on her track, and look her over from periscope depth in the morning.

Just after midnight, we'd maneuvered into another shooting setup so we decided to fire a single wakeless fish—from the stern tube and *very carefully aimed,* set at a depth of one foot. The torpedo broached about thirty yards from the tube, but ran hot, straight, and normal. *Nothing happened.* It then exploded after a timed run to the port escort. Although nothing was seen from the bridge, in two minutes one of the pips disappeared from the radar screen and her echo-ranging ceased abruptly. The port escort was gone, but the tanker and remaining escort still did nothing!

Fyfe was reluctant to give up or give in. Vexed, he alternately paced the deck and tried to stare the target down through his binoculars, all the while mouthing inaudibilities. Then he went to his bunk to "sleep it off," while the OOD started working *Batfish* up again, so as to be on the target's track at dawn.

An hour before dawn, the OOD sent word that the target group had made a confusing maneuver that he couldn't follow—we had somehow ended up 18,000 yards astern! By dawn, Fyfe, with three hours' sleep, had closed the distance to 13,000 yards. By dawn's early light, the target still looked large enough to be worthwhile, so we started an end-around for a radar surface approach. The remaining escort was working back and forth across her bow and the target was now zigzagging. In this tumultuous sea, it was obvious that this mystery ship couldn't be hit with a torpedo. We decided to close and see what she would do if we lobbed a few rounds into her from our four-inch gun.

At a range of 9,000 yards, the target speeded up a couple of knots, zigzagging more radically. Now clearly visible, she was a 300-foot MFM vessel with a high stack, bridge amidships, and a shallow draft. Her foremast was about sixty-two feet above her waterline. At 8,000 yards, the escort proved larger than the "spitkit" she had first seemed. She was a modern, sophisticated, and deadly PC boat with a clipper bow and a very low, rakish silhouette, sporting a three-inch gun forward and a large, well-filled depth charge rack aft. Nonetheless, after expending so much time and torpedoes, Fyfe was determined to get in at least a few rounds.

We closed the range to 5,500 yards. Suddenly the "target" hoisted a flag. She and the escort immediately turned upon us, increasing their speed to seventeen knots.

Q-boat! This was a ship of grim deception, disguised as a harmless merchantman. A deadly decoy on which captain, crew, and armament remained fully concealed and fully aware until the victim was inside the trap.

"Emergency! Hard left rudder, full speed! Emergency!"

Speeding toward us with no uncertainty, the Q-boat stripped herself of disguise. Hinged plates dropped, tarpaulins were whisked off, exposing her full intent and wicked armament: several first-class four-inch guns, two torpedo tubes, depth charge launchers, and a full orchestra of heavy machine guns—complete with accomplished musicians rushing to play them.

Her first salvo straddled *Batfish* so closely that our bridge party suffered the equivalent of two tidal waves at once. *Batfish* heeled left and around on all four engines, then stretched out at emergency speed to execute the well-known maneuver of "getting the hell out of there!" Outgunned by the two avengers on our tail, standing and fighting would have been suicidal.

Her second salve bracketed us neatly and even closer. This proficiency portended some very accurate depth charging because at submergence there would be absolutely no doubt about our position or course.

Wide open, we had perhaps a one- or two-knot advantage over our pursuer. But with her surprise head start, the Q-boat was closing us so quickly she threatened to run us over before our speed edge began to count. Fifteen salvos screeched and whined over and around *Batfish*— some so close they seemed to burn her paint—before we could get away to deep water. We found it and dug in in twenty-eight seconds. By diving we lost our edge of speed, praying to regain our distance in depth.

Their ashcans followed us, as if sucked down by our diving swirl. The first three were very close, the next five even closer, ramming us past our test depth at a very steep angle. The lights flickered out, then on, then out again, intermittently lighting grim, shocked faces in the eerie atmosphere. We were plunging downward at great speed.

Closer than the first pattern, the next five-charge cluster shoved us down even harder, exploding directly overhead. The next ones followed us deeper and deeper. The forward torpedo loading hatch gasket sprung, and the sea tried to come in. Nearly drowning in the dark, cold torrent, the forward torpedo crew began to dog the hatch down with a block and tackle.

We had to level out quickly, or the increasing water pressure would do for us what subsequent depth charging just might. All hands fought to check our descent. The lights continued to feebly flicker on and off in their nightmarish cycle. Wheels on valves popped off, clattered to the floor, and more water began to trickle in. The depth charging continued, but the explosions began to lighten, as if our would-be killers weren't quite sure where we now were. We could only guess at our actual depth; several instruments had lost their tongues under the pressure. But it was somewhere between her test depth and her crush depth; *Batfish* was groaning ominously by the time she returned to an even bubble.

The depth charging stopped. We waited, slowly coasting *Batfish* upward, focusing our absolute attention for any signs of the enemy above. At 390 feet we found an eight-degree temperature gradient and sought refuge under this welcome roof. We assumed the enemy was waiting, catlike, to pounce the instant we came up, or until she could get a fresh reading on our position. Every time we decided to try a run for it, we thought we heard something of her lurking presence. She was such an expert, we couldn't assume she'd give up on us easily. It was a long, silent wait.

As hours passed, the humidity in the boat grew high, the level of oxygen in our air so low that a match wouldn't light nor a cigarette burn; the slightest movement produced a sense of suffocation. But barely breathing was preferable to not breathing at all.

Eventually we began our muted run for freedom and fresh air, staying at 400 feet and gradually increasing our speed until we had it up to half. When we ascended to periscope depth, there was no one in sight in the thick, black night. We surfaced and our lookouts streamed topside. All reported nothing in sight.

The first few breaths of cool, fresh, salty night air cured most of our ills. Inside, *Batfish* smelled of our hours of sweat and muted terror. We turned out with interest to revive ourselves, air *Batfish* out, and see what damage she had sustained topside. Absolutely none.

The Q-boat had been a new and chilling experience, and we had escaped her. We'd figured we were getting good at surface gun battles, but we'd sure as hell been outdrawn in this one. How did we get away? Pure luck. We were aggressive, possibly even reckless, but we weren't crazy; it would be better to tell our grandchildren about this encounter than to repeat it. We set our course to the west and cleared the area as wiser, but still chagrined, young men.

Many small native sailboats were on the water the next day, so we passed the Tiger Islands submerged, proceeding up Macassar Strait. An unusual amount of debris was in the water, and for the third day in a row, small craft abounded.

At 6:30 P.M., 23 October, we received good news on the radio: the invasion of the Philippines had begun. We had missed it—by several days and about 1,500 miles. Our coverage of an important exit for the Japanese fleet had been hopelessly delayed. Had we departed Australia on schedule and not been set back by the Q-boat, we could have worked our way north in time.

Instead we ended up with a bad taste in our mouth—despite Perth's royal reception for us, *Batfish* had not been treated as well as her crew. It would be fair to say she'd suffered some neglect. Later that night, our spirits got a lift with orders changing our patrol area to the Sulu Sea, off the southwest coast of Mindanao, Philippine Islands. Some units of the Japanese Navy were reported to be coming our way.

Overnight, SJ picked up interference from two sister subs, no doubt pouring on as much oil as we, rushing northward into the fray.

24 October 1944

11:14 A.M. Surfaced.

1:20 P.M. Sighted two-masted ship bearing 300° true on the horizon. Commenced tracking.

1:37 P.M. Dove.

2:15 P.M. Identified our ship as a tree (complete) floating in such a position as to look suspiciously like a medium-sized ship. We had been dodging debris like this for the last two days, but this looked more like the real thing than anything yet.

The war we'd missed seemed to be sending us floating postcards. Somebody was sure raising hell upstream.

26 October 1944 _____

6:21 P.M. Surfaced. Patrolled northeast and southeast, between Negros and Mindanao. It sure looks like we missed the boat on the Jap fleet both going in and coming out.

8:45 P.M. Radar contact bearing 307°, 25,000 yards. Manned radar tracking stations. When contact started to get us wet decided we were a little desperate and trying too hard to find a Baker Baker.

27 October 1944 _____

Navy Day—I hope.

At 2:40 A.M. when we turned on the SD for a plane sweep we found that this reliable instrument was being jammed by someone who was taking a lot of pride in his work. We turned it off until we had cleared the area.

28 October 1944 _____

Patrolling area between Negros Island and Mindanao. So far we have seen nothing but a lot of debris on the water, several lights at odd intervals on the beach, and a few unidentified planes in the air. Although the Battle of the Philippines is apparently still going on, I think we must be closing this particular barn door after the horse has been stolen. However, comma.

5:13 A.M. Dove.

9:13 A.M. Sighted sailboat bearing 160° true.

1:45 P.M. Four more sailboats. Did my best to will them into men of war and ended up with a headache.

During the course of the evening of 30 October, lookouts sighted a "Black Cat"—one of our planes for a change.

_____

I guess the aviators have the situation well in hand now and perhaps we can go to more fertile fields. I hate to think how fertile this particular place apparently was the day before we arrived. A curse on all "Q" ships!

When we got word of some downed aviators we sped toward their rescue at three-engine speed, charging batteries with our fourth. On the alleged spot at 11 P.M. we commenced searching for them using standard search procedure—firing green flares every fifteen minutes, preceded by a long blast on the whistle.

At 2:30 A.M. *Batfish* exchanged recognition signals and calls with U.S.S. *Hardhead.* Within hailing distance of her an hour later, we called across, inviting her to join in the search. She was willing, taking the territory to the south while *Batfish* searched the northern half. Neither of us finding anything, *Hardhead* departed twelve hours later to rendezvous with another sister submarine. On 1 November, still searching in accordance to plan, we shifted to southward of the reported position of the rubber boat. It began to look like our sky-guys in the water were goners unless they had already been picked up by our planes.

We searched fruitlessly until dark, then secured search for these survivors and headed back toward Negros Island. Over the last two days we thoroughly covered at least 1,600 square miles, parts of it twice. In the process we investigated no fewer than one hundred objects floating in the water, all of which turned out to be logs, tree trunks, native boats, airplane belly tanks, and all kinds of flotsam and jetsam—but no aviators. Since we'd sighted a distant friendly plane three times the day before, we hoped he'd made the rescue.

Receiving orders to patrol the area west of northern Luzon, we changed course for Mindoro Strait. En route, we established three sources of SJ radar interference, but exchanged recognition signals with only two U.S. submarines. This can produce an uneasy situation. Japanese submarines had been known to tag along, biding their time, waiting their moment to strike. We cleared the area, presuming that our friends did likewise.

West of Luzon on 4 November, our orders were again modified, directing us to lifeguard off Lingayen Gulf. This is about halfway between the northern tip of Luzon and Manila Bay, circled by

Corregidor, Bataan, Manila, and Cavite—where it all began in this part of the world 7 December 1941. Our carrier strikes were expected on 5 through 8 November—good news to those who'd heard a thousand "Remember Pearl Harbors" and gotten goose bumps every single time. We reached our new area shortly after midnight, 5 November. Upon arriving, *Batfish* exchanged signals and calls with U.S.S. *Ray* on SJ radar.

Shortly after dawn, while circling on our lifeguard station, we got an SD contact at eighteen miles Keying our IFF, we got no response, but that wasn't unusual. Some of our guys up there needed both hands on the wheel, and others were not speaking when spoken to. Believing he was one of ours, we decided to let him approach closer, and at twelve miles sent the IFF again. He disappeared, still unresponding, and then reappeared on SD at ten miles. When he had closed to three miles, our lookouts dove for the deck from their perches on the periscope shears. We pulled the plug and crash-dived, but not before the red balls of the Empire were directly overhead. No bombs, no explanation. We wished for a little friendly fighter protection—that *was* part of the deal.

No sooner on the surface, we had to dive again to dodge another unfriendly two-engine bomber. It was beginning to look like this day's strike was happening farther south toward Bataan Peninsula. We decided to stay submerged on station, maintain a high periscope patrol, and surface at the first indication of a raid. Meanwhile, we maneuvered to close Lingayen Gulf, only fifteen miles east, hoping to catch something coming out of there.

Although pickings were slim at sea level, the air was teeming with oviparous birdlife, all wanting to lay eggs on us. The bomber had been our forty-first aircraft contact. The realistic implication of forty-one airplanes is forty-one dives, which is clearly exorbitant even to a submariner.

We surfaced at dusk, having seen no smoke, dogfights, ack-ack, or carrier planes all day. Even if there had been a strike, we couldn't have accomplished any rescues without fighter cover.

Before noon the next day we had sighted eight more enemy planes. The endless, tiring routine of diving to evade went on. The Japanese seemed to be determined to give us the wrong kind of air cover, so we repeated yesterday's performance, maintaining a high-periscope submerged patrol.

Shortly after submerging, we sighted two columns of smoke. Soon we glimpsed the masts of two ships hugging the west Luzon coast on a northerly course. They appeared to be heading straight for the San

Fernando Harbor. Fyfe called the crew to battle stations, submerged. On their track, he studied the charts and the targets, predicting they would zig twenty degrees right after rounding Cape Bolinao. We proceeded on that assumption, which turned out to be correct.

As we approached 10,000 yards, we could count and identify a thirteen-ship convoy—the largest we had yet encountered—including a choice target: a damaged *Aoba*-class cruiser with a slight port list. She was in column with a large AK and a medium-large AP. Seaward, nearest us, were two destroyers, an aircraft ferry, and four patrol boats. Inboard of the target column, not more than 500 yards from shore, were three small AKs. Land-based bombers furnished air cover for the convoy.

At noon, rigged for silent running, we began our submerged approach on the cruiser, running right under the outer screen of destroyers and patrol boats. Safely under the fence, *Batfish* crept up to periscope depth for a quick sweep and a firing setup. Rising, we made ready our bow tubes.

Fyfe rose with the periscope. The second destroyer of the screen completely filled the eyepiece, her slashing bow little more than 500 yards away. The DD was almost on top of us! We wanted to fire if only in self-defense, but adequate data couldn't be force-fed into the TDC fast enough. The distance narrowed dramatically.

"Take her deep! Emergency!"

Batfish surged deeper as Fyfe took from the last seconds of periscope vision what data he needed for a submerged shot at the cruiser—hopefully enough to sink her.

We barely avoided collision; Sound could almost trace the destroyer's screws on paper. On the way down to 120 feet, Fyfe decided not to fire. He had already expended seven torpedoes on the Q-boat and wanted to make this salvo count. The instant the DD passed, we would come up to periscope depth and double-check the cruiser's position. But the escort behind the DD bounced a couple of pings off our hull, then slowed down to verify contact. We laid low until she moved on.

By the time we returned to periscope depth, the cruiser had been skillfully shepherded away. The only available target was the large AK. Two escorts, one on our starboard beam and one astern, were getting too close for comfort, and intensified air cover made our periscope exposure precarious. In a quick set-up, we estimated her speed at five knots and fired six bow torpedoes on a wide spread to cover all anticipated errors.

We evidently overestimated her speed. All six fish missed ahead of the target.

This was a heartbreaker. We were now out thirteen torpedoes—an investment of roughly ten times our monthly payroll—with no tangible returns.

As a result of our intrepidity, we were also surrounded. Four escorts formed a square box above us, one escort to a side, a fifth dropping depth charges. All of them methodically echo-ranged and listened; each of them took turns ovulating depth charges. At no time did they seem hurried and—like the Q-boat—as long as they were able to track us, they were very efficient.

Once again, we were getting worked over by pros. For two agonizing hours *Batfish* was pounded with depth charges and occasional bombs from land-based planes. At 350 feet, we found a sound-deflective temperature gradient—and relative peace. When we tested the boundaries of the thermal layer, we found it much wider than the box we had been in, and crept away from the posse on padded hooves.

Within an hour of surfacing at 3:43 P.M. we sighted seven aircraft. They didn't seem to have sighted us, suggesting that, thanks to our own aviation, an increasing number of enemy pilots now spent as much time looking up as they did down.

We were exhausted and frustrated. Sunset, meant to be the time for our surface patrol, was disregarded for the time being, and *Batfish* submerged for a much-needed rest.

While lifeguarding the next day we found our thirteen-ship convoy again—moored and anchored in San Fernando Harbor. The wounded cruiser and the large AK were both tied up inside. Two patrol boats were making quite a show churning up the entrance channel waters. Behind them lined up a second string of four PCs in two columns, motors revving. We could hear their echo-ranging. Planes abounded overhead.

When we pushed pursuit of the tempting cruiser to 5,000 yards, the whole scene registered *TILT!* The PCs came directly at us, and the planes homed in. It was such a perfect maneuver we thought we must have triggered a magnetic loop or sound cable on the harbor bottom. Yesterday's performance was duplicated to perfection; again we were surrounded.

7 November 1944

4:24 P.M. Evasive tactics definitely in order! Went to 250 feet and started fishtailing.

How this team picked us up and tracked us the way they did was a mystery. As well as we could tell, we weren't trailing an oil slick or bubbling any air. Once again they were very skillful and thorough in their technique.

With not even the benefit of a temperature gradient, we lucked our way through an unlikely hole in their offenses and escaped—another mystery some of us called the "J-Factor," "J" for Jesus. Others rubbed the belly of the small bronze Buddha in the forward torpedo room until the pain went away. The rest seemed satisfied not wanting to know why; just escape was sufficient explanation.

As the depth charging faded slowly behind us, as the enemy echo-ranging decreased, and as the sun sunk below the horizon, *Batfish*—foiled again—surfaced for a star fix and a battery charge.

At 8:30 P.M. we were ordered to rendezvous with *Ray* and *Raton* the next evening and operate in a coordinated attack group as a wolf-pack—a chilling name, evocative and apt. The Germans had initiated wolfpacking in World War I with absolutely devastating effect and nearly perfected it in this war.

The wolfpack's ideal target is a large enemy convoy, where the element of confusion compounds the elements of stealth and surprise. Probably the most diabolically effective method of reducing ships to seawater, proper wolfpacking leaves no survivors, nipping around the edges of the convoy until there is no convoy left. The terror and havoc are so powerful that ships within a convoy often collide and sink each other. Wolfpacking would be a new experience for us, and we looked forward to getting some results.

At 11:55 the next night, we exchanged signals with an American submarine, which was, however, neither *Ray* nor *Raton*, apparently engaged elsewhere.

The next morning we sighted smoke on the horizon and began an end-around attack at seventeen and a half knots. Within an hour, high periscope could see an eight-ship convoy, proceeding at about seven knots in an open order, most of them smoking heavily. Although we could see two planes circling the convoy, they apparently didn't spot us, so we proceeded to move ahead of the convoy on the surface. At noon, however, the convoy radically changed its base course, causing us to lose the ground we'd gained. Since we were only twenty miles off the Luzon coast, back on their port quarter again, it would be impossible to get around them to eastward in daylight. We started a new end-around to westward—the long way.

A photo of U.S.S. *Batfish* (SS-310) taken during her crew's training off Long Island (*Navy Department*)

The Commissioning Officers of U.S.S. *Batfish*. Left to right: Ensign O. A. Morgan, Ensign W. L. McCann, Lt. (j.g.) D. A. Henning, Lt. Cmdr. Wayne R. Merrill (C.O.), Lt. (j.g.) R. L. Black, Lt. J. M. Hingson, Lt. Cmdr. P. G. Molteni (*Courtesy Lieutenant Commander Merrill*)

In *Batfish*'s control room diving station, Diving Officer H. W. Kreis, Motor Machinist James L. Garnet (on stern plane controls), and Gunner's Mate Robert T. Craig (on bow plane controls) all watch the diving plane indicator—the dive must not be too steep (*Navy Department*)

Batfish crewmen firing .50 caliber machine gun at a Japanese mine floating in the South China Sea (*Navy Department*)

Captain John K. Fyfe, who succeeded Captain Merrill as *Batfish*'s commanding officer, joining a lookout on deck (*Navy Department*)

Enroute Pearl Harbor, Quartermaster John Glace prepares a battle-flag display in *Batfish*'s forward torpedo room. Torpedoman Robert A. Collar checks warhead while Torpedoman Harry L. Coker lies alongside torpedo reading magazine (*Navy Department*)

On entering Pearl Harbor, *Batfish* raised three battle flags representing her kill: 7 Japanese warships, 8 merchantmen, and 3 submarines (*Navy Department*)

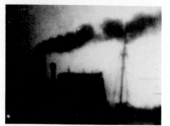

Photos taken through *Batfish*'s periscope, of Japanese ships that fell victim to her torpedoes from her First through Fifth War Patrols (*Navy Department*)

In dress uniforms, *Batfish*'s officers and crew muster on deck to receive combat awards. Submarine at right is not identified (*Navy Department*)

After 17 months in the Pacific, *Batfish* enters San Francisco harbor on
13 March 1945 (*Navy Department*)

Aground and listing in the Arkansas River. Note lines securing her bow to shore (*Lewis Jarrett*)

A postcard of the U.S.S. *Batfish* War Memorial Park in Muskogee, Oklahoma (*Storer's Cards*)

Half an hour later, Fyfe counted fourteen ships through the high periscope. This time, one of their aircraft spotted us and came in, as one of the escorts also turned at us with a bone in her teeth. At a range of twelve miles, we could have outrun the escort but not the plane, so we dove.

Within ten minutes the escort began probing for us with depth charges and was soon joined by a friend. Between the two of them they kept us away from their flock for the rest of the afternoon.

Although we had done our best to keep up with them submerged, when we finally resurfaced at 4:30 P.M., the smoke from the convoy was no longer visible. We started a surface chase after them, but two A/S vessels we hadn't seen came charging in on our starboard bow. We dove again. These two stayed on our tail for the next hour and a half, depth charging and being generally and persistently unpleasant.

When we surfaced once more at 6:52 P.M., we resumed the chase after the convoy, by now probably forty-five miles ahead. After three hours with no sign of them, we gave it up with the hope that our boats off Manila Bay would get into this outfit, and headed back to our area and our rendezvous.

At 10 P.M. we received orders from wolfpack leader *Ray* to continue submerged patrol off the Luzon coast the next day. During 9 November the wind and sea picked up drastically, making our depth control difficult. We surfaced into the midst of a violent typhoon and received orders to ride out the storm independent of *Ray* and *Raton*. Until today, we had doubted the reported frequency and severity of the November typhoons off Luzon's northwestern coast, as the weather for the most part had been light breezes and a moderate sea. Then a sudden drop in barometer brought on high, heavy seas and a thirty-five-knot wind. Even close in to the coast, Luzon Island offered no windbreak. The barometer hung at the low for two days, whipping rain and seawater about us, and we suffered the raging surface only when we had to recharge the batteries. Our lookout was maintained, but all other hazards were upstaged by nature—there was no event but the storm itself.

During the next day the storm began to weaken, but once again, our best friend was deep submergence so everyone could get some sleep. At 10 P.M., 11 November, we received orders from *Ray* that really made our day—to conduct submerged reconnaissance of San Fernando Harbor at dawn.

Submerged off Fagg Reef in a much calmer sea, we conducted

preliminary surveillance of the beach south of San Fernando Harbor, approaching cautiously with the memory of our last event in this area. At 10:30 A.M. the tops of a large AK were sighted. Evaluating the data on known and likely minefields and considering our close call during our last patrol, we decided against proceeding between San Fernando Point and Fagg Reef. We decided to enter the harbor from the northwest as we had before, arriving in position at the harbor entrance at 1 P.M..

There were no crowds today; we had a front-row seat. There was a large anchored AK and two medium-sized AKs moored to the dock. Our cruiser had slipped away. Several tugs and other small craft were milling about, but no patrol craft or airborne planes were in sight. The harbor seemed strangely wide open.

Slinking in cautiously to set up our attack, we ran in as far as the twenty-fathom curve, where the bottom began to shoal abruptly to fifty feet. Needing some slack for a quick escape into deeper water, we decided we had better fire from here: the anchored AK was 2,500 yards distant, the moored AKs at 4,800 yards. All targets were pointed straight at us, heading into a steady fifteen-knot wind. A strong current to eastward could influence not only our course but the accuracy of our torpedoes. They were going to be extremely difficult to score, fired down-the-throat at the targets' narrowest profile.

We made a very careful scan for antisub nets, close planes, and patrol boats. Finding none, we fired our last four bow fish—two at the anchored AK, the final two at one of the moored AKs.

We watched our first two torpedoes' wakes pass astern of the big AK and explode on the beach at the base of some airplane hangars, possibly doing some damage. This got their attention, and planes quickly rose to counterattack. Retreating, we heard our third torpedo connect with something solid—either the moored target or the dock— but at sixty-five feet and digging deeper, we never got a chance to confirm the hit. Eight aircraft bombs exploded around us.

Half an hour later we tried to come up to eyeball the damage, but the planes were of a different opinion. We finally surfaced after dark and proceeded on our general reconnaissance of the area shared with *Ray* and *Raton*.

During our second visit to San Fernando Harbor, we had encountered no patrol boats, dispelling any theory of a submerged magnetic loop or sound buoys alerting them to our presence. On 7 November we had probably been spotted by planes with a rambunctious backup of ready-to-go patrol boats; this time we alerted the wasps by shooting their nest. Considering the pains we took to get in for a shot, the yield was disappointing. Undoubtedly the best way to have scored hits would have been to fire torpedoes singly to observe the effect of the current, then compensate in succeeding shots. But the quick aerial counterattack hadn't left time for that. At any rate, we had fired our last bow torpedo, making us a somewhat snaggle-toothed wolf, but *Ray* and *Raton*'s presence would take the heat off if we got pinned down.

Alerted by a contact report from *Raton* shortly after 5 P.M., 14 November, we sighted smoke on the horizon and closed on it. A total of eight pips presently appeared on radar, of which at least four appeared to be *marus,* the others their escorts. We singled out the largest of the AKs and tried to close her from ahead so as to favor our stern tubes.

But being the junior of the wolfpack, *Batfish* was directed to wait until *Ray* and *Raton* made their attacks before getting our licks in: the traditional "you take the escorts, and we'll take the gravy." At 7:46 P.M. *Raton* announced she was attacking from the convoy's starboard flank, *Ray* from its port flank. The convoy's escorts were patrolling each side, two ahead and two flanking.

We attempted to stay on the largest AK while tracking her from ahead. When we had closed to 9,000 yards, *Ray* claimed a tanker, apparently loaded with gasoline. For an instant the explosion flashed from horizon to horizon like a giant flashbulb. In the returning darkness, a number of emergency lights appeared on all ships, now scattering in confusion and haste.

Minutes later, an irregular series of explosions resounded from the darkness: *Raton* was in for a kill. From our watery dugout we could see the enemy's red panic lights and large, bright searchlights frantically sweeping the dark sea. We continued to hear what we hoped were *Raton*'s hits—and then her misses: enemy depth charges.

At 10:45 it was our turn. *Ray* was clear; she radioed us to attack from the port flank. We had maintained radar contact on a loose, scattered group of four ships—two small, one medium, and one large—at 6,500 yards astern. We began approach on the largest, which was radically zigzagging on three-, four-, and six-minute legs. Within minutes we sighted her from the bridge—a heavily smoking medium-sized *maru* with quite a bit of superstructure. She appeared to be a cargo freighter or troop transport. Her near escort was at 4,500 yards. With surface haze and no moon, it was an ideal night for a surface approach by a sub sporting only stingers.

After we maneuvered into the best possible firing position—

wishing all the while for bow fish—the target zigged away from us to the left at 11:40 P.M. We set out to work up ahead of her again.

Forty minutes later, we were again ahead and in position 1,200 yards off her track. We slowed, training *Batfish*'s stern toward the nearest escort while waiting for the target *maru* to lumber into range. When she threatened to zig away again, we had a decent enough setup, so we fired four electric stingers from 3,000 yards.

Four minutes later our second and third torpedoes exploded on the AK at fifteen-second intervals. Within a minute, our fourth torpedo got her far escort—a lucky shot. The remaining escort fired two flares, then turned and made a halfhearted attempt to counterattack, but at no time came closer than 4,300 yards.

Upon aft reload, we began search for the remaining smaller *maru,* last seen headed east. Within an hour we contacted her, the reluctant escort now at her side, both zigzagging radically at a speed of nine knots.

As we closed them to 6,000 yards we suddenly picked up strong SJ radar interference at 8,400 yards. Because of the wavelength, she had to be a U.S. submarine, but she wouldn't reply to our challenge. Thirty degrees on the *maru*'s port bow, she stubbornly continued on her attack course. We asked *Ray* and *Raton* if they were making an attack; both replied in the negative. Pacing the target beam, we again challenged the sub, again receiving no answer. On the PPI screen we watched her close the target and dive to radar depth about 3,500 yards ahead of her.

When we could see no results of an attack within half an hour, we again started working up ahead of the target to do it ourselves. At this point, yet *another* U.S. sub came in for an attack from the target's bow. Challenging her on SJ with no response, we voice-broadcast blind, requesting identification of submarines attacking an enemy ship at that latitude and longitude. Again, we got no response.

This was a classic example of the need for standardized wolfpack frequency codes and calls for boats of two different task forces operating in overlapping areas. Dependence on keying SJ radar simply allowed for too many ifs, ands, or buts. Barely north of our area and slightly into the Task Force Seventeen "College" territory, we didn't know whether we were poaching or being poached. The *maru* seemed to be in skillful—though taciturn—hands. We didn't want to get hurt by our sister subs while insisting on the right of way, and certainly didn't want to lob one into either of them, so we moved out to rejoin *Ray* and *Raton.*

As the sun came up, we were running through considerable debris and oil drums—all that was left of the convoy our wolfpack had attacked. While awaiting orders from *Ray*, we searched for survivors and thought we'd found some when lookouts spotted "people in the water." On closer inspection they turned out to be hundreds of coconuts—items from the manifest of some stricken ship.

We did sight the body of one dead Japanese soldier in a lifejacket floating nearby and we brought *Batfish* alongside to salvage his pack. The only papers on him were a sort of wallet whose contents were unintelligible to us. Fyfe raffled off his bayonet, cartridge belt, and canteen for the benefit of the Welfare Fund and wrapped up his wallet for delivery to the Office of Naval Intelligence.

Later in the day we exploded with rifle fire a floating mine, no doubt cast loose by the recent typhoon. We were startled at the power of its detonation.

At midnight, 16 November, we received orders to pass back into the operational control of ComSubPac and proceed to Pearl. We had only three aft torpedoes left and were running dangerously short of provisions. On two different occasions, three hundred pounds of beef had to be thrown overboard; then we jettisoned our remaining inedible fowl. Our rice and macaroni were weevil heaven; half of each had to be thrown away. Many of our canned fruits were inedibly green, and the canned fruit juices, except for the apple juice, were so bitter that it was impossible to drink more than a swallow.

Much of our other Australian stores was of very poor quality, indigestible and totally unappetizing. Our two first-class cooks tried all sorts of culinary tricks to disguise the taste and improve the food, but many of their best efforts went to feed the sharks. Throughout our patrol, this had been a never-ending source of distress for Fyfe. And *Batfish* was in grave need of proper refit: at least fifty or sixty specific repairs and alterations were needed before she could do battle again—and the list grew as we limped home. Pearl Harbor was definitely good news.

Although we'd had a great and glorious time at Perth, Fremantle's follow-through had cost us time and more problems than we had entered with. Because of the more than a week this lag had cost us, *Batfish* narrowly missed covering one of the enemy's prime exits from the Battle of Leyte Gulf—the greatest naval engagement in the history of the world.

Shortly after MacArthur said, "People of the Philippines, I have returned," we arrived at Pearl. Ironically, our only plane contacts on the way home were several of our Liberators—headed, no doubt, whence we came. ComSubPac deemed our fifth war patrol successful, although on our fifth and final torpedo attack it was said that "the Commanding Officer should have made another attack on those ships or at least maintained contact until they were destroyed by other submarines." We certainly didn't pull away because we wanted to!

We'd sunk two cargo ships, a destroyer escort, and a patrol craft. We'd made emergency dives to escape most of our seventy-five aircraft contacts, we'd been suckered in by a Q-boat, and saved by luck— several times. We'd been bombed and depth-charged so much that by now most of us accepted that as "normal" on any war patrol with Captain Jake. But all in all, it was a reasonably satisfied crew that was bused off for two weeks of R & R at the Royal Hawaiian Hotel.

Our two-week stay flew by. Christmas in Hawaii was a cross between Christmas at home and Christmas at sea. On land, the nostalgia seemed more poignant than undersea, where there had been no real signs of the holiday. We yearned for Christmases past, but we yearned even more for the next to come; with war's end in better sight, we might be home again.

There was that inevitable loss of twenty-five of our now-veteran submariners to crew new construction submarines. Twenty-seven replacements came aboard. We were especially sad that our exec, Lieutenant Commander Jim Hingson, was among those leaving, although we were happy he was getting his own command, the U.S.S. *Diodon.* He'd been with us since Portsmouth and was the strong hand we had looked to during the troubled final days of Captain Merrill's command.

On 30 December our OOD gave the orders to take *Batfish* to sea on her sixth war patrol in company with U.S.S. *Charr* and under the escort of PC-465. Our new exec, Lieutenant Clark Sprinkle, was at the helm.

SIXTH WAR PATROL

9 January 1945

The sixty-seven alterations to *Batfish* had seriously cut into our two-week training period. Fyfe had called the confusion of simultaneous refit a "thorn in our side," and requested an extension so that we could get better acquainted with the changes in our boat before departure. Permission was not granted, so we constantly trained and drilled in transit, singly and in the winking accompaniment of *Blackfish* and *Archerfish,* our wolfpack mates for our sixth war patrol.

Ten days out of Pearl, *Batfish* approached Apra Harbor in the island of Guam. Captured by the Japanese shortly after their attack on Pearl, Guam was recovered in July and August 1944 at a heavy loss to both sides. Here now was Admiral Lockwood's headquarters aboard the tender *Holland,* about 1,300 miles closer to the receding enemy's homeland.

Mount Tenjo towered higher and higher behind Apra Harbor above Guam's rocky coastline as we made our approach. Our SJ had tracked this peak from one hundred miles away coming in. After exchanging recognition signals, the submarine net tender towed open his formidable barrier, then flashed us "go ahead," closing it behind us when we were safely inside. *Batfish* carefully maneuvered through the busy traffic in the inner harbor and moored alongside the tender *Sperry,* together with *Archerfish* and *Blackfish,* who had preceded us.

After refueling, we gained the advantage of some minor alterations to our hardware based on performance en route. For some reason we had been poorly reprovisioned at Pearl Harbor—not so badly as in Perth—here was our last chance to upgrade our larder.

When Fyfe appealed directly to Admiral Lockwood, there was a shake-up in the Commissary Department, and we were reprovisioned to our satisfaction. The food loaded aboard was the most appetizing and varied we had yet stowed away for war patrol. We submariners were the prima donnas of the fleet; the decision to volunteer for the submarine service often turned on the merits of the menu—along with the highest pay, the quickest promotion rate in the service, and a general reluctance to crawl around in foreign mud.

For this mission, our three-sub wolfpack was code-named "Joe's Jugheads," in dubious honor of Joseph H. Enright, commanding officer of our senior submarine, *Archerfish.* Our patrol area was to be in the South China Sea, between Hong Kong and Vietnam and around the Chinese island of Hainan.

With the Pacific war now in its thirty-seventh month, there were finally enough new American fleet submarines and effective torpedoes to go around. But we were running out of targets. Although wolf-packing originated for the destruction of large convoys, Japanese convoys were generally smaller now, after three years of Allied predation. Nonetheless, wolfpacking did increase our efficiency in attacking whatever we found, and it broadened our scouting range.

Joe's Jugheads were under way once more on 10 January. *Batfish, Archerfish,* and *Blackfish,* proceeding on well-separated, parallel tracks, closed our patrol area in six days of high-speed transit. On our westward course, we had passed within radar range several of the Babuyan Islands just north of Luzon. En route we practiced synchronized tracking and communication drills, with surface target practice here and there. Some unproductive lifeguarding, repeated aircraft contacts and evasion, and contacts with submarines of both varieties honed our battle edge but provided no real action.

We arrived at our South China Sea destination in the teeth of a typhoon that shook us up badly. Maintaining an efficient lookout was impossible, and heavy seas carried away several deck plates and superstructure supports. Since aircraft took advantage of the slightest lull in the storm, we maintained constant radar vigilance. The first day on station, amid the pitching effect of the high seas, we went up and down like an elevator, evading at least six planes. Our forces had recently made heavy strikes in this area south of Hong Kong, and our aerial adversaries were really stirred up. We assumed these were their planes, for not one of our IFF signals was reciprocated.

On 17 January when in desperation we escaped the angry surface, an electrical fire burst out in our after auxiliary power distribution panel. Fighting the fire and effecting repairs made this a long, hot day without lights or ventilation. The acrid burning odor seeped through every compartment, and a smoky film settled on everything. When we finally surfaced at sundown into the still-roaring storm, aching for a deep breath of fresh air, the temperature inside the boat had reached 110° and the humidity was a pungent 100 percent—all sweat.

The following morning, our lookouts sighted a mine tossing in the stormy seas. In an hour of trying, we couldn't manage to explode it with our deck guns; like shooting from a bucking horse, but good exercise.

On 19 January we got word of downed aviators and proceeded quickly to their probable location. It was doubtful that men could survive long in this violent water. All we found was another mine, which we tried to explode with gunfire as it tossed and bobbed down *Batfish*'s starboard side about seventy-five yards out. It would have been pure luck to have hit it.

At night—or under weather conditions like this—these floating hair-trigger explosives became inconspicuous, even to the keenest lookout. And then we were the target of these random weapons, cut loose by storms from their minefield moorings. If we'd spotted two of them in as many days, how many had we passed unknowingly? We would never know how many more had been as close.

All of us had felt the personal terror of complete vulnerability. A mine passes by at thirty feet; a torpedo misses by thirty yards; a depth charge curls the railing on the bridge. The sea bottom claims your boat's sound head; the water pressure makes her groan aloud in pain. Unable to reduce the deadly odds against us, which all increased in proportion to our exposure and aggressiveness, we focused instead on doing our jobs perfectly and remaining constantly alert. We rarely let our concern show, lest we contaminate our shipmates, thereby rupturing the sometimes thin membrane of composure. Your shipmate was your pillar of strength when you needed him, and you made yourself seem at least that strong for his benefit, If ever we succumbed to terror, it was singly, privately. Worry took shifts just as we did, but always missed enough of us to avoid incapacitating our boat.

And there was too much real work to do to dwell on the fear that causes fumbles. *Batfish* drew all fates unto herself, away from single jeopardies and singular deaths. We gave ourselves to her and submitted to our captain, absolutely trusting both.

We continued our search for the downed aviators, but didn't find them; neither did our sister subs. Perhaps they were rescued by a friendly seaplane, perhaps by Japanese, perhaps not at all. As a rule, we didn't dwell on what their fate might be, any more than we dwelled upon our own.

Over the next two days the weather improved as we patrolled unproductively. On the evening of 22 January, we got word from a friendly plane that a convoy in the Tonkin Gulf was headed east through the Hainan Straits. If they anchored, we could intercept them tomorrow for certain—and possibly tonight if they didn't.

Two hours after midnight, SJ picked up two pips at 9,800 yards, their speeds varying between one and three knots. As we eased in to 3,500 yards, we could see two large, vague shapes from the bridge. Having difficulty reconciling the two large shapes with the two small pips on the radar screen, we were suspicious, especially with the absence of propeller sounds or radar activity. Not wanting to hazard *Batfish* on an unfounded guess, we decided to track them and wait for some daylight on the subject.

Just before dawn, we submerged for a periscope approach to discover who they were and what to do about them. As the light increased, so did the ships. In the predawn twilight, at least twelve ships emerged within the dim outlines of two distinct groupings. We went to battle stations. By 6:39 A.M. we had counted over twenty-eight junk-type sailing vessels, varying in size to well over 100 tons.

When the light was up and fog rising, we battle-surfaced to see if they were carrying Japanese personnel or freight. Firing all deck guns, we charged in upon them from 3,000 yards. When we had hit one of the larger junks several times, all the vessels hove to, letting us approach without resistance. We ceased fire but kept our sights on them. At no time did any of them fire back at us.

Carefully maneuvering alongside a group of four assorted junks we saw that the people on these boats were topside, staring at us almost docilely, it seemed, awaiting our approach. Even though we had burst from the sea spouting loud and deadly, then attacked them at full speed, not one of them attempted to run and hide, even as *Batfish* bumped their craft to board.

Our boarding parties found them all to be harmless Chinese fishermen. Entire families of men, women, children, and babies sat in quiet groups on wooden crates or on the decks. These junks were the only homes they had. A thorough search for contraband revealed nothing but a few days' catch of various unappetizing fish. Our conscience prompted us to give them as much bread, beans, and rice as we could spare. Then we headed for the junk that had caught the brunt of our gunfire.

The boat had three holes in her hull near the waterline, a mast shot off, and partially demolished rigging. Climbing aboard, after many polite bows and lots of sign language, we discovered they weren't so concerned about their damaged boat; they simply wanted us to treat the two of their men who had been shot. Our pharmacist's mate was promptly dispatched with his little black bag.

The patients were an old man with a bullet wound in his thigh, and a younger man with one wound in his back and one in his arm. As the pharmacist's mate removed the bullets and treated the wounds, we witnessed an unforgettable demonstration of plain intestinal fortitude. The old man didn't flicker an eyelash. The man with two wounds was a rock during treatment and afterward, most amiable and active. We gave them cigarettes, stocked their larder, and parted the best of friends.

When we resurfaced at 10 A.M. after evading our first plane of the day, many of our junks were still in sight, all sails now furled but one. The damaged junk would not be far behind, the way her crew energetically set about to repair her rigging. We chose not to associate them with the plane attack, preferring to accept coincidence (also known as fate without a radio). In such a wide war in the middle of a hostile sea we had enjoyed the brief respite with these friendly strangers.

At dusk, we sighted and sank a floating mine with 20-mm gunfire. The sea was calmer now.

Patrolling to northward of Hainan Straits before dawn on 24 January, presuming the reported convoy to be long gone, we followed up on an SJ contact at 13,000 yards—which proved to be another junk fleet. We dove to evade it, resurfacing well out of sight an hour and a half later. These increasing junks were becoming as much a nuisance as the sampans had been on our first war patrol, except that the junks apparently had no radio relationship with enemy patrol planes—or so we continued to assume. We decided to patrol submerged off the Taya Islands for the day.

At dusk we hunted for another reported flyer in the water, but couldn't find him. After exchanging calls with *Archerfish* at dawn, we surfaced to look for survivors of another downed plane. Midafternoon we exploded another mine—our third, not counting the two TGBs.

Late 29 January, we radioed SoWesPac boats in our adjacent area that we were moving into their bailiwick to act on a plane report of ships anchored in Yulin Bay on South Hainan. If they had any objections, they didn't make them. The only response was from an imposter— another instance of the enemy receipting our messages and trying to fool us. These counterfeit calls were easy to spot, having a different signal note and lacking the proper authentification. En route late that night, we spotted lights on the horizon—more junks.

The next morning we reconnoitered Yulin anchorage from 6,000 yards. No shipping. At 1 P.M. we observed Gaalong Bay. No shipping. In late afternoon a bomb exploded in the water between the two bays quite far from us, more than likely just a token warning from a China Recco plane—just his way of saying hello.

At dawn on 31 January we dove again off the mouth of Yulin Bay. Initial periscope surveillance revealed only a few small surface craft and some half-sunken wrecks. But within three hours a small tug came chugging out of the harbor. We tagged along, sniffing her out. Shortly, out ventured another small tug. It looked like they might be expecting company big enough to need their help entering the narrow harbor.

Within minutes a small coastal freighter appeared about five miles out and coming in. We went to battle stations submerged and set up for an easy shot.

Presently the target closed, then paralleled the coast to join the waiting tugs. Above the AK, a single aircraft patrolled in tight circles. Now seaward of our target, we made our periscope approach. For accurate range, we took a single ping that agreed with the generated range. With a perfect setup and all data buzzing in beautiful harmony, three Mark XVIII bow torpedoes streaked out toward the small AK from a range of 1,000 yards.

Sound tracked all torpedoes to, under, and away from the target. Someone suggested writing home for some captured *German* torpedoes.

31 January 1945 _____

> I don't know when I have ever been so disappointed. I was so sure of getting this one we even had the cameras ready to start taking pictures. If there was ever a storybook setup, this was it.

We followed our target, now turning northward to enter Yulin Bay, in the hopes of getting another crack at her. Chances were the narrow entrance channel was bounded by mines, and her guardian angels—the tugs or pilot boats—protected her from a fate far worse than reefs or sand bars.

We kept her within periscope sight until she anchored within the sanctuary of the inner harbor. Then we hung around and waited, since there was no chance for another shot until she came back out. It was odd—this small AK would probably not have been worth a torpedo expenditure even weeks before. Now, with targets getting more and more scarce, she was becoming worth waiting for. If we passed this one by, we ran the risk of finding nothing better.

We moved out at night, dodging some planes at dawn. Then at midmorning we detected our little target by her approaching smoke. But she was going the wrong way! The same ship that had anchored safely within Yulin Bay was now steaming full-thrust from Gaalong Bay back toward Yulin Bay, just as she had the day before. How and when she'd moved out was a complete mystery to us. Now on her second run into Yulin, she had caught us off guard and out of position. She casually swung into the harbor entrance—this time without assistance—2,000 yards inboard of a red buoy that we took to be the channel marker.

One hour later, the little AK got under way with dispatch, heading straight out to sea. Submerged to ninety feet, we started tracking at standard speed to intercept her. When Fyfe periscoped to observe, she had turned farther east away from us, toward Gaalong Bay once more. And once again we were out of position. Maneuvering in these shallow, poorly charted, and probably mined shoal waters was as dangerous as it was irksome. Her sailors knew these waters well; perhaps she was a Judas goat, knowledgable and shallow-drafted.

Now that we had definitely established her route, we knew where to be the next time she made her milk run. There was no way she would get by us again.

Shortly after midnight, we received a radio message from Com-SubPac: "FOR JOE'S JUGHEADS 020200 X JOIN WITH CLYDE'S CANNIBALS IN THE CAMPUS X PLAICE IS TOP DOG X EXECUTE BLOCKADE ON RED SUBS IN EVACUATION EFFORT X USE SAFETY LANE X 051900 X."

2 February 1945

12:20 A.M. Hate to leave here now that we have cased the joint so well . . .

In the deteriorating weather, we dodged one more airplane and departed for greener pastures via the nearest "safety lane" to rendezvous with Clyde's Cannibals and Joe's other Jugheads in the Luzon Straits. The Japanese were not supposed to know of these safety lanes—so Japanese contact within them was random, whereas friendly fire often seemed somewhat concentrated.

The events leading to our new assignment had begun when General MacArthur's forces landed on Luzon at Lingayen Gulf. In the weeks since, they had hammered the reeling Japanese forces under the command of General Tomoyuki Yamashita—the Tiger of Malaya. We suspected that at that very moment, our artillery was shelling Japanese

161

emplacements on the outskirts of Manila. With all major air and surface sea lanes now dominated by our forces, Japanese high officials were frantically searching for the safest avenues of escape. Their remaining submarines seemed the most logical conveyances.

Ultra-informed Allied Intelligence believed that only four Japanese submarines were currently operating in northern Philippine waters—and that these were carrying on emergency evacuation from Aparri, in the middle of the north Luzon coast. Thus ComSubPac ordered us to patrol the enemy's alleged evacuation site. Our orders were to stop the evacuation; *Plaice, Seapoacher,* and *Scabbardfish* were already in the area.

As we plowed north and east, the weather again became so heavy and the seas so rough that we pondered whether typhoons came to this area to spawn. Sea and sky were as awful coming out as going in. Sleep came hard to us, as the boat would pitch and roll as much as forty degrees, and it was useless to try to keep the boat clean. Anything loose flew down off shelves and bunks and skittered across compartment decks. Eating was a major task, since everything slid off the tables, including our elbows. For two days *Batfish* slowly surged through this maelstrom before turning southeast toward the Babuyan Islands.

Just as the clouded sun began to set on 4 February, lookouts spotted an enemy landing barge on a northerly course toward Formosa, eighty miles distant. It was too rough to man the five-inch deck gun, so we battle-surfaced to see what we could do with our machine guns. The target had no visible armament except a light machine gun mounted on its bow. Guns ready, we closed from 4,000 yards, opening fire with the 40-mm at 1,200 yards. Returning light fire for heavy, the enemy effectively kept us off her stern so we were unable to use our superior speed to any advantage. Our bridge was swamped on most courses, and then it started to rain again, which in the twilit gloom made for rotten visibility. We managed to hit her forty or fifty times with our 40-mm guns; she caught fire twice and returned our fire only sporadically. At seventy-five yards, when she tried futilely to ram us, we moved in to about fifty yards and sprayed her from point-blank range with all guns. Either her gun was gone, her personnel killed, or she had lost her fight; we no longer received return fire.

Darkness enveloped our target, so we broke off action before we could sink her. This was just as well for us, as all of our 40- and 20-mm ammunition was expended, except for that in deck stowage— inaccessible in these fierce seas. Even if we didn't see her sink, she had caught more than half of the 1,100 rounds fired. It was doubtful if this very shot-up ship could ever make Formosa. For our part, we sustained no injuries or damage from the hour-long skirmish.

At 7 P.M. *Plaice* ordered us to patrol the pass between Babuyan and Calayan islands. We expected an improvement in the weather as we crossed the 20th parallel southward, but high winds, heavy seas, and horrible visibility still prevailed as we patrolled down across the Luzon Straits.

We spent 6 February on a peaceful submerged patrol between our assigned islands, making no contacts at all. A minor ailment had become chronic: from age and depth-charge abuse both our periscopes leaked badly. What began as moisture had become a steady trickle of cold seawater that tended to drip down Fyfe's arms and off his elbows. Short of overhaul, nothing could be done but bear it. The area was devoid of anything but spindrift; Captain Jake muttered a lot more than usual. The next evening we requested and received permission to patrol the Babuyan Channel between Camiguin Island and the north Luzon mainland.

Two uneventful days later, the seas began to relax. Although we were running out of flour, our baker treated us with homemade cakes. An odor as delicious as the cake itself issued from the ovens, filling *Batfish*, provoking some mild attacks of homesickness.

At dusk on 9 February we surfaced for a navigational fix before beginning the night's patrol. We had been forewarned to expect enemy boats in this area, but it looked like they had either been sunk last month by our Third Fleet activities or had withdrawn from these parts. Since the landing barge five days before, we had not contacted a single craft of any sort.

Once the sun had passed completely beyond the horizon, sky and sea knit seamlessly into a single darkness, unbroken by moon, star, or phosphorescence. For nearly four hours we had this blackness completely to ourselves. Then at 10:10 P.M. we had company. "Radar signal on APR, one five eight megacycles."

A heavy saturation signal started coming through loud and clear. The wavelength was definitely alien. For over half an hour we monitored the constant signal as it increased from strong to stronger. We were approaching or being approached by whatever it was. SJ registered no pip; neither Sound nor lookouts made any contact. The absence of SD contact ruled out a plane.

Forty minutes later, SJ got a small pip off our port bow at 11,000 yards. Our lookouts were alerted, but in the dense blackness it was doubtful they could spot anything until we were right on top of it. We went to battle stations for a night surface radar attack. Tracking the target by its own radar emissions, we sporadically checked range and confirmed bearings by keying our SJ.

Sound finally picked up a set of extremely quiet screws at 4,000 yards. With no visual confirmation, SJ and Sound put the target's speed at twelve knots. This data was fed into the TDC. Since no bearings or ranges could be fed into it from the TBT on the bridge or from periscope observations, they would derive from the PPI scope of the SJ radar, backed up by Sound. *Batfish* closed to fire four Mark XVIII torpedoes.

The target was proceeding toward the pass between Fuga and Camiguin islands on a direct course north from Aparri. The pip remained small; our target was small, low in the water—and alone. We knew Japanese radars were inferior to our own, yet this transmission's characteristics indicated a top-of-the-line set, most likely a nondirectional air-search radar more similar to our own SD than to our SJ. Certainly it would not be wasted on anything less than an expensive man-of-war; we suspected a submarine. But with five of our sister subs in the area, a nagging doubt appeared. "Radio," Fyfe called from the bridge microphone. "To be on the safe side, we'll chance a call to our other boats."

"All set, Captain."

Fyfe dictated a terse contact report. The bridge speaker clicked twice. Then he heard his message read back for his confirmation prior to transmission: "TOP DOG X SUB CONTACT X POSITION ABLE SIX TWO X COURSE ONE TWO OH X SPEED TWELVE X RED OR BLUE X CONFIRM X JAKE X."

"See if their ears are on." Fyfe called back, muttering hopes that our target was deaf.

Within minutes, all but one sub had responded; "NOT ME X GO GET HER X." Then the fifth response trailed in, same as the others.

"Kick her ahead a couple knots," Fyfe ordered.

Suddenly the target changed base course radically, with a hard zig to her left to clear Fuga Island, the nearest land before turning toward Formosa. She bore straight on her new course as if we weren't there. We closed steadily in on her from the east. Her saturation signals on APR continued without pause.

"This guy wouldn't be hurting himself any more if he turned on all his lights and played music on his deck speakers," the OOD said to Fyfe. The captain solemnly nodded. As the signal increased, the range diminished.

"Right full rudder," Fyfe ordered. "All ahead flank." As the annunciators went all the way up, the diesels rumbled louder in deeper pitch and *Batfish* swung into our final attack approach.

At 1,850 yards, still with no visual contact, we fired four bow torpedoes in twelve-second intervals at the target, now slightly off our starboard bow. All four Mark XVIIIs were set at six-foot depths with low gyro angles and two-degree spreads. The counter's stopwatch ticked off the seconds until impact—and then some.

Eight minutes later, we heard four distant end-of-run explosions. Being closer, the target must have heard them, too, but she may have taken the explosions to be a bombing run on Fuga Island. Her speed and bearing remained unchanged.

Fyfe climbed below and moved to the beckoning attack officer at the plotting board.

"We had her speed wrong, Captain," he pointed out on the plot. "She's doing fourteen knots, not twelve."

We now pulled out to 5,000 yards off her track and began a high-speed end-around while making bow reload. Still confident that our target was a submarine, we wanted to close to visual range for the next attack, hoping that wouldn't put us right in her lap.

The crew was beginning to react to our stalking one of the subs we'd been sent to kill. A tingle of excited anticipation was in the air, already taut from the miss on our first go-around. A pool on the outcome couldn't develop; we had never sunk a submarine before, much less one full of generals and top-secret documents—maybe even gold. They had to be skimming off whatever cream was left for the taking, before the whole mess curdled.

At midnight we had closed to 1,500 yards and could see our target vaguely. At 1,020 yards she was clearly visible from the bridge. Her silhouette differed drastically from any of our own submarines. It was too dark to tell whether she was an I-boat or an R-boat, which differed primarily in size, but she was IJN for sure.

Binoculars in hand, Fyfe pressed the bridge intercom button. "Japanese submarine in sight. Prepare to fire."

The word came down and went around. Sweating forward torpedomen silently awaited the final firing data to send their three Mark XVIIIs away.

Fyfe called down a swift stream of observations to the conn party below. Then, "Clear the bridge!" The lookouts scrambled below in careful haste, leaving their night vision behind. Should they return topside, the red-lit conning tower would leave them blinking in this darkness for quite a while. But Fyfe did not want anyone in the way in case of a fast dive.

Alone on the bridge, his eyes intent upon the enemy silhouette transfixed on the TBT's crosshairs, he could feel the flooding and opening of forward tubes one, two, and three.

We closed to 900 yards without spooking her; we were indeed beautifully in position. On she came, in blissful ignorance, at fourteen knots. "Ready to fire, Captain," the exec relayed to Fyfe.

For another tense moment he trained the binoculars on the submarine in case she made a last-minute move. "This is it," he called down. He pressed the button to send the final bearing below. "Bridge to conn. Fire when ready."

Through the open hatch, he could hear, "Fire one." But Fyfe stiffened with a vague malaise; he felt no recoil. A three-thousand-pound fish kicks when it leaves its tube, at twenty knots and accelerating.

"Hot run in the tube!" a frantic voice called out. "Number one failed to fire!"

Electric torpedoes don't run "hot" in the tube, but number one was stuck in its open flooded tube with its arming vane spinning. If *Batfish* traveled 350 yards with the torpedo in this position, it could arm itself, the vane aligning the detonator with the charge. Then the torpedo would explode on contact—but *could* detonate at the instant of arming!

"Fire it again—manually!" Fyfe bellowed into the phone. He didn't wait for number one to clear. Lose our setup, and we'd likely lose our target. "Fire number two when ready!"

"Fire two!" the exec repeated. Number two kicked out. If the target saw us and turned to attack, we'd have some problems evading with a "hot run" and three tube doors open. And we sure as hell were in sight, should they bother to look. Forward torpedomen wrestled to blast free the lodged torpedo with a high-pressure compressed-air charge.

"Fire three!" Fyfe roared. Number three sprang from its tube with a jolt twelve seconds after number two.

"Three away!" came up from below.

Fyfe was torn between staring at the target and preoccupation with our jammed number one torpedo. The assistant attack officer was intent on his stopwatch, accounting for the two fish on their way. Sweating, holding his breath, he was waiting to account for the third!

"Number one fired manually!" the talker shouted. But we had felt it before he yelled. That torpedo probably ran erratically—but at least it was clear of us.

"Conn, come left to two seven oh," Fyfe ordered. The course change would take us away from the target. As *Batfish* began her swing, the blackness burst with flame—a column rocketing skyward at least a thousand feet.

Fyfe tried to squint away his sudden blindness as shock waves pummeled *Batfish*. Flames swept out from the base of the explosion, for an instant silhouetting the stricken submarine. Her screws stopped. APR reception ceased abruptly. The group around the PPI screen watched as the pip fragmented into smaller pips, quickly fading. When Fyfe's vision returned, she had completely disappeared except for low rumbles as internal explosions fragmented the crumbling submarine into smaller pieces, sinking.

"Permission to come on the bridge, Captain."

"Permission granted."

The exec popped up in a hurry to see if there was anything left to see. A few sparks drifted down like slow shooting stars. It was all over so quickly. A rash of "Permission to come on the bridge" requests came up the hatch. Fyfe granted most of them, and smiles and handshakes made the rounds on the bridge.

Four minutes later, we heard one end-of-run explosion. The assistant attack officer was still tending his stopwatch. Coming down the hatch, Fyfe asked him, "How many hits did you count?"

"Just one hell of a big one," he grinned without looking up. "Number two. From the sound of it, it must have blown her out of the water. Number three tracked dead on, but must have passed under—or maybe through her. Number one unaccounted for."

Fyfe nodded. "Radio, tell the wolves we got a red one."

A few minutes later, word came up the hatch. "*Scabbardfish* sends congratulations and says, 'Welcome to the club.' " (A little over three months before, *Scabbardfish*, with "Pop" Gunn, had sunk a Japanese submarine near the mouth of Tokyo Bay.)

"Clear the bridge. Take her down and commence forward reload."

Other congratulations came through on the radio. Reload completed, we surfaced and rigged a searchlight to patrol the area. Running through a heavy oil slick coating about four square miles of water, the smell of diesel fuel was overpowering. We soon realized the searchlight was accomplishing little except ruining the bridge party's night vision and needlessly advertising ourselves. We decided to wait until daylight, then come back to investigate.

10 February 1945

1:50 A.M. . . . would still like to salvage some Nip submariners and see what makes them tick.

Within the hour before dawn, six plane contacts were made at radar depth. Rising to reinspect the area, we were driven right back under by a single patrol plane coming in low from the east. Despite heavy overcast, it was growing fairly light. Since the planes seemed determined to keep us under, we rolled with the punches and took a break in the concealing depths.

After any attack, there is always a physical and mental letdown that should be compensated, lest we lose our edge. The three-and-a-half-hour rest was welcome.

At 9:47 A.M. *Batfish* was again patrolling at periscope depth. It was still too crowded upstairs for us to satisfy our search for survivors and souvenirs. The periscope spotted a group of five U. S. Navy planes coming up from the mainland at a distance of four miles. A Black Cat torpedo bomber flew in low to investigate the oil slick. The other four fighter escorts kept their distance. Some "genuine" U. S. Navy planes for a change—how nice!

"High-speed propeller noise! Bearing zero nine zero!" came the frantic voice of Sound. "Sounds like a torpedo—I could hear it splash!" Fyfe roared the orders that sent *Batfish* down her well-worn path to deep submergence. All ears attuned to *that* sound again; there was little other noise as we waited. We'd heard rumors about a secret weapon our Dirty Tricks Department had been working on long enough to have perfected it: an acoustic torpedo guided by its own sonar, and used in some of our aircraft. Once in the water, these torpedoes would allegedly "home in" on a sub's screw sounds, making escape impossible.

At ninety feet the propeller throb passed directly overhead, then began to fade rapidly. A high falsetto pierced the air, "Stupid swabbies that can't row, they put 'em in a goddamned aer-o-plane!"

"Level off at two hundred feet," Fyfe ordered.

Batfish remained submerged for the remaining daylight hours. We surfaced at dusk, to learn that ComSubPac had ordered *Plaice, Scabbard-fish,* and *Seapoacher* to patrol elsewhere. *Batfish, Archerfish,* and *Blackfish,* reverting to our maiden wolf name of Joe's Jugheads, were ordered to continue patrol in the Babuyan Island area.

During the course of the evening we had to crash-dive twice in one hour when the Japanese A/S planes began broadcasting their now-familiar trademark. Whenever a slowly sweeping radar steadied on us, became increasingly stronger, and started being keyed, it was time to pull the plug unless we wanted to count the rivets on the plane. They were probably still searching for the submarine that killed their sub, or perhaps they were out for anything that gave their radar a return.

When we surfaced at 10:54 P.M., the planes had fled, probably to find someone else to annoy. Strangely, there were still no A/S surface craft in the area.

At 1 A.M. pack commander *Archerfish* directed us to patrol west of Calayan Island. There was no way we could reach our new area before dawn, so we continued patrolling in our present area, to make the run next evening.

At sunrise we dove to avoid a Japanese early bird and spent the day on submerged periscope patrol. At dusk, we resurfaced and shortly contacted two planes sporting radar at twelve miles; they disappeared without forcing us to dive. It was time to make a run for our designated patrol area.

Little more than a half hour later, APR reported radar inter-ference at 158 megacycles. Weak at first, the signal increased steadily. *Batfish* swung in order to find its null and determine the source's approximate bearing. Cautiously keyed, SJ probed the pitch-black void with its invisible beacon until we had a definite fix on the suspected Japanese submarine. At 8,000 yards, we found her bearing; she was on a 170° beeline for Luzon.

We began tracking. This night was as dark as the last. We would make a surface attack if developments permitted it. Assuming radar capabilities equivalent to last night's target, we would attempt to close for visual identification before firing. From the bridge Fyfe called, "Steady as she goes. Sound battle stations, torpedo."

Throughout the boat the clanging alarm roused members of the off-duty watch sections and sent them scurrying to their stations. "Battle stations manned," followed shortly.

"Another Jap sub!" "Maybe just like the other one." "Does she know we're here?" Tense, muted comments circulated throughout the

169

boat. We were no longer shiny-eyed battle virgins. Ahead was an enemy ship, by now as impersonal as the morning star.

But always before, our prey and victims had been surface vessels, a different species. We now deliberately stalked to kill another submarine. We'd had a night and a day to think about that. This was different from anything we had ever done before in all our killing—and we felt it, though no one had the words together.

The exec joined the captain on the bridge. Black sea and black sky were quiet. Water hissed along *Batfish*'s smooth sides.

"Range six oh double oh," sounded from the conn.

"All ahead flank," Fyfe called back. *Batfish* stepped up her stealthy pace, flaring a larger wake and driving spray upward across the bow.

"Got the feeling we've done this before?"

Fyfe grinned. "Hope that doesn't mean we're going to miss."

In the long minutes of silence in darkness, the throb of the diesels and the splash of the sea were all that could be heard. All eyes probed the blackness, straining for first sight. The lookouts knew all the steps to maintain the keenest night vision. A low-profile submarine would be able to see us—if its lookouts were looking as hard as we were. We believed we had the edge; our swift approach assured it. From the shears, the forward lookout called, "Jap sub dead ahead!"

Fyfe swung his glasses on the reported bearing and saw what the lookout was seeing: Japanese submarine, unobtrusive shears, very low in the water.

"She doesn't appear to be zigzagging, Captain," commented the exec.

"Radar bearing dead ahead, range one three double oh," sounded through the bridge speaker.

A moment later, the range to the target was 1,200 yards. *Batfish* was on a course for a ninety-degree starboard track. Fyfe had made up his mind to shoot when the gyro angles decreased ten more degrees to ten degrees left.

Suddenly the target disappeared from sight. APR interference changed abruptly. The sub had dived.

We changed course to the left and held our speed. It could be we'd lost this one for trying to repeat the theoretically perfect setup. Why she dove became a point of discussion—not only on the bridge. Had an alert lookout saved his ship from *Batfish*, black spider creeping across a black web? Had *Batfish*'s wheezing caught the enemy's ear? Many strains and assaults had taken their toll upon our boat, and we winced at the thought of our sound signature at any speed beyond a creep.

Half an hour later, Sound heard a swishing noise from the general direction of the target's forward track. "Sounds like she's blowing her ballast tanks, Captain," Sound added.

Sure enough, at 9:06 P.M. the target's 158-megacycle interference was back on our APR, only weaker than before. "We've regained radar contact with her, Captain," the operator relayed. "Range, eight six five oh yards."

Whether the target heard us, thought she saw us, had us on her radar, or just made a routine dive, we'd never learn. Still manning battle stations, we proceeded on a high-speed surface end-around to put us back ahead of our target's track.

"Range six thousand yards," radar reported.

"That's close enough for our purpose," Fyfe observed. "Clear the bridge!" Pressing the alarm, he hollered, "Dive! Dive!" As Fyfe cleared the conning tower hatch, *Batfish* shifted easily to electric drive and slid under the water smoothly. The target had increased her speed from seven to twelve knots, which would put us right on shooting range within a very few minutes.

"Radar depth," Fyfe ordered. "All ahead one-third. Come right to one two oh."

In a matter of seconds, we steadied at course and depth.

"Set torpedo depth at four feet. Up scope." For all the light it reflected from its upper eye, our leaking periscope might have been filled with ink. With the target approaching a generated range of 880 yards, it was still invisible to all but our SJ.

"Angle on the bow starboard one hundred. Bearing one two oh."

"We're set," the TDC operator answered promptly.

"Shoot!" Fyfe snapped.

"Fire one . . . Fire two . . . Fire three . . . Fire four."

Nervous silence settled over the conning tower and control room. The assistant attack officer counted off the running time to the enemy submarine. It was now up to the stopwatch.

From the periscope eyepiece, a bright light illumined Fyfe's sweating face A towering sheet of flame lit up the sea for miles around. At 10:02 P.M. the submarine literally blew apart and sank immediately.

"We got the sonofabitch!" sang out a lone voice from the control room.

One muffled hit—timed as the second torpedo hitting the sub, or part of it—was heard and felt by all. Eight seconds later, another muffled explosion. The attack officer conjectured it was our third torpedo hitting a piece of disintegrating submarine.

"Down scope," Fyfe said quietly. "Course one five oh."

As we leveled off at 150 feet, two loud explosions reached our ears. Three minutes later, we heard the end-of-run explosion of our final torpedo—a miss. What had there been left for it to hit?

Over the next fifteen minutes, Sound reported a variety of noises from the sunken submarine. Feeling the rumbles, we silently envisioned the small internal explosions, escaping air, shifting weights, collapsing bulkheads, scraping, tearing metal—then all was silent.

Suddenly, we were startled by an explosion so violent we thought at first it was us. But it was only the concussion of the submarine's finale on the ocean floor; she must have been carrying high explosives to General Yamashita.

At 11:41 P.M. Fyfe brought *Batfish* to the surface, into a darkness that had swallowed up the sea that had swallowed up the submarine. Slowly we searched the area, not expecting to find survivors. Yet we hoped for at least one—to let us know that survival was possible. But there was only a small froth of small brown bubbles sticking to the oil slick.

"Single aircraft bearing zero four zero! Range ten miles!"

Fyfe pressed the bridge diving alarm. "Clear the bridge!" he yelled. "Take her down!" Almost simultaneously the vents popped. Air whistled through them, casting white vapor up between the deck slats. Four lookouts tumbled down from their perches and disappeared down the hatch, Fyfe right behind them. The plane, on a southerly course for the north Luzon coast, droned on without paying us any attention. As a precaution, we stayed down for another fifteen minutes, then brought her up to radar depth. A clean SD sweep gave us the green light to surface. We reported the results of our attack to *Archerfish.*

"Come left to one two oh," Fyfe spoke. "All ahead two-thirds." This maneuver would put us back on course, following our interrupted transit, toward our assigned area—to find enemy submarines.

Arriving west of Calayan Island at 6 A.M., 12 February, we began submerged scouting in the pass between Calayan and Dalupiri islands. At dusk, Joe ordered us to search for a pilot in the water somewhere west of Sabtang and Batan islands. Changing course to northeast, we headed for the area immediately.

At about 2 A.M. on 13 February, the exec joined Fyfe in the cool, damp air on the bridge. This night was also as dark as it could be. The sea was no longer calm; around us rain squalls appeared and disappeared.

"We've got a radar interference, Captain. This one's at one five seven megacycles. A bit weaker than the other two were."

"Tell APR to pick up the null."

"Yes, sir. Battle stations?"

"Wait for SJ contact."

The exec climbed below to pass the word. *Batfish* began a long, slow swing, searching for the source's approximate bearing. Before the null in the target's radar broadcast was found, the rumor spread.

"Appears to be two two oh, Captain," the operator called through the speaker.

"Change course to two two oh. All ahead full."

Twenty minutes later, the exec relayed an SJ report to Fyfe. "Captain, we've got a solid pip at eleven thousand yards. Two two oh degrees true," he grinned. "She's all alone."

"Seems to have developed into another Nip sub," Fyfe replied. "Call the crew to battle stations."

We began tracking the small pip, her base course 120°, her speed seven knots. For a few minutes, nothing further came from the radar operator. Our position relative to this target was almost identical to our last two: we were surface-approaching with the darkest part of the dark sky behind us; we could barely see the heavy cloud cover now rolling over us.

"Contact now bears zero one five. Range eight thousand yards." The tracking party's report confirmed that *Batfish* was approaching an ideal position. The target's change in bearing and range indicated it was heading southward and that *Batfish* was off its port bow.

We had fired all but two of our remaining bow torpedoes at our last target; firing the last two would play these odds too close and leave us dry forward in an emergency. We would have to fire stingers.

"Target speed seven knots and steady, course is one two oh," called the exec from the plotting board. The fly was coming to the spider: all we had to do was move across the web a little faster. With the target's range now approaching 7,000 yards, we had to cross her course to put her behind us at a good range from which to fire down our own wake.

"All ahead flank!" Fyfe called back. "Come left to one nine oh." At flank speed, we would cross ahead of her just right and then slow to await her approach.

Fyfe pressed the bridge alarm. "Clear the bridge! Dive!" The bridge party tumbled down the hatch, Fyfe slamming it hard behind him for the quartermaster to dog down tight. *Batfish* bored beneath the choppy waves. "Up scope!" *Batfish* leveled off at forty-four feet, maintaining three knots submerged. It was working like clockwork. The only thing that could prevent us from reaping our setup would be a radical change in the target's course. Even a change in her speed could be easily compensated for, as long as her bearing remained more or less the same. But a submarine can make one radical course change that no other boat or ship can: *it can dive.*

"Target just disappeared from radar, sir!" an urgent voice called out. "Last bearing zero two zero, range seven one five oh!" Why did she dive? We weren't pinging; Sound was listening only. We were keying our SJ infrequently, and then only briefly on command; our radio was silent—there was nothing aboard they could have DF-ed. If their sound heard our screws, then their equipment was better than our own. That opened a whole range of possibilities for other gear that we had better take seriously.

"Rig for silent running," Fyfe ordered. We crept at radar depth with our eyes and ears open, our mouths shut. "Maybe she'll blow ballast in thirty minutes," someone ventured. "Could be that's their doctrine." No one replied. "You know, like the last one, thirty minutes."

Fyfe clung to the dripping periscope, awaiting whatever Sound, APR, and SJ might reveal. Minutes ticked by, then a half hour. "SJ," Fyfe said, "key your set briefly."

There was no reason for us to believe our enemy wasn't stalking us even as we stalked him. Five more minutes passed. If she knew we were here—a suspicion that her lengthening submergence could support— then we now shared the same odds with our adversary.

In a showdown between submarine and submarine, surprise takes the biggest advantage, but luck gives the biggest breaks. After all, we had sunk two submarines just like this one—and in only two days. Could that mean we were lucky! Could it mean we now strained at that luck?

"Where the hell is she?" Fyfe surfaced *Batfish* to make a high-speed run ahead of the enemy's probable attack. Thirty minutes later, we withdrew into the depths for another radar watch. A full hour passed. We listened for our enemy, for her pinging, for *her* torpedo.

"APR contact! One five seven megacycles!" The shout startled us. There she was! The pip appeared on our SJ scope, seventy minutes after it had abruptly disappeared.

"Range nine eight oh oh, Captain. Bearing one six six," radar announced.

"Take her up," Fyfe called down the control room hatch. To close for a new approach, we would need surface speed. He climbed to the bridge for our third high-speed end-around on the target. They had had their chance, such as it was. Now it was our turn again.

With the target at 7,000 yards, we dove across her forward track and leveled off at radar depth. She approached steadily. Her long submergence seemed to have been no more than a routine dive, for her radar was chatterboxing just as before. We were now back off the pass between Calayan and Dalupiri islands. We swung about for a ninety-degree track with stern tubes. The strong tide streaming through the pass was making depth control and steering difficult. The tide rips could also affect our torpedo run.

"Make ready aft tubes," Fyfe ordered. "Stand by to fire."

"Aft tubes flooded and ready, Captain." We waited, checking and double-checking our fire-control setup. The target was approaching the bull's-eye on our plotting board. The torpedoes were set to run at six feet, slightly deeper than before so they wouldn't broach.

"Stand by," Fyfe called out.

"Bearing steady at one six five. Range is now one seven double oh."

"All set," the TDC operator said.

"Fire seven!" A pause. "Fire eight!" Fifteen seconds later, "Fire nine!"

Batfish jerked under us three times. "Seven, eight, and nine fired."

"Torpedoes running straight and true," called the sound tracker from the torpedo room.

"Up scope!" Fyfe turned to the assistant. "How long now?"

"Fifteen seconds. Twelve—eleven—ten—" The ticking of the watch was joined only by the count. "Five—four—three—two—one—"

Nothing. The stopwatch went on ticking. As Fyfe started to turn to the PPI scope, the flash through the scope's eyepiece lit the conn. A yellow fireball consumed the Japanese submarine as she blew apart.

The thundering shock struck *Batfish*, resounding through her hull, hurting our ears. SJ picked up a wide diffusion of pips on the screen as the target completely blew apart. She had shattered so completely, her pieces sinking so quickly, there was nothing for the succeeding torpedoes to hit. The men around the PPI scope stared at a blank screen.

"Down scope." The periscope slid sloppily down into its well.

Once again we surfaced in the hopes of finding survivors amid the oil slick—or debris before it sank or drifted away in the rip tide. Minutes on our way, we heard in the distance the end-of-run of our second torpedo. Seconds later, a third explosion resounded through the darkness. As we ran through the oil and wreckage, the searchlight was again not effective in the surface haze. Since dawn was close, we waited on the surface for its light. Radar would alert us of danger.

The sun began to slide up behind the dark, hazy horizon, casting dim light on slimy bits of wood and paper. Running back and forth through the oil slick, our search for something tangible was finally rewarded. We recovered a wooden box containing Japanese navigation equipment, papers, and a book of tables. If this blew off the bridge, her navigator may have been waiting for a navigational fix by dawn's first light. From the positions listed in his workbook, it looked as though the enemy had come all the way from the Indian Ocean to Formosa before heading down toward Luzon to join his ancestors.

We reported our third successive strike against the IJN submarine force. At 6:30 A.M. we dove for the day's submerged patrol. Oil was still bubbling to the surface.

Captain Fyfe's voice came over the intercom loudspeaker: "Within three days, we sank three enemy submarines. There were no survivors. Those men aboard the Japanese subs who died as a result of our actions were combatant enemies. They knowingly risked their lives in war, just as we do. We attacked and sank them in the course of our duty."

A hush settled over us one by one and we listened. No one showed much expression, looking passively across the crowded compartment at nothing in particular.

"Within our good fortune that we did not lose our boat or our lives, there is of course some sadness that these submariners have died, and by our hand. The only way that could have been otherwise in this war, would have been for us to die by theirs. Thank you for your excellence, and congratulations on your success."

176

Jake Fyfe had put to words the feelings each one of us had, but had not yet begun to talk about.

As a token of the occasion, Captain Jake gave a page from the recovered book to each member of *Batfish*'s crew. Exhausted from the three days of continuous action, the success of our mission began to sink in. Before long, it was business as usual.

At dusk we surfaced and proceeded back to the area west of Calayan Island to search for one of our flyers reported to be somewhere in these waters.

Not long after midnight, 14 February, we sighted a white flare, then searched the locality in the pattern of an expanding square firing green flares every fifteen or twenty minutes for three hours with no response. Fyfe suspected that the flare might have been a shooting star, but the lookout and the OOD stuck by their guns. Giving our man in the water the benefit of the doubt, we persisted in our search for him. It was very dark.

At 4:30 A.M. we received the good news that he had been rescued by our planes. We also received a message from Admiral Lockwood and Admiral Nimitz.

U.S.S. BATFISH
Naval Message

HEADING: NUBO V NPM   GR 87 BT
FROM: COMSUBPAC   TO: USS BATFISH   INFO:
HERE'S TO YOU XX FOR BATFISH FROM COMSUBPAC X FOLLOWING
RECEIVED FROM ADMIRAL NIMITZ ADDRESSED TO YOU X QUOTE X
CINCPAC FULLY CONCURS WITH COMSUBPAC YOUR PREVIOUS
MESSAGE X UNQUOTE X WITH THE THIRD DEPREDATION REPORTED
IN YOUR LATEST DISPATCH WE BELIEVE THE HEADACHE HAS
CHANGED TO CHRONIC MIGRAINE AND AGAIN ADMIRAL NIMITZ
CONCURS XX DEAD EYE
TOR:1300/2-14-45

That was good news, too.

The next day, 15 February, passed without event as we swept the passes between Calayan and Fuga and Camiguin islands. With only one plane contact the following day, we caught up on some sleep, and surfaced at 6:20 P.M., receiving orders to depart station and head for prearranged rendezvous with *Blackfish*.

Although "social consumption of alcoholic beverages" was strictly prohibited aboard all U.S. naval vessels, there wasn't a submarine in the Pacific that didn't carry a good supply of "depth charge" whiskey to be administered medicinally if the going got too rough during an attack. Captain Jake broke out the booze and allowed his crew a celebration. Our lookouts and those on or about to go on watch were satisfied with a rain check—something to look forward to when the rest of us were merely looking back. Those who didn't drink became inordinately popular with those who did. After we drank to Captain Jake, we toasted Admiral Lockwood and Admiral Nimitz and wished them well.

A flashlight battery recovered from the debris of our third sub sinking became outrageously funny. "What's this? Their forward battery?" "Well, hell, no wonder they sank!" "Wonder how big their after battery was!" The stories of our three enemy encounters were told and retold—*whistling past the graveyard*—as we passed around and signed each of the pages Fyfe had given us out of the Japanese book. We were in high spirits, albeit illegally.

Next day we proceeded in company with *Blackfish* toward Guam. Plane contacts had grown surprisingly scarce. In fact, the first one sighted, on 20 February, appeared to be a B-25, with which we exchanged visual signs—from the bridge. What was this war coming to when your own airplanes don't try to bomb you anymore? Before dawn on 21 February, *Batfish* and *Blackfish* rendezvoused with our escort, PC-1082. Three hours later we moored portside to U.S.S. *Apollo*, Apra Harbor, Guam.

The news of our enemy submarine sinkings had preceded us. Official Navy photographers were there to greet us royally. Flashbulbs popped everywhere as *Batfish* was photographed from every angle, inside and out. Admiral Lockwood was there, beaming, to shake every hand.

Then Fyfe was whisked off for a briefing with Fleet Admiral Nimitz, Commander in Chief, Pacific Forces. Repairs to *Batfish* were begun by *Apollo* and Submarine Squadron 28 Repair Unit, but the gray lady was going to need more than these facilities would provide; her six war patrols had taken their toll. The forthcoming Mare Island Navy Yard overhaul was overdue, but would include at least a hundred outstanding alterations that would bring *Batfish* up to date. She'd never be as good as new, but the way we seemed to be winning the war, maybe she wouldn't have to be.

When Fyfe returned from his briefing that evening, he volunteered, "All the brass in CincPac—Army, Navy, Marine, and Army Air

Corps—was there. The aviator types asked the most questions. I guess I did okay after my knees stopped shaking." It's odd what makes men's knees shake. In four war patrols, we'd never seen his battle-chatter.

The next day we got under way for Pearl Harbor. In company with *Archerfish*, we rendezvoused with our escort, *PC-1078*, and arrived there on 3 March, moored at the submarine base in early afternoon. The band was playing and a large crowd had turned out to cheer us in. In the Silent Service way, we were famous.

Then came the awards. Each of us got the Submarine Combat Medal.

We received the Presidential Unit Citation with Bronze Star from an emissary of Secretary of the Navy James Forrestal. A number of us received lesser awards for specific acts. In addition, on behalf of the Philippine Government, we were awarded the "Philippine Liberation Ribbon with Bronze Star." Captain Fyfe was personally awarded the Navy's highest honor, the Navy Cross.

ComSubPac's endorsement swelled our pride even more:

> This illustrious patrol was outstanding and smart in every sense
> of the word. The splendid planning, judgment and daring
> displayed in the attacks is best characterized by the unprece-
> dented sinking of three enemy submarines. . . . The Commander
> Submarine Force, Pacific Fleet, congratulates the commanding
> officer, officers and crew on the brilliant teamwork and headwork
> displayed on this patrol and the severe damage inflicted upon
> the enemy.

On 6 March 1945, we departed Pearl Harbor without our R & R, but nobody complained: we were going home!

Also aboard were two passengers, Lieutenant Commander Walter L. Small and a *Life* magazine photographer who took hundreds of pictures en route. We didn't mind that our accomplishment was too packed with top-secret implications for the article to be published until the war was over—but then, the war was not expected to last much longer. We looked forward to seeing our pictures at the newsstands.

Arriving in San Francisco on 13 March 1945, *Batfish* went to Bethlehem Steel Shipbuilding Yards for her overhaul. We were going home for thirty-day leaves—a joyous occasion.

But once again, our joy was tempered with sadness. Captain Fyfe was detached from *Batfish* with orders to proceed to Philadelphia and join U.S.S. *Trumpetfish*, then under construction, as her prospective commanding officer. Captain Jake had come to us when *Batfish* was in difficult times. During our four war patrols with him, he'd given us far more than survival; he gave us pride. What all of us had accomplished together, none of us, in all likelihood, would ever know again. In our poignant farewells, we took this accomplishment to be the glory we had sought.

To a man, we hated to part company with Jake Fyfe, of *Batfish*.

THIRD WAR COMMAND
SEVENTH WAR PATROL

12 April 1945

WALTER LOWRY SMALL, JR.—*"Walt" "Groundhog"*—Academics had never been difficult for Walt; had he worked harder here he might have been outstanding; for his proficiency in the engineering courses was marked. Yet in his idler hours we knew him best—whether at cribbage, blackjack, or over a stag sandwich at the "Spoon." Speeding back from Baltimore in a vain attempt to get in under the deadline, or dragging to the hops, he was the ideal companion. He consistently refuted Bacon by taking his literature in one form, the Reader's Digest, but his main diversion was wrestling. Now at the parting of the ways we look back on four very pleasant years with him. As for the future, equipped with a practical intelligence and keen personality, he is bound to succeed. So, good-bye, Tarheel, and good luck! The Navy needs men like you!

U.S. Naval Academy Lucky Bag, Class of 1938

Shortly before our leaves were up, while many of us were en route across the States to *Batfish*, came the announcement of another loss: President Roosevelt had died.

The news was also distressingly bad in San Francisco, where diplomats from all the Allied nations had gathered to establish the charter for the United Nations, a worldwide organization being formed to safeguard the peace that was sure to come. Russian diplomats' obstructions to a suitable charter were making foreboding headlines.

Then, during the final stages of *Batfish*'s refit, came some good news: on 7 May Germany surrendered unconditionally and signed the formal documents the following day. With the European victory, we expected the Pacific campaign to end in a matter of days. Surely now, Russia would declare war against Japan. Against such odds, Japan's acceptance of our unconditional surrender terms would certainly follow.

Over half of *Batfish*'s officer and crew complement had changed. We were now under the command of Lieutenant Commander Walter L.

181

Small, a battle-experienced officer with a distinguished record as exec aboard U.S.S. *Flying Fish.* Our passenger from Pearl Harbor to the States, he'd come aboard as *Batfish*'s prospective commanding officer. Jake Fyfe was a damned tough act to follow, but we gave our new skipper our full confidence and our best efforts.

Batfish was scheduled to participate in one of the most exciting secret missions of the war, code-named Operation Barney. A nine-submarine wolfpack equipped with newly developed FM-sonar mine detectors would depart Guam on 27 May to penetrate *en masse* for the first time the formidable minefields of the Tsushima Strait, the southern entrance to the Sea of Japan between Kyushu and South Korea. This daring undersea raid on the "Emperor's Bathtub" was calculated to devastate the enemy's morale, map safe channels through the mine barrier for succeeding naval forces, and most certainly find and sink ships. What remained of the enemy's shrunken fleet was logically expected to be concentrated here.

With tension mounting for our last-minute departure, *Batfish* was plagued by interminable problems and setbacks during refit in the Bethlehem Steel Shipyard in San Francisco. Finally back in the water, she developed a badly leaking sea suction valve on the after engine room circulating water intake, directly beneath the maneuvering room. Being on the hull, this valve was not reparable in place; when you open this one up, you're looking directly into the sea.

Replacement was the only solution, yet waiting weeks for our turn to go back into dry-dock was a demoralizing prospect. Pressed for time, the ship and shipyard jointly devised a scheme that would never be considered under less urgent conditions.

Many damaged ships had been kept afloat long enough to make port by no more than a mattress shored firmly into place inside the damaged hull. We had an emergency—and needed a miracle.

A diver went over *Batfish*'s side with a plain Navy sleeping pillow to stuff into the sea valve opening. Since the soft patch above the engine room was off, there was no way to pressurize the compartment if the pillow didn't work. The idea of nothing but a pillow between *Batfish* and the harbor bottom prompted a last-minute improvisation—nearly as primitive, but somewhat more reassuring. We whittled a wooden plug to fit the hole.

Nervously, we wrenched the nuts off the inside hull flange. Then when it was clear, the valve was snatched off, and a clenched fist went into the hole to keep the pillow in place. Standing by was a man ready with the wooden plug and another with a small sledge hammer to drive it in at the first sign of feathers. The water that flowed into *Batfish* was no worse than had been leaking from the defective valve; there was no need for the plug. A deft coordination followed: out came the fist, on went the new valve, the lock washers and nuts were tightened down, and we were as good as new. The entire procedure had taken about fifteen minutes.

We sailed out under San Francisco's Golden Gate for sea trials. *Batfish* bore many major transplants, renovations, additions, and re-arrangements as yet unsynchronized under practical sea conditions, and in effect, this was a shakedown cruise to "harmonize" the boat. Systematically we reduced the bugs and kinks, but when hooked up for an acoustical rating, our sound signature was excessively loud. As the post-overhaul shakedown wore on, the noise worsened.

Loudest was a bad click in one of the two reduction gears that connected *Batfish*'s power to her port and starboard propellers. As with the sea valve, standard procedure would be to return to dry-dock, take out the whole gear for repair, then put it back together—which could take weeks. Impatient to join our wolfpack in time, we decided to attempt repairs ourselves.

Picking our time and our place, while cruising slowly on one propeller, we unbolted the top, then poured Prussian blue dye into the gear box. In theory, the dye would be rubbed off at the point of greatest friction, identifying the high spot causing the click. In practice, it was trial and error.

Each time we thought we'd found the point, we handstoned the spot. The cramped space allowed room for just one man at a time. But when we closed it up and got under way, the click was still excessive.

Next day we took another crack at it, determined to get off a little more metal. The results were not enough to pass a sound test—administered by either side. It was decided that the next day was to be *it*. One day more without turning toward Pearl Harbor would lose our race with time, for if we failed, we were certain to be ordered back to the shipyard.

When Captain Small said, "Go to it, and good luck," our surgical team broke its record for opening up the patient. Fingers and eyes relocated the bastard bulge, and the carborundum stones took over. But our best efforts were not enough. On war patrol we would have been the loudest submarine in the fleet—a detriment to ourselves and to our packmates.

On 26 May *Batfish* left dry-dock and entered the loading period. On 27 May Operation Barney's nine-sub wolfpack departed Guam for one of the most intimidating sea rampages in history. On 31 May we finally departed San Francisco. Our reduction gear had been quieted down to the maximum allowable noise level, but entering Pearl Harbor eight days later, our readings had increased.

All of us followed the news of the war that was winding down so ponderously, but would not end. Although Japan had absolutely no hope of winning, it seemed that only an extremely decisive stroke would paralyze her determination to continue fighting. Russia's timely presence could still save many lives. But there was still no sign that our Russian allies were going to declare war on Japan, despite their Potsdam pledge to do so thirty days after Germany's surrender.

Departing Pearl Harbor on 26 June, we arrived at Saipan on 8 July, refueled, and made minor voyage repairs alongside U.S.S. *Orion*. Two days later, *Batfish* took on the last of her sea stores and got under way.

Possibly because of our recalcitrant clatter, we had drawn lifeguard duty off the southeast coast of Kyushu for our seventh war patrol. From our hard-won bases on Okinawa, Iwo Jima, and other recaptured islands to the south, massive air strikes upon the Japanese mainland were in progress. Our people had finally worked out a deal with the air people whereby we would stand by on the surface in predesignated locations, so, if the flyers got in trouble, they could seek us out for rescue. Knowing that splash-down in enemy waters would not necessarily result in capture or death by exposure was calculated to increase their daring. In exchange, we were to receive fighter cover when and if we needed it, and immunity from friendly bombing. Despite their tendency to steal all the thunder, we submariners did acknowledge that if these gutsy guys crashed into the ocean, they would need all the help they could get.

En route to our lifeguard station, we passed two distant friendly subs, sighted and chitchatted with *Pilotfish*, and exchanged SJ with *Ronquil* and *Sea Devil* and said hello to *Case*. All surface ship and plane contacts we met with were also friendly.

At 9 P.M. on 14 July APR announced a 157-megacycle radar contact. We *knew* it was a Jap sub. Finding nothing on Sound of SJ, we swung the ship to find the null in the signal, and set out upon a 225° true course to sink number four.

Wrong null! Forty-three minutes later, the signal was fading rapidly, so we reversed course. Two hours later we had followed the interference to its source—a shore radar station scanning at 157 mega-cycles from Aoga Shima. If we'd had a tank on board, we could have silenced him.

Daily, we could hear the roaring squadrons overhead, occasion-ally glimpsing our high-altitude bombers through breaks in overcast. We saw no Japanese aircraft and not one enemy ship or boat of any kind, not even a sampan. We had begun to probe close in to shore, hoping to stir up any kind of target. We did, however, sight another friendly sub.

16 July 1945 _____

2:10 P.M. Okinawa based PBM and four fighters were very friendly. They liked to play around and zoom sub after identity was firmly established. It was very hard to make myself stay on the surface.

Log of U.S.S. *Batfish* (Small)

At about 3:30 P.M. a plane reported sighting a man in a rubber boat. We said we'd get him. The plane told us that *Argonaut* was also headed for him. When we sighted *Argonaut* two hours later, she was recovering the aviator. After some chitchat, we followed her to rendezvous with *Quill-back*, who then took him aboard. Then we transferred to *Quillback* a crew member suffering from chronic renal colic.

So far, it looked like the zoomies had the area pretty well cleared out. When we surfaced at dawn on 17 July, the enemy made his first appearance—a Rufe float plane. At dusk, another Rufe. Then, at 9:45 P.M., a friendly PBM. We evaded all three.

Next day at dawn, a Japanese patrol plane was contacted, then one at dusk, the same as the day before. During the day we got an SD contact at eleven miles, verified by APR. Lookouts could hear friendly planes apparently shooting up some small boats, but saw nothing. We considered helping out, but decided we'd probably be in the way.

On 19 July we surfaced to lifeguard a strike that was due to come over. By midmorning we had contacted no planes and received no news of cancellation. A typhoon reported raging near Okinawa could explain the lack of planes or news. Shortly after dusk, we sighted a green flare not far astern. Thinking it was a man in a boat, we reversed course, and within a minute we had SJ contact at 2,000 yards.

The surfacing submarine certainly had the drop on us. We pulled the plug and tried to challenge her, but had no luck. Within an hour, we surfaced to further SJ interference. Testing, we exchanged recognition signals with *Blackfish,* then closed to talk. To our consternation, she said that while we were surfaced, we had passed over her once today and twice yesterday. A conference was held with Sound and lookouts.

Next day, with the typhoon coming our way, we patrolled close to shore. By noon, the seas had picked up considerably and were increasing. Expecting a strike, we patrolled within 8,000 yards of Noma Misake and Bono Misake. Nothing happened. There had been no message from Okinawa one way or the other.

21 July 1945

4 A.M. Still nothing from Okinawa, and the weather is fine. We wondered if we had missed a message, so opened up and asked; got a negative answer. It would certainly help if we could get the dope on days that there are no strikes so that we would feel free to patrol. As it is we can't get far enough away from our lifeguard station to feel that we are actually patrolling. But perhaps just our presence keeps shipping from coming through here. We did feel pretty conspicuous.

At 10:03 P.M. a lookout's warning pierced the wind. "Torpedo wakes on the starboard bow!"

The bridge party sighted one wake ten yards ahead across our bow, another a little farther out.

"Hard right rudder! Clear the bridge!"

We dove after the torpedo tracks had streaked by at a very narrow margin, then listened for the sub that had fired them. Ironically it was probably a "friendly" since they seemed to abound in the area. It would be a mistake to assume that our sound signature was familiar just because it was loud. Although our targets were far fewer, our own people were a constant threat to our existence—and the Japanese were sure to be as willing to kill us as ever—when and if they appeared.

Shortly after midnight, 23 July, we spent an hour trying to get radio dope for today's lifeguarding, but with their operator, it wasn't easy. He truly missed his calling—as a boilermaker. Immediately after we signed off without gaining any real insights into what was happening, a Jap called *us* using our correct call number. A real party line!

Okinawa wasn't fooling anyone by giving "aircraft" calls to lifeguard submarines. When we were called, we were expected to answer

186

receipting the message in a plain-language call—and the enemy immediately knew there was a submarine fifteen miles off southern Kyushu. This time, though, we didn't answer.

We had also been missing messages, which contributed to our less than perfect understanding of the situation. More often than not, the Japanese had a daily dawn and dusk patrol, rarely appearing at other times. As this coincided with our scheduled communications, we were often evading when we should have been copying. Complicated by nearly continuous radio jamming, we never knew whether we missed the message or whether there was to be no strike the next day. Too often, the enemy ended up knowing more than we did. If Okinawa had only broadcast in code an hour later and repeated it before dawn, we might have a chance to be more helpful.

Then we received new communication instructions that rendered the above comments obsolete except for historical interest—all of our wishes had been granted. Thank you, Okinawa!

For several days we had been acting as diversionary cover for *Sennet* and *Pogy*, to draw attention from their scheduled penetration of Tsushima Straits. Patrolling close to shore, we brazenly looked over Kusuhaki Shima, giving them every opportunity to look us over. The Japanese had progressed remarkably in antisubmarine detection, but no longer had the means to follow through effectively. Their dawn and dusk patrols were token tigers of little consequence. Generally, we had more bullets than targets; they had more targets than bullets.

Batfish and her many sisters covered Japan's only remaining link to extraterritorial supplies: the Sea of Japan. To get there, we had traveled almost 9,000 miles. If Russia, with a coastline on this sea, were to clamp off this final transfusion from Manchuria and Korea, Japan's prolonged resistance could mercifully end. But still Stalin made no move.

There was no air strike for 24 July. Submerged for the day, we caught up with minor repairs. Lacking anything constructive (or destructive) to do, scouting fruitlessly while waiting for someone to fall into the water, we became restless and ill at ease. We scanned our sketchy area-intelligence books for a shore target worth shooting up; anything that would help end this stubborn war, but not so involved or distant that we could not effectively respond to lifeguard call.

On the chart we picked Nagata, a village on the northwest coast of Yaju Shima, about fifty miles south of Kyushu's southern tip. At first sight, Nagata was asleep; the two lookout stations north and south of it seemed to be sitting there at ease. We maneuvered to within 3,500 yards of the south beach, then barrelled to the surface, manning all guns.

Before we got off our first salvo, about twenty people on the beach vanished from the shore. Spotted for the barrage by high periscope and from the bridge, our 40-mm went to work putting practically all its shells into the town. The five-inch gun opened fire on the squat lookout tower within a small encampment with beach defenses, demolishing a barracks and putting a big hole in the barbed-wire barrier. The first ten rounds, three of which were duds, raised smoke and dust so thick that further hits couldn't be observed. The five-incher shifted to the business district of the town, but after nine rounds into it, smoke and dust again prevented spotting. A direct hit destroyed one of the larger shore-front buildings.

By now the dust at the camp had settled a little, so our five-incher swung to bear on it once again. One round burst directly over the remaining barracks, probably exploded by hitting an overhanging tree limb. Both areas were obscured by smoke and haze. Flames licked here and there through the gloom. It was certain we had made other direct hits that couldn't be observed.

Then, as swiftly as we came, we left the scene before their artillery could become effective. Behind us, more of the town and camp had caught fire, but there were no large explosions usually associated with fuel or munitions dumps. Perhaps we could have knocked out the north lookout tower, but what shore defenses they might have there would surely be ready for us.

Other than exchanging recognition signals with *Pomfret*—joining *Batfish*, *Sandlance,* and *Spikefish* in the "Texas League," the code name for our lifeguard pack—25 July passed without event as we patrolled northwest along the Takao-Sasebo route. Early in the afternoon, we tried to sink an empty life raft with gunfire—but it was made of cork!

Now we were getting our requested two radio communications each night from Okinawa, and for the first time thought we were on top of developments. We had been lifeguarding ten days now; there hadn't been any air strikes we knew of. Perhaps this meant we would have one soon. We submerged and closed Noma Misake.

Midmorning the next day, we sighted a PBM and eight P-51s— our air cover for a strike just beginning. To our surprise, they told us that there had been six or seven strikes within the past ten days. We'd had no dope on any of these, only on the ones canceled on 19 and 23 July.

They left us behind at 1 P.M. No strike! Other than the Japanese dusk patrol, we saw nothing further in the sky or sea, until an hour before midnight, when three searchlights slashed the sky over Kyushu. We stuck around, surface patrolling at the eastern edge of Kagoshima Wan, a long bay with a narrow mouth. From this vantage point, we could keep watch on both the seaward and bay side coasts at once. A Japanese naval base was known to be deep up in the bay. Since anything coming or going from there would have to pass in front of us, we camped on this crossroads.

Shortly after midnight, an IFF was flashed at us from the northeast off the ocean coast. A Japanese submarine, mistaking us for her sister, was saying hello. Not illogical. Then we sighted a dim red light on the coast, probably put on so that our challengers could enter Kagoshima Wan. Or maybe it told her who *we* were. Speechless, we dove and sped away, across the mouth of the bay and abeam her probable route to base.

Around the cape she came, tracked by our SJ radar. Running within 300 yards of the beach at about twenty knots, she entered the bay. We tried to close in a northeasterly approach. Just as Sound was getting a reading on her smooth, quiet screws, she dove.

Submerged, we ventured across the bay—which *had* to be mined— to intersect her assumed course. She knew the paths of safety, and we didn't. Now, where would *we* have laid a minefield if this were *our* bay?

Our charts were so bare of data that our best navigation was pure hunch, our best chart probably a prayer book. But we wanted to get a shot at her so badly we proceeded with the unknown minefield probably on our left, the unseen submarine probably on our right.

At dawn, our target surfaced abruptly on predicted course and began heading for her barn at flank speed. Submerged at five knots, we closed her to within 7,000 yards, but she beat us to the pass and cleared out ahead of us. We watched her wag her tail until she was out of sight, then headed back to lifeguard station.

One uneventful day later, we intercepted a distress signal on the emergency aviation channel we monitored. Apparently this bomber had believed he could make it home to Okinawa and had ditched well beyond us, ninety miles to the south. Subsequent messages sounded like a PBM would land and pick up the three men in the water. But since we were the nearest sub, we set out at flank speed to attempt rescue anyway.

At about 4 P.M. we heard that a B-17 had dropped a life raft to his people in the water. Good news, for there was no way we could make it there before dark. Then two hours later, we learned the men were in the boat, but the circling PBM couldn't set down because of increasing wind and seas. We alerted Okinawa that we were heading down and gave them our estimated time of arrival.

Many friendly planes were in the air, high and low. Some tried to give us a hard time, causing delay by forcing us under. At one point we had to whisk down our high periscope to save it from a zoomie skimming the waves.

Running low on fuel, the PBM left the flyers behind at about dusk. Slowed considerably by high wind, heavy seas, and exasperating crash dives, we were now an hour and a half from reaching them. We asked Okinawa if there would be a relief plane to orbit the survivors. Negative. Had they a light and flares in the raft? Again, negative.

Running south at full speed, we arrived at their reported position in pitch-blackness. Unless they had a light to show, we would never find them. Lookouts doubled up on the periscope shears, but in these dark waters a life raft would be as hard to spot as a drifting mine. After sending off flares every fifteen minutes or 8,000 yards for most of the night, we knew we should probably give it up. The weather was miserably rough but not yet a typhoon; we were pitching and rolling and making so much spray we could definitely be better lifeguards with some daylight on the subject. But although they were known to be in the raft—the best of a bad situation—they could be bleeding to death. So we persisted in the search.

At 10:10 P.M. we picked up a distress signal on our lifeguard wavelength, and followed its bearing to the west. The signal increased in intensity as we chased it for forty miles, until it was saturated all around the dial. When we were two miles south off Akuseki Jima, the signal disappeared. This had to be intentional deception; no doubt the enemy knew the search was on. The rules exempting hospital ships from attack should apply in a rescue situation, but the Japanese obviously disagreed.

Back on location, we continued the search throughout the night assisted by a passing friendly patrol plane. It could have been no more than a well-intentioned gesture—they couldn't see anything either.

Come first light, our search pattern was the familiar expanding square, starting outward from their last reported location. The PBM came back at dawn, covering more territory more quickly than we could. After he relocated them and homed us in with fresh directions, we sighted the raft at 9:30 A.M. and were within a hundred yards of the survivors before they knew we were there.

Crowding on the bridge, we were close enough to see an expression of utter astonishment on their faces when they looked up and saw us. Two swimmers dove into the water to secure a line to the raft so we could draw them in. All three were injured; our pharmacist's mate supervised their removal to our deck. The man least visibly banged up complained of back pain and numbness in his legs. He was carefully strapped to a stretcher and lowered vertically down the hatch. The others made it with a little less help.

The flyer with back pains was taped to a flat board and laid upon Captain Small's bunk, then closely watched. His injury most alarmed our "doctor." Another flyer had a severe headache—probably a concussion, but not extremely alarming, since he remained conscious. The pharmacist's mate eased his pain with narcotics, and he was put to rest in a two-man state-room. The third had a tremendous gash on his leg, opened from the knee to the ankle with the bone laid out. It was treated with a thorough coating of sulfa powder, then wrapped with bandages and splinted. Fortunately there was no sign of infection as yet. All three had numerous minor lacerations and bruises and were suffering from shock and exposure. Each was given a liberal ration of "depth charge" whiskey to relax and warm him up.

29 July 1945

We don't know the situation on Okinawa and are not criticizing, but at 7:45 P.M. the survivors were definitely located with us 1½ hours away. If this base could possibly have provided a plane to drop a couple of one-hour flares for the boat to stay close to, three badly injured and shocked men would have been saved a cold, wet, miserable twelve hours in a boat with a twenty-five-knot wind and a force five sea.

We destroyed their raft with gunfire and began the eight-hour surface run back north. *Batfish* was by now about 140 miles south of lifeguard station, inside the island chain. Sighting the usual friendly planes throughout the day, at midafternoon we received a report of a fighter plane down and headed for his position. But before we got there, we heard that the pilot, the plane's only occupant, was definitely dead.

By sunset the three aviators had recovered from their ordeal enough to tell us what had happened to them. Dropping their bombs in the vicinity of Sasebo, just above Nagasaki, they had been well on their way back to Okinawa when ack-ack tore their plane in half. The tail section with three men in it spun down, disintegrating when it hit the water at 125 knots. Aflame, the forward section with these three men in it half spun and half glided into the sea. Unable to clear a life raft from the sinking wreckage, they swam like hell to escape its final explosions. Their aircraft located them within minutes and dropped a raft. They were very fortunate.

We asked them why they had looked so amazed at spotting us. They said they didn't know the United States had lifeguarding subs out here—at first they'd thought we were Japanese! Either they weren't briefed for their own rescue, or these particular flyboys had been goofing off during the briefing.

Just before dawn, we submerged and closed Suwanose Jima from about 10,000 yards. Coming south yesterday on our survivor hunt, we thought we had seen an anchored seaplane and a large sampan. Probing the coast, we were caught in a swift tide rip and pulled within 500 yards of the beach before we could turn and head back out. There was no enemy craft of any kind in that area.

We surfaced to proceed to station, the thunder of our bombers high above us in the sky. The sky was full of friendlies all the way back, but also a few enemies here and there. We witnessed no dogfights, but on five occasions we had to dive to avoid.

On the morning of 1 August, we could see our bomber squadrons flying north toward the Kyushu mainland, five miles off our starboard beam. Visibility was excellent for a change, and many of us were granted permission to witness the awesome spectacle from the bridge. We'd come a long way in this war. Surely with all this unrestricted might streaming northward with such little obstruction, we wouldn't have to wait much longer.

"Flash them an IFF," Small directed.

The quartermaster snatched up the light and passed the recognition code. "IFF acknowledged, Captain," he replied in a moment.

Then, from the ordered ranks of the lethal air armada, one single plane peeled out of formation in a graceful turn and flattened out directly toward us. We thought the squadron was splitting up for separate targets, but no one followed him. Maybe he was coming over to thank us: the Army Air Corps knew we had their men. Dropping altitude and coming in at two miles, apparently we were in for some close harassment by a pilot with a warped sense of humor.

"Aircraft is opening his bomb bays!" a lookout screamed. "He's coming right up our tail!"

"Clear the bridge! Emergency! Move it!"

We cleared the hatch without touching a rung. In grim determination, the quartermaster stayed topside flashing our identification at the equally determined friendly.

"Clear the bridge!" Small shouted. "You, too!" The quartermaster leaped from the shears and in one bounce was down the hatch, with both hands and full weight slamming it shut as *Batfish* broke her own record going under.

A cluster of American bombs walked toward us. *Batfish* trembled as they rumbled past our port beam, before our stern had cleared the surface. At 200 feet, fishtailing away from the attempted fratricide, word came up from the rattled aviators. Although not hysterical, they were unabashedly unnerved by the noise and unseen commotion and wanted to know what was happening. Apparently flyers need to *see* what's going on.

When things had settled down, Captain Small went below to speak with them. "It seems that some of your people don't like us," he responded. "We were nearly bombed."

"But don't they know we're here?" an incredulous pilot blurted.

Small gave him a moment to find the answer.

"Did you?"

The pilots looked at each other. "I'd report him, sir. Did you get his number?"

Small nodded.

"You get us back to base," the third pilot called from across the narrow corridor, "and we'll back you up. I mean solidly, Skipper."

Captain Small agreed that he would report the bomber—standard operating procedure in any case.

"One thing more, Captain. Could you get us off this submarine?" Despite the best accommodations in the house, they were not comfortable aboard our boat. Small said he'd see what he could do, then returned to the conn.

Once these three got back in the air, it wasn't likely that they would forget who we were. They, at least, had learned a lesson that could do with some passing around.

When we surfaced an hour later, we monitored more friendly planes on SD at seven miles but couldn't see them; the sky was darkly overcast with heavy brown clouds and the wind and sea were rising. However, they did see us. One plane said that there was a "bogey in the water." "You drop," another replied, "I'll spot for you." We dove and rode this raid out submerged. Even though our contract with the Air Corps said we should be visible like a beacon, we'd had enough target practice at our expense.

We surfaced just after dark to report our near-bombing and request ComSubPac's permission to transport our passengers to Okinawa, a three-day round trip to the south. Permission was granted to discharge our injured pilots, but our destination was changed to Iwo Jima, twice as far away. We proceeded southeast at best speed in a typhoon.

Just before dawn, we passed a floating mine. The sea was too rough to play with it; but it missed us by twenty feet! We passed another one in the early afternoon, but it was still too rough to do anything but gingerly avoid. That evening we received an unprecedented message: "PILOT ADMITS BOMBING YOUR SUB X DELIGHTED THERE WAS NO DAMAGE X PILOT APOLOGIZES X PILOT NO LONGER A PILOT X"

Well, hallelujah! Our aviators seemed almost as pleased at this news, as with our ETA at Iwo Jima of about noon on 4 August.

They disembarked cheerfully, grateful to be back on dry land. This seemed curious to us, who had never considered the Wild Blue Yonder to offer very secure footing. Our pharmacist's mate accompanied his patients in the small boat that would transport them safely into the care of the Flight Surgeon, Seventh Fighter Squadron of the U. S. Army.

Our doctor-striker reported back with a smile on his face. The flyboys were in good hands and reasonably good shape, but the back injury had turned out to be a broken spine.

We were thankful that we had been able to accommodate him so gently, except for the one crash dive.

We tied up at Iwo a little over twenty-four hours to top off *Batfish*'s tanks and repair the master and auxiliary gyros that had gone on the blink coming there. We got a new five-inch gun seat and fresh provisions, "borrowed" some green flares, then got under way at 6:30 P.M. under escort of *PC-1259*.

On 6 August we were back on lifeguard station—about halfway between Iwo Jima and Tokyo, near Lot's Wife. The evening's radio reception carried a cryptic piece of news. Earlier the same day, an American bomber had dropped a single bomb on Hiroshima, which *completely* destroyed the city. The radio-press report called this incredible weapon an "atomic" bomb.

As inconceivable as this secret weapon was to us, it was not likely that we had only one of them. It was illogical that the Japanese would permit any more of their cities to be totally incinerated. Surely now they would surrender.

The next day all thoughts were on the evening news ahead. We learned of further Allied victories along the island chains leading to Japan, and on isolated outposts cut off from the war. Operation Barney had been successful beyond expectation. No details were transmitted, but our imagination went to work, picturing them sweeping through the Sea of Japan like a school of hungry sharks on an incoming tide; then, triumphantly exiting through the northern La Pérouse Strait between Hokkaido and Karafuto, a few miles off the coast of Russia. But there was not one word of Japanese intention to surrender.

During 8 August, we lifeguarded west of yesterday's station. We weren't sure who our air cover was, but a B-24 using a call that was not our cover circled us much of the day. Since he seemed to know who we were, we decided he'd do.

The evening news of 9 August was sweet and sour. Nagasaki had been destroyed by a second atomic bomb. And finally, on this ninety-first day since Victory in Europe, neutral Russia had formally declared war on Japan, obviously entering only for the spoils.

For the next four days we did nothing but zigzag unproductively on station with our eyes and ears open. Each day, we thought, *this* has to be the last day of the war. It was tense and dull, relieved only by the sighting and sinking of drifting mines.

At eleven minutes before noon, 15 August, we received a message from ComSubPac, sent to all naval units—the message we had all been waiting for.

U.S.S. BATFISH
Naval Message

HEADING: NUBO V NPM -OP-A-NPM1 15φ124 ADFU COUP TART GR 26 BT

THE PRESIDENT HAS ANNOUNCED THAT JAPAN HAS ACCEPTED OUR
CONDITIONS AND THAT V-J DAY WILL BE PROCLAIMED UPON FORMAL

SIGNING OF THE SURRENDER TERMS BY JAPAN BT 15ϕ124 AR
TOR:ϕ232/LR-VAR/355KCS/15AUG'45
FROM: RDO HONOLULU, T.H. (1)   15AUG'45
TO: ALL US NAVAL AND SHORE ACTIVITIES   OPERATIONAL PRIORITY

There was no spontaneous jubilation aboard *Batfish*—probably because we had overrehearsed for it.

Then we copied:

"Cease offensive operations against Japanese forces. Continue search and patrols. Maintain defensive and internal security measures at highest level and beware of treachery or last-minute attacks by enemy forces or individuals."

The peace wasn't yet signed; there were always some who didn't get the word—or didn't want to hear it. Remnants and stragglers from the Japanese fleet had been ordered to come home; their passage would take them through these waters. We didn't relax our guard.

At 4:43 A.M. two diverging torpedo wakes were spotted, bubbling through the water toward *Batfish*'s bow. We zigged hard right at emergency speed and rigged for collision. Bulkhead doors and hatches clanged shut, and the bridge party tumbled down the hatch. The air induction valves closed and the engines cut off. Our motors whirred as our propellers drove us into the sea.

At 250 feet we listened silently for half an hour. Although Sound reported nothing and our ears had not picked up any sound through our hull, the OOD, JOOD, and forward lookout all swore to their sighting. The skipper hadn't seen them, but no man aboard was going to doubt the sudden cry of a lookout sighting danger!

We surfaced cautiously into the warm, moonlit night. That evening's Fox schedules confirmed our scheduled departure. The war and our seventh war patrol had ended the same day! U.S.S. *Tigrone* was to relieve us on station; we were ordered to rendezvous with her to take aboard an aviator she had rescued. This was accomplished before midnight. As *Tigrone* cast off for southern Honshu, we flashed, "Be careful." Her reply was, "You, too."

At midnight we crossed the eastern boundary of our patrol area—homeward bound. In a moderately choppy sea, *Batfish* stood to the southeast toward Guam, leaving Honshu and the rest of the war-ravaged Empire Islands at the end of her lengthening wake. The following day found us well out of Japanese waters.

196

That evening we were ordered to change course for Midway. Sensing our need for celebration, Captain Small told the pharmacist's mate to break out some "depth charge" whiskey from the safe—two ounces per man. Not a hell of a lot, but the wave of smiling and shouting and backslapping and handshaking that swept *Batfish* was truly marvelous. We toasted everything good we could think of—a tiny sip at a time—and ended up clinking glasses with our flyboy, toasting the damned Air Corps while he toasted the damned submariners. With the last drops of the whiskey, we toasted *Batfish*—she was three years old this week.

The next day brought no hangovers, but "Wouldn't it be nice to have one?" The day and sea were pleasant, so Captain Small let some of the enginemen come up to stand watch, for sun and fresh air.

Jittery, one of these lookouts was hyper-alert for danger upon his unaccustomed perch. His sudden cry of a plane zooming in on us from the west broke the calm. The OOD punched the alarm and we scurried below. Last lookout down the hatch, the nervous kid snagged the inflation ring to his Mae West and it blossomed out wedging him tight in the opening. Planing under the water, *Batfish*'s decks were awash. Still topside, the quartermaster jumped on the kid's shoulders, as men below pulled on his legs. He popped into the conn like a cork, followed by the quartermaster and a torrent of seawater.

The sprawl of bruised humanity sprang for the hatch, slammed it shut, and dogged it down. We went deep, maneuvering to the left to give the plane time to lose our swirl. Slowly, we crept back up to periscope depth and saw our plane—an albatross soaring as peaceful as the moon.

Sometimes skippers think OODs and lookouts see things that aren't there, and sometimes OODs and lookouts just about shit a brick waiting for the skipper's "Dive, Dive, Dive!" When you make thousands of dives, you're bound to goof on one or two.

It was all the same to us: we dove without question and sought concealment's options; fight, or flee and fight a little later. And this is why we were still alive—and why the war was over.

Half an hour later we were back on the surface, heading for home—with a new lookout.

On 22 August *Batfish* entered the lagoon at Midway, her wartime mission accomplished. Here, our aviator was transferred ashore suffering a chronic case of seasickness. The following day we departed, arriving at Pearl Harbor on 26 August.

As MacArthur and Nimitz signed the formal Japanese surrender aboard the battleship *Missouri* in Tokyo Harbor, *Batfish* departed Pearl on 2 September 1945—for home, for peace, *for good.*

EPILOGUE*

Batfish arrived in San Francisco on 9 September 1945. World War II was over! All of *Batfish*'s men went home on thirty-day leave, and all but her career submariners would shortly be mustered out of service to begin their reentry into civilian life. For most of us, coming out of this war was as abrupt as going in. The homes and lives we'd left were not the same ones to which we now returned; and we certainly weren't the same people coming back. Four years of war had intervened—on a submarine! After that, very little seemed familiar; nothing was the same.

Batfish herself went into the Mare Island Shipyard for "inactivating overhaul," to prepare her for peacetime service.

Then on 6 April 1946, she was decommissioned from the Regular Navy and assigned to the Pacific Reserve Fleet as a training vessel.

Following war's end, teams of American investigators had gone into Japan to tally and evaluate her wartime shipping losses and damage claims to *her* enemy. At about this time, the Joint Army-Navy Assessment Committee (JANAC) had tortuously arrived at an estimate of the war's toll, combining whatever Japanese records had survived destruction with American claims of damage inflicted and sustained. Their conclusions were impressive.

Many American claims weren't credited because the Japanese had no records of ships we claimed to have sunk, much less of their sinkings. Apparently many Japanese died anonymously on ships that didn't exist, sadly losing their identities along with their lives. (As a possible insight into the state of available records, the navigator of *Batfish*'s third submarine victim—whose log we fished from the water—had made no entries for *over two months*.) Also, a number of completely or partially sunk Japanese ships were refloated, refitted and sent out to fight or freight again. In some cases, salvaged bows or sterns were reconstituted into "new" vessels with altered identities and missing or misleading papers.

Although JANAC credited only sinkings substantiated beyond a doubt by both sides, the verified Japanese losses from all war causes— planes, surface vessels, mines, shore bombardment, and submarines— were nonetheless extremely heavy. Before these results were finally

---

*Portions of the Epilogue are reprinted with permission of Major Books, from the book *I-Boat Captain* by Zenji Orita with Joseph D. Harrington, © 1976 by Joseph D. Harrington.

tabulated, no one had fully realized the cumulative effectiveness of the American fleet submarine, and the awesome value of concealment and tactical surprise in naval warfare.

The final JANAC figures are eloquently explicit about the part U.S. submarines played in what many historians refer to as the "Air War." Combined U.S. forces sank about 10 million tons of Japanese shipping, of which approximately 8 million tons were merchant vessels; the rest, warships. Submarines sank more than half of this combined tonnage (54.6 percent to be precise)—a total of 1,314 ships, or 5.3 million tons of shipping, *credited by JANAC.*

Land-based and carrier aircraft sank about a third of the total: 929 ships for 3 million tons. The remaining 1.4 million tons of Japanese shipping were sunk by mines, miscellaneous causes, and surface craft—in that order.

American subs sank 60.4 percent of all merchant vessels lost by the Japanese: 1,113 ships for 4.8 million tons, although aircraft claimed 41 more Japanese warships than did submarines (by a 247,000-ton lead). The combined American air forces sank 687 merchant ships totaling 2.25 million tons. The JANAC tonnage figures and cargo inventories sunk in the Pacific are but educated guesses, reinforced by hindsight, and minimized by missing Japanese records.

Few nations were more dependent on shipping exchange than Japan, who even in peacetime had to import huge quantities to survive, let alone prosper. Japan's population density was double that of India. At peace or war, she had to import at least 20 percent of her basic food supplies and about a third of her industrial raw materials. And there was no way Japan could internally provide the metal necessary to her war effort.

Absolutely dependent on foreign trade, Japan's principal cities were seaports. Coastal shipping carried most of her intra-island freight, and inter-island steamers linked the main ports. Thus the sinking of *any* Japanese merchant ship produced a manifold loss: the ship itself, her cargo, the loss in manpower and time. Delays to shipping caused by bottlenecked ports under submarine blockade, time lost to convoying and evasive routing, damage to cargoes water-soaked but not lost, damaged ships unable to return to war, lives lost or incapacitated—all these are unobtainable figures.

And so the submarine attrition of Japanese shipping, however disconnected it seemed in its specific applications, was overwhelmingly disconnecting in its overall effect.

Despite the JANAC statistics, the discrepancy in many history books initially reflected the secrecy necessary to preserve the security and effectiveness of the Service's operation. But this silence about the Submarine Service persisted long after most World War II records had been declassified.

But the achievement of the submarine force was considerable. This Silent Service, which in 1,700 separate war patrols caused more than half of Japan's sea losses, numbered *less than 1.6 percent of the total U.S. naval strength* during the war. These sinkings, which took almost half a million Japanese lives, were made at the heaviest relative cost of American lives of any branch of the U.S. Armed Services, including the Marines. For every American surface sailor killed in action, six submariners lost their lives. One out of every seven American submariners died: 3,505 officers and enlisted men. The Service lost one out of every five submarines: fifty-two sunk or "missing, presumed lost."

Batfish, in seven war patrols, claimed a total of fourteen sinkings that *we* were sure of, for 37,000 tons, and damaged two other ships. JANAC officially credited *Batfish* with only six and a half sinkings, for a total of 11,248 tons. This accreditation was par for the statistical course. Generally, American submarines were credited with only half of what they sank—or claimed twice as many ships as were later substantiated.

At any rate, JANAC accorded *Batfish* the definite sinkings of three enemy submarines. But even here the records are confused, particularly as to the identity of the first submarine *Batfish* sank on 9 February 1945.

Some records indicate it was the *I-41,* others the *RO-115,* and still others, something else. To the best of available knowledge, there is general agreement about the second and third submarine victims: *RO-112* and *RO-113.*

I-Boat Captain, by Zenji Orita (one of the few surviving Japanese submarine skippers) with Joseph D. Harrington, states "U.S.S. *Batfish* claims to have sunk a third submarine before getting these two, but I think American crewmen interpreted a premature explosion as a hit. We lost no other boats in that area at that time. . . ."

Elsewhere, Orita states generally of *RO-35* (and succeedingly numbered) class submarines, and specifically of *RO-55*: "This type submarine was much favored by Japanese captains. [They] proved highly maneuverable and seaworthy, so eighty improved versions ... were authorized. Only eighteen were actually built. They were 280 feet long and could make 19.7 knots on the surface, eight submerged. Range was

5,000 miles at sixteen knots, or 11,000 miles at twelve. Underwater endurance was forty-five hours at five knots. They mounted four bow torpedo tubes and . . . a high-angle 80-mm gun forward, plus a twin 25-mm on the after end of the conning tower. All but one of these boats (*RO-55*) were lost in the war. . . ."

Later, it is stated that *RO-55* went down on 7 February. "Lieutenant Commander Koichiro Suwa and his crew were not long out of a shakedown training when they left Kure on January 27. The last word received from Suwa was on February 2. Five days after that, west of Manila, he tried to attack a convoy of ships heading for Leyte Gulf. The destroyer escort *Thomason* picked him up on radar and sank his ship. . . ."

Although not otherwise identifiable at the time, the total destruction of a Japanese submarine was clearly visible from *Batfish*'s bridge and definitely registered on SJ radar, APR, and Sound. The loading list of *RO-55* was since recovered by our Office of Naval Intelligence.

In the final analysis, our *first* Japanese submarine sinking seems to have been the *RO-55*—definitely in our area at the time of our definite sinking of a Japanese submarine. "At the end of January, four submarines were ordered to northern Luzon for this [evacuation] work. *RO-46* was the only submarine that successfully brought passengers home."

Newest of the three IJN submarines, *RO-55*'s keel had been laid on 5 August 1943 at the Mitzu Zosen Shipyard in Tama. Launched 23 April 1944, she was commissioned on 30 September the same year, Lieutenant Commander Koichiro Suwa commanding. Mechanical failures plagued *RO-55* as her captain attempted to get his inexperienced crew into fighting shape. Her extensive shakedown finally completed, *RO-55* departed Kure, Japan, on 27 January 1945.

After passing the west coast of Luzon, she proceeded to her patrol area on 1 February, but was rerouted later the same day to Formosa, where she was loaded with ammunition. Two days later she proceeded to Aparri, North Luzon, to exchange cargoes.

In the early morning hours of 7 February, *RO-55* was unloaded. High-ranking military and civilian officials fleeing MacArthur's return from the south crammed aboard her, along with considerable cargo. Early evening on 9 February, *RO-55* departed for the relative safety of Formosa.

Unaware that *Batfish* stalked her from the dark eastern horizon,

IJN submarine *RO-55* moved toward the pass between Fuga and Camiguin islands at a speed of fourteen knots, on a direct route north. Here she was attacked and sunk by *Batfish* on 10 February 1945, with Captain Suwa, a crew of forty-five, and forty-two passengers aboard. There were no survivors.

The keel of *RO-112* had been laid on 20 June 1942 at the Kawasaki Juko (Kobe) Shipyard. She was launched on 25 March 1943 and commissioned 14 September, Lieutenant Commander Jun Yuji commanding. After shakedown training in Japanese waters, she patrolled the areas of Surabaja, Australia, Truk, Saipan, and the Philippines. During May 1944, she served in an eight-boat sentry line north of New Britain and New Ireland.

On 16 June *RO-112* began war patrol in the Marianas around Saipan. Returning home in early September, she departed for the Leyte Gulf area via Bungo Suido on 26 October. Her final patrol before her evacuation assignment took her to the China coast.

On 9 February *RO-112* arrived at Kao-hsiung, Formosa, from Kaoyu, China. There, like *RO-55*, she was loaded with fuel and supplies for General Yamashita's beleaguered forces and sailed immediately for the evacuation staging area of Luzon to unload her cargo and rescue stranded airmen whose planes had been destroyed. En route,

> She ran into the prowling American submarine, *Batfish*. Lieutenant Toroo Yuchi was taking *RO-112* to Aparri, and was just entering Babuyan Channel when another technique new to us was used against him—radar-controlled torpedo fire.... U.S.S. *Batfish* had radar so dependable she could use its ranges and bearings in solving the ballistic problem associated with firing of torpedoes, while the radars on our submarines even at the end of the war, were so primitive that they might be referred to in American slang as the "Model T" brand.

Fatally encountered by *Batfish* on 11 February 1945, *RO-112* went to the bottom with all hands.

RO-113 had been somewhat more successful than her sisters in offensive warfare, according to her log records. Her keel also was laid at the Kawasaki Juko Company, on 11 July 1942. Launched on 24 April 1943, she was commissioned 12 October, under the command of Lieutenant Commander Kiyoshi Harada. After shakedown training in home waters, she performed antisubmarine operations around the Ryuku Islands. During May and June of 1944, she patrolled around

Saipan and New Ireland. Then on 25 October she departed Penang to participate in operations in Bengal Bay, where she sank an unidentified Allied merchant ship on 6 November. Little more than a month later she reported sinking two more unidentified Allied ships. Departing Singapore on 20 January 1945, *RO-113* arrived at Kao-hsiung, Formosa, on 9 February, shortly after *RO-112.*

Having taken on cargo for delivery to Luzon, like her sisters, she departed for Aparri on 11 February 1945. Before reaching her destination, *RO-113* was intercepted and destroyed just before dawn on 13 February, by U.S.S. *Batfish.* There were no survivors.

"By the middle of February 1945, the (IJN) 6th Fleet was down to a total of seven RO-boats ... and six I-boat *Kaiten* carriers (midget suicide submarines). One of these had to be put into use as an underwater tanker, so critical was the shortage of fuel in Japan at the time. The situation seemed hopeless, our problems insurmountable."

During the war the Japanese lost a total of 134 submarines, not including midgets or *kaiten.* Accidents claimed 10 of them; of the remaining 124, American submarines sank 23. Approximately 10,000 IJN submariners died aboard Japan's diverse fleet of submersibles—roughly three times American submarine fatalities, with far short of American sinkings in recompense.

Japan had produced many different types of submarines—the smallest, largest, slowest, and fastest submersibles, including a series that carried aircraft upon its decks—instead of perfecting one and concentrating on using it effectively. Coupled with the waste of these "side shows," more than two thirds of Japan's submarines became increasingly engaged in defensive and supply missions, in a sense becoming the equivalent of underwater *marus,* often devoid of armament. For the Japanese to supply their distant outposts, concealment was critical, particularly when so many of these island bases were cut off from direct support. As the war progressed they had to be serviced by submarines if they were not to be left—as many had been—to "die on the vine." As a consequence, most Japanese captains never learned how to fight their subs aggressively to best advantage; and what once ranked with the world's best in submarine forces had by April 1945 deteriorated to "one lone submarine (*RO-50*) left to fight the enemy in the old manner with conventional torpedoes only."

Ironically, American submarining took an opposite course during World War II. Initially the Japanese invested great faith in their own submersibles, but American naval policy and shipbuilding held submarines in low priority until our great surface fleet was lost on 7 December 1941. By necessity, America suddenly concentrated on perfecting one standard model and was consequently able to mass-produce and train subs at an increasing rate.

Also by contrast with the Japanese, who began the war effectively fighting their submarines, U.S. subs started out performing a diversity of nonaggressive duties. An example of U.S. submarining at the time of the war's outbreak is here described by retired Rear Admiral John Kerr (Jake) Fyfe, present aboard U.S.S. *Dolphin* at the Pearl Harbor attack.

> *Dolphin* had just returned from "patrolling" off Wake Island—if patrolling can be defined as submerging for a day and night following a ship contact, and surfacing to report only after enough time elapses to render that report obsolete.
>
> *Dolphin* is a part of my life I would like to forget. We spent more time fighting the ship than we did the Japanese. I was the chief engineer and . . . it was a constant struggle just to keep her operating. The boat leaked water in and fuel oil out, dove like she was built to fly, and you never knew whether she would start down stern first, or bow first, or just sink on an even keel! In addition to all that, we had a skipper who was ready for Saint Elizabeth's, although they sent him out one time. . . . He was the classic example of the peacetime skipper who couldn't cut it when the chips were down.

By war's end, a saying circulated among the Japanese in Singapore that they could walk home on the tops of U.S. submarine periscopes. In actual fact, our numbers had so increased that we became extremely cautious lest we shoot each other. In *Batfish*'s seventh war patrol, for instance, we made twenty-one friendly submarine contacts and encountered only one Japanese naval vessel. In almost every way, *Batfish* was typical of her sister submarines. She had three skippers—average for the submarine service during the war period. Many submarines sank more enemy ships than *Batfish*: quite a few sank fewer. In our second and seventh patrols, we sank nothing. But on our sixth patrol we sank three submarines within seventy-seven hours.

Not simply a curiosity for the Book of Records, this unique achievement epitomized the JANAC conclusions so instrumental in the strategic reorganization of the postwar Navy. Regardless of the fact that

Batfish's victims were on the surface, did not detect our presence, and consequently did not evade or counterattack, the name *Batfish* resounded through the highest Navy chambers until her exploit had crystallized an idea that had only vaguely been considered before: a submarine was potentially the most effective weapon against other submarines.

Atomic energy, of course, was necessary for the true *submersible,* breaking forever its umbilical dependence on the surface for air. Heretofore, a submarine had been a surface vessel that could submerge, but must resurface. Aerial "torpedoes" with nuclear warheads could theoretically render battleships, aircraft carriers, planes, and stationary missile bases obsolete. As we now know, the effect of these revelations has changed the very nature of warfare and cast the longest shadow upon the future of mankind: invisible mobility with infinite firepower!

After six years of reserve duty, *Batfish* returned to active duty as the Korean War gained intensity. She received her reactivation overhaul in January 1952, and was recommissioned in March, Lieutenant Commander Robert J. Jackson commanding.

After six weeks of readiness training, she set course via the Panama Canal for Key West, arriving there 9 May 1952. As a unit of Submarine Division 122, U. S. Atlantic Fleet, she served the remainder of her commissioned career in training operations in the Caribbean and along the eastern seaboard. Inactivated for good on 5 May 1957 in the Charleston Naval Shipyard, she was decommissioned on 4 August the following year and assigned to the Charleston Group, U. S. Atlantic Reserve Fleet.

In the summer of 1959, *Batfish* was assigned as a naval reserve training ship at New Orleans, there redesignated in 1962 as an auxiliary submarine (*AGSS 310*).

United States submarine production was now exclusively of nuclear-powered types, built nearly as commodiously as ocean liners. The tie with the sea's surface severed, these "nukes" were capable of indefinite submergence and virtually unlimited range. The last fleet sub, U.S.S. *Bonefish II,* had been launched in 1959; no sisters to *Batfish* would ever be built again.

Batfish continued to serve at New Orleans until her name was struck from the Naval Vessel Registry on 1 November 1969. She was twenty-six years old. Obsolete, remembered by few, unknown to most,

Batfish's hatches were sealed. Empty of submariners for the first time, her fate was uncertain, limited to three possibilities: She could be given or sold to a foreign country. United States fleet submarines were now serving in the navies of Canada, Argentina, Brazil, Chile, Venezuela, Spain, Greece, Turkey, Italy, the Netherlands, Pakistan, and Japan.

She could be scuttled or cut up for scrap. Or she could become a permanent war memorial as a few of her sisters had—if someone would ask for her.

THE "EIGHTH PATROL"

If you spent enough money, you could put a submarine on Pike's Peak.

Dr. Glen Berkenbile,
Vice-chairman,
Oklahoma Maritime Advisory Board

In 1956 the United States Submarine Veterans of World War II formalized their unique bond by incorporating as a national fraternal organization with chapters in every state. As the Navy began to retire the obsolete fleet submarines in which these men had served, SubVet chapters in coastal states began acquiring them as war memorials for their communities—and themselves. The Navy was willing to give these men their old boats, so long as they could be afforded respectful upkeep to promote interest in the history, traditions, and contributions of the U. S. Navy.

Upon completion, the Arkansas River Navigable Waterway system, under way since the early fifties, would provide waterway transportation from the Mississippi River at its confluence with the Arkansas northwesterly into Oklahoma. Within twenty years, the dredging, widening, and lock-and-dam construction along the Arkansas would link Oklahoma with the Gulf of Mexico—and the oceans and ports of the world.

By 1969 the Oklahoma SubVets were particularly impressed with the U.S.S. *Drum* installation in a war memorial park alongside the battleship *Alabama* in Mobile, which drew over 300,000 paying visitors in its maiden year—ample to make the project solidly self-supporting, according to the Oklahoma SubVets' state commander, Albert C. "Ace" Kelly, a former lieutenant (jg) who had served during World War II on four submarines including the legendary *Wahoo*.

A delegation from the Oklahoma City and Tulsa chapters asked the Navy if they could adopt a retired submarine. On hand at the New Orleans Naval Yard was the U.S.S. *Piranha*, which the Navy agreed to turn over to them if they could fulfill the donation requirements. An undertaking of this magnitude would need funding and political support at state level.

Wanting the *Piranha* for his hometown, Republican State Senator

James Inhofe agreed to sponsor a bill accepting this gift for Oklahoma.

BE IT ENACTED BY THE PEOPLE OF THE STATE OF OKLAHOMA:
Section 1. For the purpose of operating a state memorial park to honor Oklahomans who participated so valiantly in World War II, the Korean campaign, and the Vietnam campaign, there is hereby established the Maritime Advisory Board, a state agency, to function as an advisory board to the Industrial Development and Park Department.

The bill made the *Piranha* a general responsibility of the Industrial Development and Park Department, which had come into existence when Oklahoma decided it ought to be enticing industry to the state while generally increasing and upgrading its state parks to entice industry's families.

The Maritime Advisory Board, although paper-clipped to Nigh's department by protocol, would have the "duty and authority . . . to acquire, transport, berth, renovate, equip and maintain the submarine U.S.S. *Piranha* and any other military equipment which may be obtained and used as a war memorial park" as well as "any additions thereto, labor, material and equipment therefore and any such purpose or others approved by the Maritime Advisory Board."

Once they had gotten the submarine, the board was empowered "to select and improve [an] appropriate" site for the vessel and "hire such laborers, artisans, caretakers, technicians, stenographers and administrative employees and supervisory personnel as may be necessary." A "Maritime Advisory Board Revolving Fund" was to be set up in which any money received would be deposited for use by the Industrial Development and Park Department for the Maritime Advisory Board's purposes. But the board itself didn't have any money. To raise the money they'd need to get the submarine situated as a paying attraction, the Industrial Development and Park Department *could* cause revenue bonds to be issued. Having detailed every imaginable power to the board, the bill concluded that "all obligations incurred by the Industrial Development and Park Department on behalf of the Maritime Advisory Board and all bonds issued by it shall be solely and exclusively an obligation of the Maritime Advisory Board and shall not create an obligation or debt of the State of Oklahoma, or any county or municipality therein."

209

The bill—which specified only where its funding was *not* to come from—was signed into law on 23 April.

When the brand-new Maritime Advisory Board convened for the first time, it elected as chairman ex-*Gabilan* Captain Karl R. Wheland, and Dr. Glen Berkenbile, a Muskogee surgeon, as vice-chairman. With over a year and a half before the waterway's opening there was plenty of time to form committees to acquire the park site, arrange for the donation of the submarine, and cost the project.

Nominally, Williams Brothers Engineering Company—one of the nation's largest oil-pipeline conglomerates—agreed to take on the engineering task. The initial reports claimed it was impossible to get a submarine as far upriver as Tulsa; it was because the Arkansas River Channel above Muskogee was not deep enough, and there were a couple of turns a submarine couldn't make because of its length. Senator John Luton stepped forward to claim the submarine for Muskogee. However, a later report also ruled out a direct tow upriver, even to Muskogee. The Army Corps of Engineers would maintain the waterway at a minimum depth of only nine feet; a fleet submarine draws at least 12 feet forward and 14½ feet aft—therefore a method of transport other than direct towing would have to be devised.

On 2 October 1970 the Muskogee City-County Trust Port Authority agreed to donate five acres of prime waterfront real estate—worth about $90,000 an acre—for the submarine berth and memorial park.

Then the submarine procurement committee met to transact preliminary arrangements with the Navy for *Piranha*'s transfer. The Navy would not hold *Piranha* unless the board made formal application for her, and they would have to take immediate possession once the donation contract was approved. Since the waterway would not be open for at least a year, interim docking charges would be prohibitive.

They decided to wait and take their chances. In September they inspected *Batfish*, an alternative. Although both submarines had suffered considerable neglect, *Piranha* ("out of commission, in reserve" since 1947) had been almost completely cannibalized. *Batfish* was much cleaner and better outfitted.

Nearly a year passed before the board made formal application—for *Batfish*, now mothballed beside *Piranha* at the Naval Inactive Ship Facility at Orange, Texas. She had a far better war record. Commissioned in February 1943, *Piranha* had made five war patrols, claiming

210

seven sinkings for 19,300 tons; JANAC, however, credited her with only one sinking—on her first patrol. The board was very impressed with *Batfish*, and the Navy made no objection to the last-minute swap. However, the change of names never made its way into the language of the Oklahoma legislation.

The donation contract was drawn up 24 June 1971. The Secretary of the Navy approved the transaction and on 26 August forwarded the contract to Congress for consideration. After a compulsory period of sixty days of continuous session without adverse action, congressional approval became automatic on 8 November.

Board Chairman Wheland signed the contract on 22 November 1971, and returned it to the Navy on 9 December. *Batfish* now belonged to Oklahoma—at least on paper. The board agreed to accept delivery at the Orange Naval Inactive Maintenance Facility on an " 'as is, where is' basis . . . without warranty of any kind."

Energetically at the forefront of the engineering and submarine procurement, Ace Kelly had also generated an estimate of the cost of getting *Batfish* to Muskogee—"about $100,000," he told the Maritime Advisory Board.

Brilliant and eloquent, Kelly had a degree in economics from Harvard and a graduate degree from the Wisconsin Graduate School of Banking. By the time the board finally got around to arranging *Batfish*'s funding, the waterway had already opened, and Ace Kelly was scurrying to combine *Batfish*'s arrival with the Muskogee Azalea Festival in April. He invited the Secretary of the Navy to be the principal speaker and arranged to have the Navy Band provide the music.

The board solicited three Muskogee banks for an aggregate loan of $100,000, to be secured by a bond issue once Kelly's estimate could be corroborated. The banks, however, said they wanted some time to think it over.

The towing was to be divided into two phases: a direct offshore tow from Orange to the Avondale Shipyard at New Orleans. Then, after Avondale raised and cradled *Batfish* between two pairs of baredecked barges on steel lifting straps, the 1,350-mile upriver tow would proceed.

Of the three marine surveyors bidding on the first phase, only the U. S. Salvage Corporation insisted on an expensive initial drydocking at Orange to prepare *Batfish* for the ocean tow—she was too wide for the Intercoastal Waterway. But only Lloyd's of London would accept coverage of the Navy's stringent insurance requirements (at a cost of nearly $11,000). Lloyd's required that *Batfish* be dry-docked near the

Navy Yard so that U. S. Salvage—the high bidder—could inspect her hull and prepare her for the voyage.

Karl Wheland resigned his job as an airlines executive and the chairmanship of the board to become the board's first salaried executive director on 24 January. He was succeeded as chairman by Ace Kelly. The Maritime Advisory Board took possession of *Batfish* on 18 February. The day before *Batfish* was scheduled to come out of the water, the Orange drydock went on strike. Since *Batfish* had a date with the Azalea Festival, Kelly forced the decision to tow her to the Bethlehem Steel drydock in Beaumont, Texas, seven hours upriver. There, after general inspection of her hull and compartments, all air salvage valves were made operable, fuel, oil, and most of her ballast were removed, and all her tanks were flushed clean. Then her hull openings were sealed. Thus lightened and safeguarded for the journey, she was towed on 1 March to the Avondale Shipyard in New Orleans. The board's credit was good for her $36,000 bill.

On 2 March Williams Brothers presented its formal feasibility "Study"—and an estimate. The cost of transporting and installing *Batfish* into her inland berth at Muskogee, exclusive of park development and modification of the boat for public viewing, would be about a quarter of a million dollars. It was anticipated that the Avondale Shipyard work would cost $25,000, followed by $18,000 for the tow to Muskogee and $11,000 for thirty days' barge rental and return. The estimate of Williams Brothers' feasibility study, engineering fees and project-supervision was approximately $44,000. Although services so far had cost more than twice their estimates, there was general confidence that everything would work out for the best.

At Avondale, it soon became obvious that the specified four barges would not provide enough buoyancy to reduce *Batfish*'s draft. The revised flotilla design, incorporating six 120-by-32-foot bare-deck barges, would be ballasted to the outside, bound together by steel stabilizing and breasting cables. Her periscope shears would ride roughly 39 feet above the water.

Avondale fabricated the steel lifting straps to suspend the submarine between the barges. Then an enormous crane partially lifted first *Batfish*'s bow, then her stern, so that divers could tack them to her hull. One of the lifting straps was discovered to be a foot or so shorter than the other five, and it was hastily lengthened to match the others. But when *Batfish* settled into her sling, it appeared the shorter strap had

212

been the right length—the other five had been too long! Avondale had to back up and reengineer the steel cradle. Rental equipment, steelworkers, welders, riggers, and dock workers all labored at time and a half and double time to meet Kelly's deadline.

On 13 March, the barges were partially secured to *Batfish* by lifting straps, but no cables had yet been placed to bind them together. At 3:32 P.M. an English tanker, the *Silvermain,* sped by at eleven knots in a five-knot zone. Her wake smacked the flotilla broadside at Avondale's Wet Dock #2. Two barges were seriously damaged and a third went to the bottom. The deck of the only barge not torn away from *Batfish* by the breakup was buckled by the strain, though *Batfish* herself escaped serious mangling. A tugboat Kelly had dispatched from Helena, Arkansas, to bring *Batfish* upriver had been standing by with its meter running.

While the Coast Guard investigated, Avondale conferred with the board's representatives. Pending the outcome of the claim against *Silvermain*'s insurers, *Batfish*'s new owners were expected to foot the entire bill. Avondale estimated the board's additional costs for replacement barge rental, salvage, repair, and its third assembly of the flotilla. For the time being, the sunken barge was left on the bottom–and on rental—at $900 a month.

Karl Wheland telegrammed the shipyard: "OKLAHOMA MARITIME ADVISORY BOARD GRANTS AUTHORITY TO PROCEED WITH REPAIRS TO SUBMARINE AND SUBJECT BARGES AS DISCUSSED TELEPHONE CONVERSATION THIS DATE. BOARD WILL ACCEPT CHARGES OF APPROXIMATELY FORTY THOUSAND DOLLARS"—payable within six months, plus 8 pecent interest.

The board had started out on a note of good luck and optimism. When they'd taken possession of *Batfish* barely a month before, the Muskogee banks had come through, primarily due to the influence of Ora Lamb, president of the First National Bank and Trust Company of Muskogee. Skeptical when board members first approached him in January, he listened thoughtfully and became convinced that the sub would be good for Muskogee: *Batfish* would be the first ocean vessel to test the maritime accessibility of this inland channel extending nearly to the center of the country. Her unprecedented voyage would enhance the waterway and the waterway would enhance Muskogee, as would *Batfish* herself.

The board had persistently asked its guardian, Industrial Development and Park Department, for the necessary bond issue. Bartlett's

213

defeat by three thousand votes had deprived the board of the only official influential enough to get things rolling in *Batfish*'s favor. Governor Hall now seemed disinclined to help them.

As the *Batfish* flotilla moved slowly up the map, propelled by two tugs at four knots, it was imperative that the bond issue be expedited—and obvious that it would have to be increased, to at least $300,000. On 3 May she passed with ease through Lock-and-Dam Number Six, but her superstructure would not clear a bridge on the way into Little Rock. The Army Corps of Engineers spilled enough water through Dam Number Six to drop the river level about three feet and *Batfish* squeaked under the bridge—clearing it by inches.

The tugs stopped at Little Rock to refuel and one then returned downriver. Then, under single tow, *Batfish* proceeded cautiously and even more slowly toward Fort Smith. Her signal flags were furled as she crossed the state line into Oklahoma.

Looking gray, rusty, and battered, *Batfish* crept alongside her temporary berth at the Will Brothers Port of Muskogee Terminal on the overcast Sunday afternoon of 7 May. A small convoy of gaily decorated pleasure craft had escorted her along the final leg of her thirteen-day journey. Several thousand curious spectators watched from bankside or moved in close to have a better look at her from the dock. Jubilant, Ace Kelly and friends cheered *Batfish* home from the sea from the deck of the yacht *Goodwill,* loaned for the occasion from the Helena Marine Company. The estimated thirty-day voyage had taken nearly three months.

Chilly winds and drizzle thinned the onlookers to about a thousand who lingered for the brief docking ceremony that began with the presentation of the colors. Master of ceremonies Kelly told the small crowd that *Batfish* "is immaculate inside and will be in fine shape by mid-June. It will take thirty-three days to refurbish" her. The public could not be safely permitted aboard until *Batfish* had been thoroughly ventilated; a strong petroleumlike odor made it impossible to stay inside for more than a minute or two. A lot would have to be done to the "old gray battler": sandblasting, repainting, refitting with steel plates and stairways to replace her ladders and sea hatches, replacement of rotten decking, and much more—all expensive. For now, *Batfish* remained captive to her seven barges—including the one on the bottom and its replacement—at the rate of $6,000 a month.

The department voted to authorize the $300,000 bond issue. As

214

an interim measure, they agreed to back the bank loans by signing a $200,000 promissory note for their temporary security.

In response to Avondale's request for authorization to salvage and inspect sunken Barge U-714 in order to determine the extent of its damage. Approval was then telegraphed in Kelly's name: FOR YOUR WORK, YOUR COMPANY SHALL BE PAID $8,000 WITHIN THIRTY-ONE DAYS AFTER RECEIPT OF INVOICE. This estimate didn't include the repair necessary to get the barge off rental and add its total damages to the hovering insurance claim.

With only $26,000 left in its bank account, the board would have to stretch these dollars until the bonds materialized. On the strength of the department's commitment, they contacted Midwest Dredging Company to dig a quarter-mile trench from the main channel to the foot of *Batfish*'s park site, north of the city cargo piers. The 120-foot-wide groove through the muddy shallows would be just deep enough to permit the intact flotilla to reach the bank, to which *Batfish* would be temporarily moored. Only then could the tug and barges go off rental.

While this dredging operation was under way, the Oklahoma Industrial Development and Park Department went out of existence. *Batfish*'s latest guardian—the newly formed Tourism and Recreation Commission—was headed by none other than Lieutenant Governor George Nigh.

The Maritime Advisory Board also underwent its own departmental shakeup. Since Kelly had control of the SubVets, who could outvote the more conservative board members, he had been running matters as he saw fit without consultation with Wheland or the board. A special meeting was called in Tulsa for the purpose of relieving Kelly of his chairmanship. But the SubVets felt this was Ace Kelly's submarine, and they backed him. He won by a single vote. The eminently capable Captain Karl Wheland then resigned as executive director.

Shortly after *Batfish* was moved into her temporary mooring, a metal ramp was borrowed from the Naval Supply depot at McAlester—courtesy of its commander, board member Captain Joe Chambliss—and at noon on the Fourth of July, *Batfish* was unofficially opened to the public.

Succeeding Wheland as executive director, retired naval officer Roy Smallwood cosigned a check for $13,000—more than half of the board's remaining money—to Midwest Dredging Company as first payment for the implacement of *Batfish* at the end of the trench; an equal amount, plus interest, was due on or before 1 October. Avondale had also billed an additional $13,000 for "ballast, disconnect, and repair" of five barges and strongly urged that someone come to New Orleans to settle their burgeoning bill. Still the new Tourism and Recreation Commission offered no information about the bonds, and Avondale's letters went unanswered.

Captain Smallwood was ruefully aware that *Batfish*'s bookkeeping, which he had inherited, had been chaotic. In late September he put together an optimistic budget for the coming fiscal year, predicting receipts of $136,000 including admissions, profit on souvenirs, sale of bonds, and the *Silvermain* settlement. *Batfish* had grossed nearly $8,000 during the two months she had been open, but her operating and restoration costs had exceeded that. There were no funds for the proposed ship's store with office space; there wasn't even enough income to restock souvenirs. Buyers were reported ready to purchase the entire $300,000 bond issue being prepared for sale by the end of September, but this money was largely already spent. There would be nothing left to reduce outstanding debts during the oncoming winter when admission receipts would be low or nil.

Indeed, it was encouraging that over eleven thousand visitors from all across the country and many foreign lands had found their way (via a rutted dirt road, a dusty weedy parking lot, a sand ramp, and a borrowed gangplank spanning twenty feet of muddy water) to pay their dollar to go aboard. In the dry language of accountancy, state examiners revealed payroll taxes to be $1,500 in arrears; and in addition to the $200,000 bank loan, there was owing to various suppliers, creditors, and engineering firms the amount of $188,000, nearly all past due. (The accountants could also not understand why the U.S.S. *Piranha* was now called *Batfish*!)

The balance of the Midwest Dredging bill had become overdue on 1 October. Doubly concerned because of the audit's conclusions, their attorneys met with Nigh. The lieutenant governor made it abundantly clear that his commission had no liability for *Batfish* and absolutely no intentions of incurring any. As a result, Midwest argued that if Oklahoma was not responsible for the $13,000 debt, and if the Maritime Advisory Board had no money, then the board members must be individually liable.

Avondale was sure to be next in line to sue for its $95,000 bill. At this point, Williams Brothers—with a $57,000 bill of its own—couldn't decide whose side it was on, for it had been the board's "company representative" in both the Midwest and the Avondale arrangements.

216

Nigh and the attorney general boiled out a damning press release. Beneath newspaper headlines declaring *Wrong Sub in Memorial? Debt Not Authorized, Either,* Nigh said "Legally, we are not obligated for one penny. Embarrassment-wise, we are in a pretty bad situation. . . . It's just this technical: they are an advisory board to us. They never advised us. I advised them that they could not go into debt. . . . We authorized them to sell $200,000 of the bonds with this instruction in our agreement that every bond sold had to have a personal guarantor on it at the bank. In other words, if the bonds default, there is a private citizen in Muskogee who has to pick up the tab. At no time can the banks look to the Tourism and Recreation Commission for money."

Until *Batfish* had a chance to become self-supporting, the only way to pay off her debts was through revenue bonds which the Tourism and Recreation Commission had voted to issue. But upon learning the extent of the debts, the commission balked, which led the banks to believe the department's promissory note had no value. The banks wanted to attach *Batfish* as something more tangible. The Attorney General concluded that "the undersea boat was brought to Muskogee at considerable expense before anyone in state government knew much about the details."

Ace Kelly was quick to tell the press that "the memorial's financial prospects are excellent." In fact, "the bonds are in the final 'mechanical stages' of preparation and should be issued anytime."

A *Batfish* conference, chaired by Admiral Kirkpatrick, was held on 30 October at the Muskogee Civic Center to discuss a financing program for the boat's continuing custody. It was agreed to seek a Muskogee Authority to own, operate, and develop the *Batfish* park. A committee was delegated to approach the City-County Park Authority. They also agreed to investigate ways to develop sound financial backing for the owner-operator-to-be.

As winter settled in on Oklahoma, without enough money in the operating fund to make it to the beginning of the tourist season in March, Executive Director Smallwood issued a press release. The Muskogee paper announcing, *"Batfish Needs to Hurdle Financial Crisis"* asked the headlined question, *"Naval Hall of Fame Here?"*

Captain Smallwood stated that by March *Batfish* would be relocated in an inland berth surrounded by a moat "if financing is provided." Landscaping, walks, lighting, and fencing would be completed by May. The following year a museum would be constructed and outfitted. In lieu of a battleship like they had in Mobile, the park museum would have a combat art exhibit, documents, and memorabilia.

Phase two of the development called for a motel and a 400-slip marina. Phase three would expand the museum building and marina complex to an eventual thirty acres. A Williams Brothers engineer estimated the total package cost at $1.4 million, plus some possible extras.

"It has been indicated that an EDA grant in the amount of $240,000 can be made available within the next few days if an adequate financial plan can be developed," Smallwood said. But the EDA funding did not materialize; nor did another application to the Ozark Regional Commission for $75,000. The Muskogee Port Authority declined the prospect of taking *Batfish* with so many dangling debts attached.

On 9 December Kelly wrote Nigh that he was notifying the Department of the Navy that they were unable to fulfill the obligations of the donation contract and asked that Nigh's commission immediately take custody and assume responsibility for operating and maintaining the memorial park. Serious vandalism had already taken its toll, requiring an unarmed security guard during *Batfish*'s dark hours. And there had been theft by person or persons unknown. Earlier that month, the Arkansas River had suddenly risen an ominous six and a half feet, damaging *Batfish*'s access ramp and loosening her tether seriously enough to force her closing for a week to effect repairs. The SubVets took the precaution of anchoring her to a sandbar by flooding her ballast tanks.

On 20 December the Tourism and Recreation Commission accepted custody of *Batfish*, mandatory under State Bill 650. Nigh's first move was to close *Batfish* down and disenfranchise her manager and crew. Before being "relieved of command," Smallwood had gotten from the Army Corps of Engineers an extension of *Batfish*'s permit for temporary mooring in the river. No one was even allowed aboard except rarely visiting officials and a security guard, whose arm was broken when a hatch cover fell on it.

On Monday, 12 March 1973, heavy spring rains flooded the Arkansas River. *Batfish* gave the appearance of tugging so violently at her mooring cables that the Army Corps of Engineers feared she would rip loose and crush the Muskogee port docks or the new U.S. Route 62 bridge downriver, blocking the channel. *Batfish* listed precariously to port in the rain-swollen Arkansas and her list increased as she opposed the current. Shifting sand and mud increased her tilt even more to nearly forty degrees.

Panicked into existence, a Chamber of Commerce Task Force met in emergency session. They felt that most of the money to save the sub might be raised locally, but it was critical that some government funds be found. "But with present money policies," the spokesman said, "I'm not holding my breath."

Nigh called a press conference to go over the latest developments. "Actually," he said, "there haven't been many . . . it's taken $400,000 to get *Batfish* this far along, which is either too far or not far enough. It would take another $400,000 to get the sub permanently moored in the proper surroundings. I think the Navy should take it back and make an agreement with somebody else. . . ."

Despite Nigh's comment that, "nobody is crazy about having her the way she is right now," Fort Smith gave some signs that it might be interested in taking *Batfish*. Roy Smallwood told the press there was considerable feeling among most Muskogee residents to keep her. A Chamber of Commerce spokesman declined to comment further until some definite plan was developed.

On 16 March Nigh flew to Muskogee to take a firsthand look at *Batfish*—and to meet a CBS television news crew. Extensive local coverage had escalated via the press services to the national media, which focused on *Batfish*'s desperate plight.

Muskogee Attraction/Batfish Listing in Flooding Arkansas. Woes Continue Piling Up for Batfish Submarine. Batfish Stew Brews/$400,000 Bill Provides Heat. Oklahoma Tries to Disown Noted Sub. Abandoned Sub Once Tourist Lure, Now River Menace.

For the first time, *Batfish* had the world's attention.

Nigh pitched his position to the world over national television: "Good men used bad judgment. . . . When this snafu surfaced, I told them not to spend another penny. But of course, I had told them not to spend the first penny, and they spent almost $400,000. The state maritime board brought *Batfish* to Oklahoma without permission of the state Tourism and Recreation Commission." But "I think this has done one thing—it has proved that the Arkansas River is navigable." His commission had unanimously voted to write the Navy requesting that the state be relieved of the ownership of the submarine. Asked what the Navy would do, Nigh quipped, "They can insist, but I don't think they will attack."

The Navy replied that it expected Oklahoma's continued conformance with its contract. *Batfish* was clearly an Oklahoma problem, not a Navy problem, and the Navy wouldn't respond officially until the state made official proposals. Nigh said he had arrived at three alternatives: The state could pay the debt and berth the boat. Another state, municipal, or private agency could do the same. Or Oklahoma could give the boat back to the Navy, though should that drastic alternative result, the Navy would require Oklahoma to return *Batfish* at its own expense.

Feeling that the most important thing was to save the boat, the Oklahoma SubVets offered to reinstate *Batfish*'s expired insurance coverage, dig the slip for her final berth and sand-dredge her into it, prepare her for public display, and proceed with construction of the museum building—at no cost to the Maritime Advisory Board, Muskogee, or the state. They contracted to pay the board one dollar a year for the lease of *Batfish*, with the understanding that the board itself would retain "total responsibility for all indebtedness prior to the date of the Agreement." They agreed to maintain the required bookkeeping and records and after covering operating expenses, to pay the old bills off from profits, should there be any.

Unbeknownst to the general public, there was a benign plot brewing. On 2 April Admiral John Kirkpatrick issued an emphatic directive that included a careful, clean plan that would get the job done—and an offer to carry it out—provided there was no interference. Upon *Batfish*'s public disgrace, Kirkpatrick had resigned from the board, but had been working effectively behind the scenes with the SubVets and Ken Meyer. Kirkpatrick said that as soon as evidence of the new Authority had been established, he would start proceedings at his own expense to move *Batfish* inland into a secure berth, giving the SubVets more time to develop her potential. Meyer told Nigh that he was prepared to take *Batfish* off his hands. No doubt had Kirkpatrick's plan been formally submitted for official approval through all the undredged channels of Oklahoma's molasses bureaucracy, his backing—which was "not to exceed $60,000"—would prove inadequate to get the job done. But as long as the river was still up, it wouldn't be necessary to dig such a big expensive hole in its bank. To rescue *Batfish* before the advantage of the flood was lost, Kirkpatrick simply announced his intention and went on with it.

The Admiral's move was tendered as a loan, not a gift; he expected to be repaid by the first gross revenues from the boat's operation, or from any other refinancing such as bonds.

Accepting these terms, the SubVets signed a contract with the Madden Construction Company from whom Kirkpatrick had obtained a firm estimate. The contractor would also put SubVet Bruce Weaver on his payroll to monitor the operation. The work was to be paid on behalf of the SubVets by Kirkpatrick at the end of each week.

In conformance with these developments, the Port Authority replaced its original donation of five acres with a long-term lease of nearly nine acres at one dollar a year, effective upon the Oklahoma legislature's confirmation of the Park Authority.

On 4 April, as earthmovers, D-7 bulldozers, draglines, and winches began biting a hole in the riverbank, a union put a picket line around the job site. Their main concern was that local workers were not being employed. When this problem was resolved, the picket line was removed and work resumed. The Muskogee City Council signed the documents creating the Muskogee War Memorial Park Authority. Ken Meyer was appointed to head its five-man board. By 19 April an additional 35,000 cubic yards had been excavated; and an amendment (to a $4.1 million appropriation for the Tourism and Recreation Commission) by Senator Luton to transfer *Batfish* from Oklahoma to Muskogee had passed the Senate. Then Oklahoma headlines proclaimed: *"Bulldozer-Boat Teamwork Eases Batfish into Berth"* and *"Batfish Finally Has Place of Her Own."*

At 6 A.M. on 21 April about twenty-five hardhats and SubVets began dredging away the sand and dirt "plug" between the slip and the river. The flooded slip was too shallow for *Batfish* to enter; the Arkansas had been dropping for days. But as the workers cleared away the throat of the slip, the Army Corps of Engineers released a bank of water they had thoughtfully stored behind a dam upriver. By the time the water in the slip had risen to the requisite fourteen feet, *Batfish* had been pumped out and floated into alignment with the slip, secured broadside to the strong current by cables. Then four bulldozers began to tug at her with 300-foot cables as a Port of Muskogee tug pushed from behind.

Her actual move from the river into the slip took only thirty minutes. By 4 P.M. *Batfish* was in, with nowhere to go but up. As the SubVet commander commemoratively rang a bell fifty-two times, the workers and spectators cheered, and the tugboat blew its whistle jubilantly.

Over the next week, the "plug" was replaced and the slip flooded to float *Batfish* twenty-four feet up to her final elevation. By 1 May *Batfish* had been realigned to overlook the Arkansas, thirty-six feet below her deck and zero degrees off her bow. Backfilling continued to displace

221

the water in her pond until she rested firmly upon the rising bottom. When her keel lay in four feet of firm sand, enough water was left in her holding pond to make her appear normally afloat.

The contractors' final bill had exceeded Kirkpatrick's budget by $246.50. When he sent the SubVets his last check, Kirkpatrick advised that someone else would have to provide the overage to the contractor and suggested a drive for donations. He cautioned the SubVets to adhere closely to all contracts, verify and substantiate all obligations, plan all moves with a definite time schedule and careful budget, and make especially certain they had a source of money *before* they spent it.

The SubVets worked hard to prepare *Batfish* for her Memorial Day reopening. Sandblasted, primed, and painted the year before, the flood had dulled her; they spruced her up with a fresh coat of paint. They repaired wooden decking, replacing sections that had rotted through, and straightened her bent propeller guards. She had taken in a lot of sand and muck, and many of her parts had gotten rusty, but under her original lighting (recircuited to outside power), she began to sparkle and gleam. Now Ace Kelly—chairman of a defunct Maritime Advisory Board with no assets, no liabilities, and no submarine— insisted on running the project his own way. Ken Meyer, on the other hand, was directly responsible to Muskogee's City Council.

Kirkpatrick was concerned that proper authority be clearly established before the coming Memorial Day weekend's opening ceremonies. He wrote the SubVets, "Albert Kelly has certainly devoted more time and energy to this project than anyone else, but that does not give him the right to confuse the management that is now in existence." Dreading the adverse publicity of a public scene, *Batfish*'s owners did not attempt to attend the opening ceremonies. Approximately fifty people turned out in the crisp, windy weather for the Memorial Day services. For the time being allowed the run of the deck, Kelly announced that the SubVets "had irons in the fire to acquire a PT boat and a Sherman tank to put alongside *Batfish* at the park."

On 13 June Admiral Kirkpatrick wrote the SubVet commander, to request again that his note be signed, and repeated his recommendation that a statement of the current financial status go to Ken Meyer, who had yet to receive any accounting. Kelly had even refused to take admission tickets. At the height of the tourist season, large crowds had been noted daily, visiting *Batfish*. Although it was not their wish to alienate the other SubVets, the authority requested police assistance to possess the *Batfish*, in case of trouble.

222

Although the Maritime Advisory Board ceased to exist when its successor was legally created, the SubVets' current newsletter stated that "the governor's Maritime Advisory Board met June 30, 1973 . . . for annual election of officers. A. C. Kelly was reelected as chairman. . . . This should quell any rumors that the board does not exist. Quite honestly, the board was set up by governor authority. If it ever ceases, it will be through the same authority."

The Navy had made it implicitly clear that if Oklahoma could not afford *Batfish* due respect, she would be put out of her misery by being honorably cut up for scrap. Another stream of negative publicity could do it.

Kelly made a last-ditch effort to hold on to his submarine. Under occupation, *Batfish* produced $1,176 in admissions over the next eight days, demonstrating that whenever she got any publicity at all, hordes of people would come to see her—for a few days. Conversely, when she received no publicity, even local people wouldn't turn out. True to form, the following six days produced only $425. On 13 July the SubVets canceled *Batfish*'s insurance. Perhaps realizing that *Batfish* would fare the worst for it, Kelly departed the scene the same day without fanfare.

Two weeks later the SubVet commander wrote Kirkpatrick, "In reply to your letter concerning the notes, the SubVets . . . voted to relinquish their lease on the *Batfish*. I personally discussed the notes with Mr. Ken Meyer. Since he now has assumed the assets and liabilities of the boat, he assured me he would take care of the notes." *Batfish*'s financial survival would depend on her first two years' income being used exclusively for interest payments, site improvements, and good publicity.

By the end of August, *Batfish* was steadily attracting a thousand visitors a week. Over the seven-week period, income from paid attendance had doubled.

Just before Memorial Day, all twenty-two members of the defunct Maritime Advisory Board had been summoned to respond to Midwest Dredging Company's suit—claiming it had been told it would be paid from a "revolving fund within the State Treasury" for the board's uses but that "no monies were appropriated to said fund."

On 21 December 1973 the Tulsa District Court sustained the demurrer of all board members except Albert C. Kelly and Karl R. Wheland, ruling that "the plaintiff's cause of action against said defendants is hereby dismissed." In June 1974 a Tulsa judge freed Kelly and Wheland, agreeing that they could not be held personally liable for the balance of the contract. However, the judge noted that the debt was "still owed by the board if and when funds are available." *Batfish* continued to attract about a thousand weekly visitors whenever weather was fair.

The outcome of the *Silvermain* matter, which had been tried in September in New Orleans, was finally revealed in November: *Silvermain*'s insurers had settled for $133,000, of which *Batfish*, et al., wouldn't see a penny. Although no commitment had been made to pay Avondale with this money, the shipyard had successfully filed an entrevenor for $110,000 including interest. The sunken barge's owner received $3,000, and the attorneys claimed the rest. Although this substantially reduced *Batfish*'s indebtedness, an accurate determination of the remaining debts became hypothetical, as an updated total would be meaningless.

Later in November, the Memorial Park Authority requested its attorneys to issue bonds in a reduced amount. In December 1974—nearly five years after Oklahoma approved *Piranha*'s acquisition—*Batfish*'s first revenue bonds were issued. Not only were they worthless when issued, but there was very little chance of their ever being redeemed. So that there would be no black mark on any other Muskogee bonds, each bore the conspicuous *caveat: "Bonds are in default when issued."* Although Muskogee came up with some money when the first interest payment came due, the city couldn't keep it up. The bonds became souvenirs.

Kirkpatrick took his share with a smile: "I look on it as money well spent getting the boat moved into position because of the humiliation to see this warship laid on her side and abandoned. In nearly every aspect it was a poorly conceived project—from beginning to end. But, like war, once started it had to be ended, regardless."

The deepest regret was that there was no real money to pay at least a reasonable settlement to those who had furnished goods or services. Some creditors like the Beaumont Texas shipyard accepted bonds as final payment so they could close their books; most of the others had simply written off the debts. There had been no fraud, only good intentions betrayed or led astray.

Although most Muskogeeans are vague on the issues, they believe *Batfish* is not costing them any money unless they buy a dollar ticket. Most SubVets say "Hell, yes, I'd do it all over again. We all would. And

224

we'd probably end up electing ol' Ace again. You know, *Batfish* wouldn't be here if it wasn't for him. He was a good ol' boy . . ."

On 3 January 1977 Albert Kelly, aged fifty-four, was killed as a result of a car-train collision near Depew, Oklahoma. He was alone in his car. Although Kirkpatrick was *Batfish*'s last admiral, Ace Kelly had been her final skipper. It was an amazing accomplishment that one man could motivate so many of his diverse fellows to move the "wrong" submarine 1,350 miles up an untested barge canal to an inland pond that wouldn't hold water, 490 feet above sea level, with no real authority and no money, against determined opposition. With a population of only 45,000, Muskogee is located off the beaten path in the middle of the prairie. Its economic base is farming and cattle; its industry is not significantly increasing.

Batfish continues to pay her way during the good weather of each tourist year. During the tight months, *Batfish*'s succession of managers have customarily taken pay cuts just to stick with her. Muskogee donated an old building and moved it to the park to be her museum, but it has yet to be renovated. Her current manager works on it when he can find time, and materials are available. Of the artifacts and memor- abilia accumulated for the Museum, the taped sound effects Karl Wheland furnished were stolen, and the Silent Service film Jake Fyfe donated walked away. One winter was so bleak the manager was forced to sell some of her lead ballast to pay bills; 1977 was the first winter there was enough money to take care of *Batfish* with no outside help.

Vandals were using her for target practice, so Muskogee police try to keep an eye on her. Except for her conning tower, she has been restored very well. More or less intact, she draws the awe and respect of her thousand or so visitors a week from late March to November. But unlike an art museum, she is not the kind of exhibit that draws regular return visits.

Batfish can be seen from the main road if you know where to look, but there are still no funds for local billboards to pull tourists in from the freeway, nor even clear directional signs. Nonetheless, one Japanese visitor who said that *Batfish* had sunk his training ship off Shimanoura Shima came two thousand miles out of his way to take her picture. But only so many people can go through a submarine at one time. There is very little in the park to occupy those waiting to go aboard. Many, having come that far to see her, go no farther than the parking lot, and don't return.

The lot is now paved to keep the dust down, and a trailer serves as a temporary office and ship's store; *Batfish* has been repainted and could make a little more money from the sale of souvenirs, but it takes a winter investment to stock them far enough in advance.

She is perhaps the only submarine in the world one can view almost from the bottom up. And with her keel four feet into the moist sand, electrolysis works like acid upon her bottom. Unless lifted onto a drydock, she'll be rusted through in twenty years or so.

Two of her wartime skippers converged in Groton, Connecticut, on 1 September 1973 for the commissioning of a new nuclear attack submarine—*Batfish II* (SSN 681). Rear Admiral Walter Small, then Assistant Deputy Chief of Manual Operations (Plans and Policies), was the principal speaker, Rear Admiral John K. Fyfe an especially honored guest.

Walter Small had a lot to do with the decisions that were to transform *Batfish*'s submersible successors. Upon his retirement from the Navy, Admiral Small, whose post-*Batfish* service included being Nimitz's personal aide, Commander Middle East Forces, and Com-SubPac, circulated an impressive resume which included managing a "ninety-man engineering organization including annual budget of $80,000, two and a half years"—*Batfish*.

After recalling how this latest "nuke" had come to be named after "the champion antisub submarine of World War II," Small turned over the podium to Jake Fyfe who lives in Newport News, Virginia, in content retirement at the end of a long and satisfying naval career. Like most old salts whose exploits are no longer classified material, he enjoys conjuring up the past.

Wayne Merrill was honorably discharged in 1949 as a lieutenant commander. He was an extraordinary engineering and training officer who could operate a submarine blindfolded and delighted in teaching others how. After a successful postwar engineering career, he married his childhood sweetheart and retired in the town in which he was born, and of which he is now acting mayor. Of all those bound to *Batfish* during those bloody war years, his memory is perhaps the clearest. He can tell anyone everything there is to know about *Batfish*, whom he truly loved—and lost.

Following a tie in Oklahoma's 1978 election, with 53 percent of the runoff vote, George Nigh became Oklahoma's governor. *Batfish* might have to wait at least until November 1982 for the assistance she desperately needs. Meanwhile, the Citizen's Guide to Muskogee lists her neither under "Museums" nor "Parks and Recreation." And *Batfish* never got her formal dedication.

APPENDIX: ROSTER OF U.S.S. Batfish

Abel, A. F.
Adams, Joseph L., Jr.
Allen, Thomas F., Jr.
Anderson, Richard W.
Athen, Donald D.
Baldes, Raymond O. J.
Beck, George T.
Becker, George (n)
Belcher, Harold W.
Bell, William G.
Benfield, Fred, Jr.
Bennett, James A.
Berman, Gerson I.
Birdsall, Raymond A.
Bohreer, John C.
Box, Clifford E.
Black, Robert
Breslin, Joseph J.
Bristol, H.
Brockway, Randall S.
Bruce, Robert D.
Burnett, Glenn G.
Burns, Sherman E.
Butterworth, James T.
Callanan, James B.
Campbell, William W., Jr.
Carter, Charles W.
Cartmill, Charles L.
Cassidy, John T.
Cavalli, Armand W.
Cherowbrier, Edward, Jr.
Cleppe, John B.
Coker, Harry L.
Coleman, Milton (n)
Collar, Robert A.
Comfort, Kenneth E.
Comstock, Wallace E.
Cornwell, Edward E.
Cosmijo, Juan E.
Cousins, Thomas E.
Cox, Clifford B.
Craig, Robert T.
Cramer, Edwin "J"
Crockett, William I.
Crue, Jose P.
Cutshall, Robert J.
Davis, Wiley V.
DeGrotte, Henry C., Jr.
Delworth, Edward (n)

Dennis, David L.
Ditewig, John W.
Dougherty, Edward J.
Drzewiecki, Albert J.
Duefrene, Edward W.
Elliott, William L.
Escarilla, Paterno (n)
Evinger, Albert J.
Farnsworth, Joseph M.
Fitzgerald, Pierce T.
Fontenot, Ivan (n)
From, John L., Jr.
Fulton, Robert E.
Fyfe, John K.
Garnet, James L.
Galiher, Clifford O.
George, Roy "D"
Gerhardt, Manuel A.
Gibson, William M.
Glace, John (n)
Gnitka, George R.
Goldfarb, Adolph (n)
Goodman, Malcolm E.
Grant, Wallace B.
Gray, William H.
Grimes, Homer E.
Hall, Glen C.
Hammond, Lewis T.
Hayes, Francis J.
Henning, D. A.
Hill, Richard R.
Hingson, James M.
Hoffman, Carl C.
Hosler, Richard F.
House, Richard E.
Hubbard, Robert T.
Huey, William B.
Hyde, Donald A.
Isbell, William J.
Javorski, Stanley J.
Johnson, Charles R.
Kelly, Nathaniel L.
Kerns, Fred R.
Kilrain, Joseph R.
Kost, Michael (n)
Kreis, Herman W.
Labrecque, Leon E.
Lamb, Richard W.
Landbeck, Frederick A.

Larch, Lynus J.
Laughlin, David W.
Lawrence, Virgil W.
Leasure, Russel E.
Lechner, Kermit L.
Lee, Dewey A.
Littell, Edward O.
Loader, Arthur F.
Longfellow, E. H.
Lowder, Hughston E.
McCann, Wayne L.
McDonald, Joseph E.
McGill, Emmett N.
Mac Kay, Kenneth B.
McKinney, Everett G.
McLarney, Howard R.
McNamara, Edward J.
Madden, James A.
Maxwell, Richard J.
Mayhew, Francis J.
Merrill, Wayne R.
Miller, Edgar V.
Mitchell, William J.
Mobbs, Harold V.
Mohr, Jacob (n)
Molteni, Peter G.
Moore, Joe R. Jr.
Morgan, O.
Morin, Henry J.
Morreale, Pete V.
Morrill, Numeriano G.
Mossman, John H.
Murphy, Arthur C.
Nelson, Ralph W.
Newton, David W.
Norris, James R.
O'Brien, John P.
O'Donnell, Eugene C.
Olson, Douglas H.
Oswald, Robert F.
Owen, Richard S.
Palmer, Everett A.
Paolo, Domenic A.
Parzych, Henry B.
Pepper, Reuben H.
Persico, Donato (n)
Peterson, Wesley P.
Pope, Joseph F.
Powell, William O.

227

Randolph, William W.
Record, Donald W.
Ricketts, Ray A.
Robare, Charles J.
Robinson, Leroy (n)
Rogers, Walter S.
Rollison, Daniel E.
Ruffin, J. L.
Rush, William G.
Ruthven, John R.
Sanks, Raymond L.
Schlief, Marius M.
Schuldheisz, Fred (n)
Sheats, Charles B.
Simson, Paul L.
Slunaker, Vernon R.
Small, Walter L.

Smith, George L.
Smith, Lyford O.
Snow, Robert G.
Sogoian, Ara A.
Sprague, Wilbur G.
Sprinkle, Clark K.
Stoinski, Raymond M.
Strauss, William M.
Sweet, Robert S.
Tamani, Felix (n)
Teeter, Lewis H.
Thibodeau, J. E.
Thomas, Charles R.
Thomas, Thomas A.
Thompson, Robert E.
Trimble, George H.
Tuma, Joseph R.

Van Leuven, Franklin A.
Vicari, Arthur F.
Wade, Charles L.
Walker, Richard H.
Waller, Emory A.
Warnick, Hubert M.
Warren, Martin C.
Wasleske, Alfred P., Jr.
Waterhouse, John W.
Weiler, James L.
Weis, Adelbert F.
Wightman, Earl C.
Witte, Ernest R.
Wood, Grover C.
Yankovich, John J.
Zimmerman, Edward J.

INDEX

Acoupa, U.S.S., 16
Alabama, U.S.S., 208
Apollo, U.S.S., 178
Archerfish, U.S.S., 155, 156, 169
Argonaut, U.S.S., 14, 185
Arizona, U.S.S., 10, 37
Atomic bomb, 195
Australia, 131, 134–36
Avondale Shipyard (New Orleans), 211, 212–13, 216

Bartlett, Governor of Oklahoma, 213–14
Batfish, U.S.S.
    awards received, 179
    decommissioned, 199
    description of, 17–18, 20–21
    dimensions of, 16
    enemy contact, first, 56–59
    enemy sinking, first, 68–71
    Equator crossing, 131–34
    Japanese submarine, first sunk by, 169–72
    in Korean War, 206
    becomes memorial, 210–16
    Pacific, assigned to, 27
    rest and recreation, Australia, 134–36
    rest and recreation, Hawaii, 154
    shakedown cruise, 17–26
    as tourist attraction, 1–2
    in typhoon, 45–48
    war patrols
        first, 41–77
        second, 78–92
        third, 93–118
        fourth, 119–36
        fifth, 137–54
        sixth, 155–80
        seventh, 181–98
    wartime record, 6
    Yamato, contact with, 61–66
Bathythermograph, 28–29
Berkenbile, Glen, 208, 210
"Black Panthers of the Pacific," 102
Blackfish, U.S.S., 155, 156, 169, 177, 178
Blind, Howard J., 136
Bonefish II, U.S.S., 206
Brown, W. S., 41, 45
Bumpus, Dean, 28, 29, 31–32, 34–35
Bushnell, U.S.S., 45

Cachalot, U.S.S., 12, 13
California, U.S.S., 9, 37
Case, U.S.S., 184
Cassin, U.S.S., 9–10
Chambliss, Joe, 215
Charr, U.S.S., 154
Christie, Ralph W., 135, 136
Clyde's Cannibals, 161
Coconut Grove (Panama City), 35
Commander Submarines Atlantic (ComSubLant), 26
Concal, U.S.S., 137
Coral Sea, Battle of, 43
Corvina, U.S.S., 44
Crevalle, U.S.S., 136
Curtiss, U.S.S., 10
Cutter, Slade, 6

Darwin, Australia, 137
Daspit, Dan, 44
Davy Jones, 132–33
Dealey, Sam, 6
Dempsey, Jack, 76
Diodon, U.S.S., 154
Dives, submarine, 21
Dolphin, U.S.S., 12, 13, 45, 98, 205
Domei News Agency, 102–3
Dorado, U.S.S., 29, 30
Dornin, Dusty, 6
Downes, U.S.S., 9–10
Drum, U.S.S., 208

"Emperor's Bathtub," 182
Enright, Joseph H., 155–56
Enterprise, U.S.S., 10

Finback, U.S.S., 53
Flasher, U.S.S., 6
Flying Fish, U.S.S., 181
Food, 153, 155
Forrestal, James, 179
Fortier, Nellie W., 16
Fremantle, Australia, 134–35
Fyfe, John Kerr (Jake), 3, 91–92, 93, 94, 95–100, 101–2, 104, 105, 106–7, 109, 111, 112–17, 123, 124, 126, 131, 135, 136, 139, 146, 153, 155, 161, 163, 164–67, 168, 169–72, 173–77, 179–80, 205, 225, 226

Germany surrenders, 181
Goodwill (yacht), 214
Gooneybirds, 73–74, 76
Grampus, U.S.S., 19
Griffin, U.S.S., 37, 38, 136
Guadalcanal, 43
Guam, 155, 178
Gudgeon, U.S.S., 14, 45
Guitarro, U.S.S., 134–35, 137
Gunn, "Pop," 167

Hall, Governor of Oklahoma, 214
Harada, Kiyoshi, 203
Harder, U.S.S., 6
Hardhead, U.S.S., 121, 144
Helena, U.S.S., 10
Helena Marine Company, 214
Hingson, James M., 2, 154
Hiroshima, Japan, 195
Hutchinson, Edward Shillingford, 89

I-Boat Captain (Orita and Harrington), 201
Industrial Development and Park Department (Oklahoma), 209, 213
Inhofe, James, 209
Instructions for the Navy of the United States Governing Maritime and Aerial Warfare, 13

Jackson, Robert J., 206
Japan, military advances of, 42–43
"Joe's Jugheads," 155, 161, 169
Joint Army-Navy Assessment Committee (JANAC), 199–201, 211

Kelly, Albert C. (Ace), 208, 211, 212, 213, 214, 215, 218, 222, 223–24, 225
Kimmel, H. E., 11
Kingfish, U.S.S., 93
Kirkpatrick, John, 220, 222, 223, 224, 225

Lamb, Ora, 213
Laysan albatross, 122
Lifeguarding, 144, 157, 177, 184, 185, 188, 189–92
Lloyd's of London, 211–12
Lockwood, Charles A., 37, 44, 118, 155, 177, 178
Longfellow, E. H., 2
Lowder, Hughston E., 6–7, 14
Luton, John, 210, 221

MacArthur, Douglas, 11, 43–44, 136, 153–54, 161
McCann, Wayne L., 2
Madden Construction Company, 220–21
Mare Island Shipyard, 199
Maritime Advisory Board, 209–10, 215, 216
Mark XIV torpedoes, 24, 25–26
Maryland, U.S.S., 37
Merrill, Wayne R., 17, 18–19, 22, 25, 26, 27, 28, 29, 30, 33, 34, 38, 39, 44, 49, 50, 52, 54, 58, 60, 61, 63, 64–65, 67, 68–70, 72, 75–77, 78, 81, 82, 85, 89, 90–91, 93, 154, 226
Meyer, Ken, 220, 221, 222, 223
Midway, Battle of, 43
Midway Island, 42, 73–77, 118
Midwest Dredging Company, 215, 216
Mines, 25
Morton, Mush, 6
Muskogee, Oklahoma, 1, 6, 210
Muskogee City-County Trust Port Authority (Oklahoma), 210, 218
Muskogee War Memorial Park Authority, 221

Nagasaki, Japan, 195
Nagata, Japan, 187–88
Narwhal, U.S.S., 12, 13
Naval Ordnance, Department of, 44
Neptunus Rex, 131–32, 133
Nevada, U.S.S., 9, 10, 37
Nigh, George, 209, 215, 216, 217, 218, 219, 220, 226
Nimitz, Chester, 44, 177, 178

Oglala, U.S.S., 10
O'Kane, Dick, 6
Oklahoma, U.S.S., 9
Old Pan American Hotel (Midway Island), 75
Operation Barney, 182, 184, 195
Orange (Texas) Naval Inactive Ship Facility, 210, 211
Orion, U.S.S., 184
Orita, Zenji, 201
Ozawa, Admiral, 108

Panama Canal, 35
Parker, H.M.A.S., 137
Parks, Lew, 90–91
Peabody, Eddie, 76

Pearl Harbor, Hawaii, 27, 36–37, 154
  attack on, 8–11
  rest and recreation at, 89
Pelias, U.S.S., 12
Pennsylvania, U.S.S., 10
Perth, Australia, 135
Philippines, Japanese invasion of, 11
Pilotfish, U.S.S., 184
Piranha, U.S.S., 208–11
Plaice, U.S.S., 162, 163, 169
Plan position indicator (PPI) scope, 37, 38
Plunger, U.S.S., 14, 45
Pogy, U.S.S., 187
Pollock, U.S.S., 14
Pomfret, U.S.S., 188
Pompano, U.S.S., 14
Proteus, U.S.S., 118, 119

Quillback, U.S.S., 185

Radar, 37–38
Radio-Sound School (Groton), 15
Raton, U.S.S., 148, 149, 151, 152
Ray, U.S.S., 145, 148, 149, 151, 152
Reardon, E. E., 210, 212
RO class submarines (Japanese), 201–2
RO-55 (Japanese submarine), 202–3
RO-112 (Japanese submarine), 203
RO-113 (Japanese submarine), 203–4
Ronquil, U.S.S., 184
Roosevelt, Franklin D., 8, 181
Royal and Ancient Order of the Deep, 131
Royal Hawaiian Hotel, 154

Salmon, U.S.S., 53
San Fernando Harbor (Philippines), 147, 149–50
Sandlance, U.S.S., 188
Scabbardfish, U.S.S., 162, 163, 169
Sea Devil, U.S.S., 184
Seahorse, U.S.S., 6
Seapoacher, U.S.S., 162, 169
Sennet, U.S.S., 187
Short, W. C., 11
Silent running, 22
Silvermain (tanker), 213, 224
SJ radar, 37–38
Small, Walter L. (Walt), 179, 181–82, 183, 193, 197, 226
Smallwood, Roy, 215, 216, 217, 218, 219
Sonar, 22

Sperry, U.S.S., 155
Spikefish, U.S.S., 188
Sprinkle, Clark, 154
Steelhead, U.S.S., 60
Submarine warfare directive, 13
Submarines
  dives, 21
  pre-World War II, 14–15
SubVets, *see* United States Submarine Veterans of World War II
Suwa, Koichiro, 202, 203

Tambor, U.S.S., 14
Tang, U.S.S., 6
Tautog, U.S.S., 12, 13
Tennessee, U.S.S., 9
"Texas League," 188
Tigrone, U.S.S., 196
Tinosa, U.S.S., 44
Tojo, Eiki (Hideki), 8
Tokyo Rose, 49, 102, 103
TDC (torpedo data computer), 23, 24
Torpedoes, 23–26
  deficiencies of, 44
  practice, 23, 24–25
Tourism and Recreation Commission (Oklahoma), 215, 216, 217, 218
Trigger, U.S.S., 6
Trout, U.S.S., 14
Trumpetfish, U.S.S., 179
Typhoon, 45–48

United Nations, 181
United States Submarine Veterans of World War II (SubVets), 208, 215, 220, 222, 223
Utah, U.S.S., 9

Velasco Reef Task Force, 122–23, 126, 127, 128
Vestal, U.S.S., 10
V-J day, 195–96
Vulnerability, feelings of, 157

Wahoo, U.S.S., 6
Wake Island, 11
Walker, Richard H., 2
Weaver, Bruce, 221
West Virginia, U.S.S., 9
Wheland, Karl R., 210, 211, 212, 213, 215, 223–24, 225
Whitaker, Reuben, 6

Williams Brothers Engineering Company, 210, 212, 216

Wills Brothers Port of Muskogee Terminal, 214

Wolfpacking, 148

Woods Hole Oceanographic Institute, 28

Yamamoto, Isoroku, 11, 42, 61

Yamashita, Tomoyuki, 161

Yamato (Japanese battleship), 61–66

Yuchi, Toroo, 203

Yuji, Jun, 203